ESSENTIALS
OF GERMAN

by **ERNST KOCH**
BROOKLYN COLLEGE

and **FRANCIS J. NOCK**
UNIVERSITY OF ILLINOIS

Illustrations by JOHANNES TROYER

New York OXFORD UNI_____ _____ 1957

Printed in the United States of America

ESSENTIALS OF GERMAN

FOREWORD

The pursuit of a foreign language on the college level deserves a serious and at the same time practical text. We have endeavored to meet this requirement with the present volume.

The presentation is based on the conviction that a sound study of the fundamentals of grammar and syntax is imperative if the student is to develop facility in reading comprehension or to gain even an elementary skill in expressing correctly *his own thoughts* in the language. We recognize, of course, that oral-aural work is vitally necessary, and so we have provided ample opportunity for *both* imitative and constructive oral-aural drill.

The presentation of grammar is here based on the assumption that most students have had no contact with a language in which syntactical relations are expressed through grammatical forms, and also on the assumption that, for most at least, grammatical terminology is a great unknown. Hence, every effort has been made to explain and exemplify grammatical principles, starting with English usage whenever possible.

In preparing the *Gespräche,* we kept in mind the fact that the great majority of students in the elementary classes will probably not go to Germany and that, consequently, the most useful conversation piece is one that teaches the student how to talk about things that he is likely to talk about in his native tongue. Thus, the student will feel more natural in his conversation exercise and perhaps may even be tempted to use German outside of the classroom. Such students as may subsequently go to Germany will learn quickly enough how to rent a room in a German *Pension,* how to purchase a railroad ticket, how to ask about the route to take with their Volkswagen to go from one place to another, etc. And the cultural benefit derived from, let us say, a conversation in an art gallery is, to say the least, minimal. Therefore, without placing the locale in any country (although some are obviously in the United States, others might be in Germany) we have written the *Gespräche* around natural themes.

[v]

Foreword

The *Lesestücke* are designed not only to give adequate reading drill for both narrative and expository prose but also to stimulate an intelligent awareness of fundamental characteristics of Germany, German life, and German culture by providing the instructor with subjects for constructive elaboration in the natural frame of the work.

In both the *Gespräche* and *Lesestücke*, grammatical forms are used which are not explained until later in the book. These are either elucidated in notes or given as entries in the vocabulary of the lesson. While the principle is not strongly stressed, there has been a slight anticipation of the grammatical points of the next lesson.

The problem of vocabulary is always a troublesome one, and to avoid limiting ourselves in the *Gespräche* and *Lesestücke* we did not restrict ourselves numerically. We have, however, made an effort to keep the vocabulary from assuming mammoth proportions and have also made use of the principle of repetition. A word appearing in the AATG *Minimum Standard German Vocabulary* (Morgan-Wadepuhl) is listed in the lesson vocabulary the first time it occurs and also in the general vocabulary. A word not in the AATG list is given in a footnote unless the meaning is obvious from the form: it is then listed in the lesson vocabulary. In either case it is included in the general vocabulary.

In preparing the exercises we adhered as far as possible to the words from the AATG list. The exercises, however, are in the main based on the *Gespräche* and *Lesestücke*, and we have therefore not hesitated to use other words from the selections of that lesson in which the exercises occur.

Our thanks are due to Professor Ernst Philippson of the University of Illinois and to Professor Helmut Rehder of the University of Texas, both of whom read the manuscript in an earlier version and gave many valuable suggestions and corrections; to Dr. Richard Seymour of Princeton University for assistance in reading proof; and to the Oxford University Press, whose patience and helpfulness have made possible the preparation and publication of this volume.

E. K.

March 1957   F. J. N.

CONTENTS

Contents

ESSENTIALS OF GERMAN

INTRODUCTION

0.1 The German alphabet. Although most printing in Germany is done today with roman type, literary works and many other items printed before 1940 were usually done with one or another of various types commonly referred to as "German type." In this text, the German of the first twenty lessons is printed in roman type; in the remaining lessons, it is done in German type.

A	**a**	𝔄	𝔞	*ah*	**N**	**n**	𝔑	𝔫	*en*
B	**b**	𝔅	𝔟	*bay*	**O**	**o**	𝔒	𝔬	*oh*
C	**c**	ℭ	𝔠	*tsay*	**P**	**p**	𝔓	𝔭	*pay*
D	**d**	𝔇	𝔡	*day*	**Q**	**q**	𝔔	𝔮	*koo*
E	**e**	𝔈	𝔢	*ay*	**R**	**r**	ℜ	𝔯	*air*
F	**f**	𝔉	𝔣	*eff*	**S**	**s**	𝔖	ſ 𝔰	*ess*
G	**g**	𝔊	𝔤	*gay*	**T**	**t**	𝔗	𝔱	*tay*
H	**h**	ℌ	𝔥	*hah*	**U**	**u**	𝔘	𝔲	*ooh*
I	**i**	ℑ	𝔦	*ee*	**V**	**v**	𝔙	𝔳	*fow*
J	**j**	ℑ	𝔧	*yot*	**W**	**w**	𝔚	𝔴	*vay*
K	**k**	𝔎	𝔨	*kah*	**X**	**x**	𝔛	𝔵	*ix*
L	**l**	𝔏	𝔩	*ell*	**Y**	**y**	𝔜	𝔶	*üpsilon*
M	**m**	𝔐	𝔪	*em*	**Z**	**z**	ℨ	𝔷	*tset*

In German type the following letter combinations are printed as single characters:

𝔠𝔥	*tsay-hah*	ß	*ess-tset*
𝔠𝔨	*tsay-kah*	𝔱𝔷	*tay-tset*

In roman type **ß** is used for the *ess-tset* combination. The American student is usually permitted to use ss for this. If **ß** is used, however, the simple rule is that ss is used only between vowels if the first of these is short. Thus, **ß** is used after a long vowel, after a diphthong, before a consonant, and at the end of a word.

Although many older Germans still use German script when writing, it is not necessary in the great majority of cases for the American student to learn it, and the alphabet in script is omitted here.

0.2 Pronunciation. The correct pronunciation of German can be acquired only by imitation. In the following paragraphs, suggestions are made which may be helpful, but the student must bear in mind that to pay careful attention to his teacher is his best way to learn German pronunciation.

0.3 Vowel length. In German, long vowels are held longer than short ones. What we call long and short vowels in English, as far as the actual sounds are concerned, are different vowels. In German, **hacken** and **Bann**, with short *ah* sounds, are different words from **haken** and **Bahn**, with long *ah* sounds.

A vowel is long: (1) if it is followed by silent **h**, as in **Bahn**; (2) if it is in the accented syllable and is followed by no consonant or by a single consonant, as in **haken** or **Plan**; (3) if it is doubled, as in **Paar** or **Beet**. Long **i** is frequently spelled **ie**, as in **Miene**.

A vowel is short: (1) before a double consonant, as in **Zimmer**; (2) usually before two or more different consonants, as in **alt**; (3) in an unaccented syllable, as in **Monat**.

If the stem form of a word has a long vowel, this vowel remains long when endings are added. Thus, **legst** has a long vowel because the stem form **leg-** of the infinitive **legen** does.

There are exceptions that can be learned only as the student advances with his study of the language. For example, **Osten** has a short **o**, **Ostern** has a long **o**.

0.4 Sounds and letters of German. Long **a** (spelled **a, ah, aa**) is pronounced like the a in **father.**

Ader, Bahn, Paar

Short **a** (spelled **a**) is the same vowel as the preceding, but cut short.

Acker, Mann, kalt

Long **e** (spelled **e, eh, ee**) is pronounced like the vowel a in **name**, but without the -*ee* glide after it which occurs in American pronunciation.

Degen, Ehre, Beere

Short **e** (spelled **e**) is pronounced like the **e** in **met.**

   Keller, nennen

Unstressed **e** is pronounced like the unstressed vowel in **Cuba** or **sofa.**

   Ehre, bekannt′

Long **i** (spelled **i, ih, ie, ieh**) is pronounced like the **i** in **machine.**

   Liter, Rui′ne, ihnen, tief, flieht

Short **i** (spelled **i**) is pronounced like the **i** in **hit.**

   finden, immer

Long **o** (spelled **o, oh, oo**) is pronounced like the **o** in **hope,** but without the -*oo* glide after it which occurs in American pronunciation.

   Boden, Kohle, Boot

Short **o** (spelled **o**) is pronounced like the **o** in **often** and **office** and is cut short.

   folgen, Koffer

Long **u** (spelled **u, uh**) is pronounced like the **oo** in **noon.**

   gut, tun, Kuh, Uhr

Short **u** (spelled **u**) is pronounced like the **u** in **put.**

   Mutter, unter

au is pronounced like the **ou** in **house.**

   Haus, Baum

ei and **ai** (and in names **ay** and **ey**) are pronounced like the **i** in **fine.**

   fein, beide, Mai, Bayern, Meyer

eu and **äu** † are pronounced something like the **oi** in **oil,** but with much greater conciseness.

   † The ¨ is called the "umlaut sign" (**Umlaut** is a German word meaning *change of sound*) and indicates that the vowel or diphthong so marked has a different sound from the one without it.

Leute, teuer, Bäume, läuft

ie in some words of Latin origin is pronounced like **ya** in **How are ya?**

Fami'lie, Ferien

Long ä † (spelled **ä, äh**) is pronounced either like a long-drawn-out **e** in **well** or like long German **e.**

Läden, Nägel, Nähe

Short ä (spelled **ä**) is pronounced like short German **e.**

Äpfel, Kälte

Long ö (spelled **ö, öh**) is rendered by pronouncing long German **e** and rounding the lips while doing it. The sound should be more like German long **e** than anything else. Many German poets have rhymed ö and e, as **hören—leeren.**

hören, mögen, Höhe, Röhre

Short ö (spelled **ö**) is rendered by pronouncing short German **e** with lips rounded. Short ö and short **e** are often rhymed, as **können—brennen.**

können, Löffel

Long ü (spelled **ü, üh**) is rendered by pronouncing long German **i** with lips rounded. Long ü and long **i** are often rhymed, as **kühl—fiel.**

hüten, Tür, kühl

Short ü (spelled **ü**) is rendered by pronouncing short German **i** with lips rounded. And again, short ü and short **i** are often rhymed, as **Küste—Liste.**

dünn, Küste

y occurs in Greek words and is pronounced like long and short ü.

Lyrik, Lymphe

b is pronounced like English **b** at the beginning of a word or in the middle of it.

Baum, beide, neben, über

If **b** occurs as the final letter in a syllable or before final **s, st,** or **t,** it is pronounced like English **p.**

Dieb, Diebs, lebt, lebst, ablegen

c by itself is used only in foreign words and names. Before **i, e, ä,** and **ö** it is likely to be pronounced like **ts,** otherwise like **k.**

Cicero, Cäsar, Café, Cato

ch, except in foreign words and names, is the spelling for two German sounds. The first of these is the sound produced at the beginning of the word **human** by breathing into it as hard as possible. It is also the sound produced by getting the mouth and tongue all set to pronounce the first sound of **year** and then breathing out. It is a sound produced without interrupting the passage of air out of the mouth. In practicing it overdo the breath pressure; it will always be easy to cut down to normal. This sound occurs after **i, e, ä, ö, ü, ei** (ai), **eu,** and **äu,** and also after **l, n,** and **r.** It also occurs at the start of a syllable.

ich, mich, nicht, fechten, Dächer, Löcher, Bücher, leicht, feucht, Gebräu′che, Milch, Mönch, Storch, Märchen

The second sound is pronounced similarly, but further back in the mouth. It occurs after **a, o, u,** and **au.** It is also a sound produced without interrupting the passage of air and should be practiced with overdone breath pressure.

lachen, noch, suchen, Gebrauch′

ch in French words is pronounced like **sh,** in Greek words it is either pronounced like German **ch** or like **k.**

charmant′ (sh), Mecha′nik (ch), Chaos (k)

chs is pronounced like **ks** if the s is part of the stem of the word.

Achse, Lachs

But if the s is an ending, then the pronunciation is of **ch** plus s.

lachst, Gebrauchs′

ck is pronounced like English **ck.**

Glück, Ecke

d is pronounced like English **d** at the beginning of a word or in the middle of it.

    danken, drei, nieder, oder

If **d** occurs as the final letter in a syllable or before final **s** or **st**, it is pronounced like **t**.

    fand, Mondlicht, Bads, lädst

dt is pronounced like **t**.

    sandte (*s* like English *z*), Stadt (*S* like English *sh*), lädt

f is pronounced like English **f**.

    fest, hoffen, auf

g is pronounced like the "hard" English **g** at the beginning of a word or in the middle of it (except after **n**).

    gegen, Gift, legen, mögen

If **g** occurs as the final letter of a syllable (except in the combination **ig** and **ng**) or before final **s**, **st**, or **t**, it is pronounced like **k**.

    Tag, Tags, legst, legt

Final **ig** is always pronounced like German **ich**.

    König, wenig

The **g** is never pronounced in the **ng** combination. The two letters together are pronounced like the **ng** in English **sing, song, singer.**

    Gang, Finger, England, Hunger

h at the beginning of a word is pronounced as in English. Otherwise it is silent and denotes that the preceding vowel is long.

    Hunger, gehen, Höhe, früh

j is always pronounced something like the **y** in **year,** but with the tongue pressed a little more firmly against the roof of the mouth.

    ja, Jahr, Joch

[8]

k is pronounced like English **k**. Before an **n** it is pronounced.

kalt, Haken, Knaben, Knie

l is pronounced about as in English.

leicht, helfen, fühlen, Ball

m is pronounced as in English.

Mann, kommen, Kamm

n is pronounced as in English.

Nachbar, lohnen, kann

For **ng**, see above under **g**.

p is pronounced as in English. It is pronounced before **f**.

Paar, Papier′, knapp, Pfeife, tapfer

ph is pronounced as in English.

Phantasie′, Physik′ (*s* like English *z* in both)

q is always used in combination with **u** and the two are pronounced like English **kv**.

Qualität′, Quantität′, Quelle, bequem′

r has two pronunciations possible, neither of which exists in English. One, generally used in the southern part of Germany, is a slight trill of the tip of the tongue against the upper edge of the upper front teeth. It is most pronounced at the beginning of a word and least pronounced at the end.

The other, used in the rest of Germany, is formed either by a trill of the uvula, the little tip hanging down at the back of the soft palate, or by making a scraping noise in the same region, similar to the back **ch** sound, but pronounced with the vocal cords vibrating.

rot, Brot, hören, hier, Bruder

s is pronounced like the **s** in English rose when it occurs before a vowel or between vowels. In German type the long **s** is used.

singen, Rose

When between a vowel and **t** or **p**, or at the end of a syllable, it is pronounced like the **s** in English sit. When final the round **s** is used in German type.

Gras, ist, Wespe (*w* like English *v*)

Before **p** or **t** at the beginning of a word it is pronounced like English **sh**.

sparen, Spiel, still, Stoff

ss and **ß** are both pronounced like English **s** in sit. See § 0.1, next to the last paragraph.

besser, daß, Straße

sch is pronounced like English **sh**.

Schiff, Busch

t is pronounced like English **t**.

Tag, Miete, gut

In words from Latin **ti** is pronounced like **tsi**.

Nation′, Patient′

tz is pronounced like **z**. See below under **z**.

th occurs mainly in names and in words of Greek origin. It is always pronounced like **t**.

Goethe (**oe** = **ö**), Thea′ter, Theorie′, Pathos

v is pronounced like **f**.

Vater, von, Vogel, brav

In a few of the words from Latin it is pronounced like English **v**.

November, Universität′

w is always pronounced like English **v**.

Wasser, Löwe

x is rare and is pronounced like English **x**.

Axt, Hexe

z is always pronounced like **ts; tz** is also pronounced thus.

Zeit, sitzen, Herz, zwei, zwischen

0.5 Accent. In native German words the accent is usually on the stem syllable, as in **le′gen** and **bele′gen.**
A certain type of prefix, which will be studied in the grammar, always has the accent. An example is **auf′machen.**
Words of foreign origin usually follow the accentual pattern of the original language. The student must, especially at the start, learn the accent for each word. A particular source of trouble is that English has borrowed a large number of words from French, Latin, and Greek and shifted the accent; German has borrowed the same words and retained the original accent: **Coura′ge, Student′, Philosophie′.** One large group which the student can easily remember consists of verbs ending in -ieren and their derivatives. These words are always accented on the -ier-, as **studie′ren, Studier′zimmer.**

0.6 Syllable division. A single consonant and certain groups of consonants which represent a single sound begin the ensuing syllable: **le-gen, la-chen, wa-schen.**
Of a consonant group, other than one of those suggested above, the last consonant begins the ensuing syllable: **sin-gen, Man-ne.**
Double **s** is always divided: **Was-ser; ß** always goes with the second syllable: **Stra-ße.**
If a word with **ck** is divided at this point the spelling changes to **k-k: Stük-ke** from **Stücke.**
Compound words are divided into component parts, regardless of the statements above: **Ver-ein.**

0.7 Capitalization. All nouns in German are capitalized: **der Mann, das Fenster.**
The pronoun of the first person singular **ich** is not capitalized within the sentence. **Sie** is always capitalized when it means **you** (see § 1.7), as is also its possessive adjective **Ihr.**

Adjectives of nationality are usually not capitalized: **die deutsche Stunde.**

0.8 Punctuation. Except that commands, requests, and exhortations are more frequently punctuated with an exclamation point in German, English and German agree in the final punctuation of a sentence.

Infinitive phrases of any length and subordinate clauses are always set off by commas.

In an enumeration **und** and **oder** are used without a preceding comma: **Tag, Monat und Jahr.**

A direct quotation is preceded by a colon. The first of a pair of quotation marks is placed below the line. **Er sagte: „Hier bin ich."**

PRONUNCIATION DRILL

The words of these rhymes and verses are not included in the vocabulary, since this is a pronunciation drill, not a reading drill.

1. Schlaf, Püppchen, schlaf!
    Da draußen gehn die Schaf,
        Die schwarzen und die weißen,
    Die wollen mein Püppchen beißen,
        Die braunen und die gehlen,
    Die wollen mein Püppchen stehlen.

2. Was kann Hänschen?

    Kann trampeln und strampeln
        und rumpeln und poltern
        und purzeln und stolpern
        und kegeln und klettern
        und Türen zuschmettern.

3. Ringel, Ringel, Reihe!
    Wir sind der Kinder dreie,
    Sitzen unterm Holderbusch,
    Rufen alle husch, husch, husch.

[*12*]

4.   *Im Vogelnest*

In den Hecken, auf die Ästchen
baut ein Vogel sich ein Nestchen,
legt hinein zwei Eierlein,
brütet draus zwei Vögelein,
rufen die Mutter: Piep, piep, piep,
Mütterchen, piep, hab' dich so lieb.

5.   *Abendgebet*

Müde bin ich, geh' zur Ruh,
schließe beide Äuglein zu!
Vater, laß die Augen dein
über meinem Bette sein!

Alle, die mir sind verwandt,
Gott, laß ruhn in deiner Hand!
Alle Menschen, groß und klein,
sollen dir befohlen sein.

6.   *Wandrers Nachtlied*

Über allen Gipfeln
Ist Ruh,
In allen Wipfeln
Spürest du
Kaum einen Hauch;
Die Vögelein schweigen im Walde.
Warte nur, balde
Ruhest du auch.

(Goethe)

7.   *Wiegenlied*

Singet leise, leise, leise,
Singt ein flüsternd Wiegenlied
Von dem Monde lernt die Weise,
Der so still am Himmel zieht.

Singt ein Lied so süß gelinde,
Wie die Quellen auf den Kieseln,
Wie die Bienen um die Linde
Summen, murmeln, flüstern, rieseln!
(Brentano)

8. *Frühlingssehnsucht*

Leise zieht durch mein Gemüt
Liebliches Geläute.
Klinge, kleines Frühlingslied,
Kling' hinaus ins Weite.

Kling' hinaus, bis an das Haus.
Wo die Blumen sprießen.
Wenn du eine Rose schaust,
Sag' ich lass' sie grüßen.
(Heine)

9. *Der Tag klingt ab*

Der Tag klingt ab, es gilbt sich Glück und Licht,
Mittag ist ferne.
Wie lange noch? Dann kommen Mond und Sterne
Und Wind und Reif; nun säum' ich länger nicht,
Der Frucht gleich, die ein Hauch vom Baume bricht.
(Nietzsche)

LESSON 1

*Nominative case; gender; present tense of **sein** and **haben**;
use of personal pronouns; **der**, **ein**, **kein***

1.1   Inflection. German is an inflected language. This means that,
to a certain extent at least, the function of a word is indicated by
endings attached to the word.

To a slight extent English is also an inflected language. The
possessor is indicated by *'s* or *s'* attached to a word: *father's
book*. The ending *s* without apostrophe denotes the plural: *books*.
If *-ed* is added to certain verbs, we know that the past tense or
participle is indicated: *played*. We still have case difference in
pronouns; *he* is used as the subject of a verb, *him* is used as the
object of a verb and after prepositions, and so forth.

1.2   Number. In German we have **singular** and **plural,** as in
English.

1.3   Cases. In German there are four cases: **nominative, genitive,
dative,** and **accusative.** Each of these is used in a variety of ways.

1.4   Genders. German nouns generally have one gender, i.e.
masculine, feminine, or **neuter.** However, since natural and gram-

[15]

matical gender do not always coincide, the gender of each noun must be learned. Thus, while **der Student,** *male student,* **die Studentin,** *female student,* and **das Wasser,** *water,* are masculine, feminine, and neuter as one would expect, **der Tag,** *day,* **die Nacht,** *night,* and **das Fräulein,** *young lady* (masculine, feminine, and neuter, respectively) do not follow the principle of natural gender. In the plural the distinction of gender has been obliterated: **die Tage,** *days,* **die Nächte,** *nights,* **die Fräulein,** *young ladies.*

1.5 Articles. The **definite** article and the **indefinite** article exist in German just as in English, e.g. **der Tag,** *the day;* **ein Tag,** *a day;* **die Nacht,** *the night;* **eine Nacht,** *a night;* **das Jahr,** *the year;* **ein Jahr,** *a year.*

There also exists in German a third important word, **kein,** which in the singular means *not a* or *no* and adds the same endings as **ein: kein Tag,** *not a day, no day;* **keine Nacht,** *not a night, no night;* **kein Jahr,** *not a year, no year.* In the plural it means *not any* or *no* and has the same form for all genders: **keine Tage, keine Nächte, keine Jahre.**

1.6 Use of the nominative case. The nominative case is used for the **subject** of the clause:

> **Der Tag ist warm.** *The day is warm.*
> **Warum kommt der Mann nicht?** *Why doesn't the man come?*

The nominative is also the case of the **predicate nominative.** A predicate nominative is by definition a noun or an adjective (usually called "predicate adjective") which stands after the verb of the clause and describes or limits the subject of the verb. Predicate nominatives and adjectives are most commonly found after the verbs **sein,** *to be,* and **werden,** *to become.*

> **Das Wasser ist eine Verbindung.** *Water is a compound.*
> **Das Gemisch wird ein Gas.** *The mixture becomes a gas.*
> **Die Tinte ist flüssig.** *The ink is liquid.*
> **Das Kind wird wieder froh.** *The child becomes happy again.*

1.7 Personal pronouns. English and German personal pronouns differ in usage in certain ways. In the first person singular and

[*16*]

plural and in the third person plural there is no difference. **Ich**
means *I*, **wir** means *we*, and **sie** means *they*.

In the third person singular there are three pronouns, just as
in English, **er, sie, es**, which can mean *he, she, it*. However, in
referring to a thing the masculine, feminine, or neuter form of
the pronoun is used, depending on whether the noun replaced is
masculine, feminine, or neuter. Thus, when referring to **Tag** the
pronoun **er** is used and the translation is *it*. When referring to
Nacht the pronoun **sie** is used and the translation is again *it*.
Es usually means *it*. In other words, it is important to remember
that **er, sie**, and **es** may all be translated *it*. (Speaking of **der
Wasserstoff**, *hydrogen*) **Er ist ein Element.** *It is an element.*

The pronouns of the second person, used in addressing another
person or other people, have different forms according to the
degree of familiarity between the speaker and the others. To a
single individual with whom he is on familiar terms the German
says **du**, to two or more he says **ihr**. If he is not on familiar terms
he uses the polite form **Sie**—always capitalized in writing—whether
he is addressing one or more than one. This pronoun is always
used with the verb form ending in -(**e**)**n**. While no absolute rules
for difference in pronoun usage can be given, the following may
be said:

(a) Use **du** and **ihr** for members of the family, relatives, children, and the deity.

(b) Use **du** and **ihr** for friends with whom you are well enough
acquainted to use first names.

(c) When in doubt use the polite form.

1.8 **Sein**, meaning *to be*, and **haben**, meaning *to have*, are conjugated in the present tense as follows:

ich bin	I am	ich habe	I have
du bist	you are	du hast	you have
er ist	he, it is	er hat	he, it has
sie ist	she, it is	sie hat	she, it has
es ist	it is	es hat	it has
wir sind	we are	wir haben	we have
ihr seid	you are	ihr habt	you have
sie sind	they are	sie haben	they have
Sie sind	you are	Sie haben	you have

These forms are so important to the verb system in general that the student must learn to recite and write them without error and without hesitation.

Note. There is only one form of a verb to be used with a given pronoun in German. Whereas in English the present tense may be either *I have* (simple), or *I am having* (progressive), or *I do have* (emphatic), in German only one form is used for all three: **ich habe.** This holds true for all German verbs. Thus, **er kommt** may mean *he comes, he is coming,* or *he does come.* The same principle holds for the other tenses.

GESPRÄCH

(When an adjective stands in front of a noun it always has an ending. This will be discussed in Lesson 9.)

Otto: Guten Morgen, Margarete.

Margarete: Grüß Gott*, Otto, bist du schon auf?

Otto: Ja, ich gehe heute morgen zur* Universität.

Margarete: Ich bin auch früh auf, denn ich habe eine Stunde
5 um acht.

Otto: Was für eine* Stunde ist das?

Margarete: Es ist eine Deutschstunde.

Otto: Dieses Semester nehme ich kein Deutsch. —Ah, da ist Rudolf.

10 **Rudolf:** Guten Morgen, Kinder*. Warum seid ihr schon so früh auf?

Margarete: Ist er nicht frech*? Wir sind keine Kinder, und wir sind auch keine Faulpelze*, sondern fleißige Studenten.

Otto: Grüß Gott, Rudolf. Grete hat eine Deutschstunde, und ich
15 gehe zur Bibliothek. Und du?

Rudolf: Ich bin auch fleißig.

(Professor Stuber kommt.)

Margarete, Otto und Rudolf: Guten Morgen, Herr Professor.

Stuber: Guten Morgen, wie geht es Ihnen*?

20 **Margarete:** O, es geht uns gut. Und Ihnen*?

Stuber: Auch gut, danke. Sind Sie alle drei dieses Semester wieder in meiner Klasse?

[*18*]

Rudolf: Otto und ich nicht. Freuen Sie sich*?
Stuber: Nein, nicht besonders*. Also, Fräulein Schroeder, Sie
sind immer noch eine Studentin von mir*. Das freut mich*. Auf   25
Wiedersehn*.
Margarete, Otto und Rudolf: Auf Wiedersehn, Herr Professor.

*Grüß Gott Hello *or* goodbye
  (God greet you—*a familiar*
  greeting in South Germany and
  Austria)
*zur to the
*Was für eine What kind of
*Kinder (*frequently used in fa-*
  miliar speech when not *ad-*
  dressing children)
*frech fresh

*der Faulpelz, -e lazybones, slug-
  gard
*wie geht es Ihnen? how are you?
*Ihnen? = wie geht es Ihnen?
*Freuen Sie sich? Are you glad?
*besonders especially
*von mir of mine
*Das freut mich I am glad
*Auf Wiedersehn Goodbye

LESESTÜCK

Wir sind hier im College. In Deutschland gibt es* keine Colleges.
Da gibt es nur Universitäten und verschiedene Arten von Spezial-
Hochschulen*, wie z. B.* Technische Hochschulen*, Bergakade-
mien*, Landeswirtschaftliche Hochschulen*, Wirtschaftshoch-
schulen*, Kunsthochschulen* und Musik-Hochschulen*.   5
  An den deutschen Universitäten hat der Student viel mehr
Freiheit als bei uns*. Er wählt sich* von Beginn seinen eigenen
Studienplan*. Das darf er in den meisten Colleges in den Vereinigten Staaten nicht. Hier sind die Kurse in den ersten Semestern
vorgeschrieben*: Fremdsprachen*, Mathematik, Englisch, Ge-   10
schichte* und Naturwissenschaften*. Erst in den späteren Semestern hat er mehr Freiheit. Aber nicht einmal in den „Graduate
Schools" hat er so viel Freiheit wie der deutsche Student.

*gibt es there are
*die Spezial'-Hochschule, -n spe-
  cialized institute of higher
  learning
*z. B. = zum Beispiel for example
*die Technische Hochschule, -n
  polytechnic institute
*die Bergakademie, -n school of
  mines

*die Landeswirtschaftliche Hoch-
  schule, -n school of agriculture
*die Wirtschaftshochschule, -n in-
  stitute of commerce and finance
*die Kunsthochschule, -n acad-
  emy of art
*die Musik'-Hochschule, -n acad-
  emy of music
*bei uns with us

[*19*]

*wählt sich chooses for himself
*der **Studienplan,** ⸗e course of studies
*vorgeschrieben prescribed, required

*die **Fremdsprache, -n** foreign language
*die **Geschichte** history
*die **Natur'wissenschaft, -en** natural science

EXERCISES

I. Answer each of the following questions with a complete German sentence: (1) Wann hat Margarete eine Stunde? (2) Was für eine Stunde hat sie dann? (3) Ist Margarete ein Faulpelz? (4) Wohin geht Otto? (5) Wie heißt (what is the name of) Margaretes Professor? (6) Hat Rudolf dieses Semester eine Deutschstunde? (7) Gibt es Colleges in Deutschland? (8) Gibt es nur Universitäten in Deutschland? (9) Wählt der Student bei uns in den ersten Semestern seinen Studienplan? (10) Hat der Student in den „Graduate Schools" so viel Freiheit wie der deutsche Student?

II. Conjugate **sein** and **haben** in the present tense.

III. Fill in the correct form of the definite article: (1) Herr Stuber ist ___ Professor. (2) ___ Klasse ist gut. (3) ___ Student ist in der Klasse. (4) Wo ist ___ Bibliothek? (5) Da ist ___ Universität. (6) ___ Kind ist schon auf.

IV. In exercise III rewrite sentences 2, 3, 4, and 6, filling in the blank with the correct form of the indefinite article.

V. In exercise III rewrite sentences 1, 2, 3, and 5, filling in the blank with the correct form of **kein**.

VI. Replace each underlined noun with the correct form of the personal pronoun: (1) Die Studentin ist Fräulein Müller. (2) Die Universität hat viele Studenten. (3) Ein College ist keine Universität. (4) Der Professor ist ein Deutscher (a German). (5) Der Morgen ist schon da. (6) Die Mathematik ist schwer (difficult).

VII. Translate into German: (1) Margaret and Otto are students. (2) Otto is going (geht) to the university this morning. (3) Margaret has a German class. (4) Does Otto also have a German

[*20*]

class? (5) Mr. Stuber is the professor. (6) Professor, have you a
class today (today a class)? (7) In Germany there are no colleges. (8) The student in the United States does not have as
much freedom as the German student.

VOCABULARY

There are several ways of forming the plurals of German nouns. These
will be studied in detail in Lesson 7. The plural form of a noun, however, is indicated in the vocabulary from the start. The hyphen alone
indicates that the plural is the same as the singular; the hyphen plus
a letter, or letters, indicates that the letter is to be added to the nominative singular. **Der Tag, -e** means that the plural is **die Tage.** If an
umlaut sign is placed over the hyphen it means the umlaut is to be
added to the stem vowel, or to the stem vowel of the last noun in a
compound noun. **Die Nacht, ⸗e** means that the plural is **die Nächte,
das Handbuch, ⸗er** means that the plural is **die Handbücher.**

acht eight
all, alle all
also so, well
an at
die Art, -en type, kind
auch also
auf up, at
der Beginn beginning
das Beispiel, -e example
die Bibliothek', -en library
das College, -s college
da there, here
danke thank you
darf may (do)
das that
denn for
deutsch German, das Deutsch
  German
die Deutschstunde, -n German
  class
(das) Deutschland Germany
dieses this
drei three
eigen own
englisch English
erst first, only, not until

fleißig industrious, diligent
das Fräulein, - Miss
die Freiheit, -en freedom
froh glad, happy
früh early
für for
gehen go
das Gespräch, -e conversation
gewöhnlich usually
gibt gives
gut good
haben have
der Herr, -en Mr. (*not to be translated before a rank or title*)
heute today; ___ morgen this
  morning
hier here
ja yes
das Kind, -er child
die Klasse, -n class (*in the sense
  of form or class group*)
kommt comes
der Kursus, Kurse course
das Lesestück, -e reading selection
die Mathematik' mathematics
mehr more

mein my
die meisten most
der Morgen, - morning
muß must
nein no
nicht not; ___ einmal not even
noch still
nur only
der Profes'sor, -en professor
sagt says
schon already
sein be
sein his
so so, thus
sondern but (*after a negative*)
spät late; später later
der Staat, -en state

der Student', -en student
die Studen'tin, -nen (female) student, co-ed
die Stunde, -n hour, class (instructional)
um at (*in a time expression*)
und and
die Universität', -en university
uns us
vereinigt united
verschieden various
viel much; viele many
von from, of
warum why
wie how, as
wieder again
zu to, too

LESSON 2

Present tense of regular verbs; imperative mood; accusative case; position of the verb

2.1 Present tense. The forms of the present tense of German verbs are derived from the stem. The stem is found by dropping the ending **-n** or **-en** of the infinitive, the form of the verb listed in a vocabulary or dictionary. To the stem are added the endings which form the conjugation of the present tense:

ich	.... e		wir	.... en
du	.... (e)st		ihr	.... (e)t
er	.... (e)t			
sie	.... (e)t		sie	.... en
es	.... (e)t			

The polite (or formal) form of the pronoun **Sie** is always followed by the verb form ending in **-en.**

Just as an *-e-* is added in English in such words as *he passes* but not in *he looks,* in order to facilitate pronunciation, so the connecting **-e-** (indicated above in parentheses) is used when necessary for pronunciation, for example after **d** and **t** and after **m** and **n** when preceded by one or more consonants.

Lernen, *to learn,* **warten,** *to wait,* and **öffnen,** *to open,* are conjugated as follows:

[23]

ich lerne	ich warte	ich öffne
du lernst	du wartest	du öffnest
er lernt	er wartet	er öffnet
sie lernt	sie wartet	sie öffnet
es lernt	es wartet	es öffnet
wir lernen	wir warten	wir öffnen
ihr lernt	ihr wartet	ihr öffnet
sie lernen	sie warten	sie öffnen
Sie lernen	Sie warten	Sie öffnen

2.2 Contracted forms. If the stem of the verb ends in a sibilant, that is, an s, z, or sch sound, the ending in the second singular is regularly -t. Setzen, *to set,* and genießen, *to enjoy,* are conjugated:

ich setze	wir setzen	ich genieße	wir genießen
du setzt	ihr setzt	du genießt	ihr genießt
er setzt	sie setzen	er genießt	sie genießen
sie setzt	Sie setzen	sie genießt	Sie genießen
es setzt		es genießt	

2.3 *Werden.* It should be evident that sein and haben are irregular in the conjugation of the present tense. Another very important verb that is irregular in this respect is werden, *to become:*

ich werde	wir werden
du wirst	ihr werdet
er wird	sie werden
sie wird	Sie werden
es wird	

2.4 The imperative mood. The imperative forms of a verb are used to express a request, an exhortation, or a command. In English the stem of the verb is used: *go, work, read,* etc. In German there are three forms, corresponding to the three forms of address. The ending -e is used for the familiar singular, -(e)t for the familiar plural, and -en plus the pronoun Sie for the formal. The imperative forms of machen, arbeiten, setzen, and sein (irregular) are:

mache	arbeite	setze	sei
macht	arbeitet	setzt	seid
machen Sie	arbeiten Sie	setzen Sie	seien Sie

The first of the three forms is used in speaking to a person who would be addressed with the pronoun **du,** the second to people who would be addressed with **ihr.** The third form is the formal form and is both singular and plural. While pronoun subjects are customarily omitted with the first and second forms, the pronoun **Sie** must be used with the formal form.

The -e of the **du** form is often omitted. This is sometimes indicated by an apostrophe: **mach', sag'.**

2.5 The accusative case. The accusative case of a noun is always identical with the nominative except in the masculine singular. In the masculine singular the words **der, ein,** and **kein** become **den, einen,** and **keinen.†**

N. S.	der Tag	ein Tag	kein Tag
A. S.	den Tag	einen Tag	keinen Tag
N. P.	die Tage		keine Tage
A. P.	die Tage		keine Tage
N. S.	die Nacht	eine Nacht	keine Nacht
A. S.	die Nacht	eine Nacht	keine Nacht
N. P.	die Nächte		keine Nächte
A. P.	die Nächte		keine Nächte
N. S.	das Jahr	ein Jahr	kein Jahr
A. S.	das Jahr	ein Jahr	kein Jahr
N. P.	die Jahre		keine Jahre
A. P.	die Jahre		keine Jahre

2.6 Accusative forms of the personal pronouns. The accusative forms of the personal pronouns are:

mich *me*	dich *you*	Sie *you*	ihn *him, it*	sie *her, it*	es *it*
uns *us*	euch *you*	Sie *you*		sie *them*	

2.7 Direct object. A direct object is the word indicating the direct receiver of the action of the verb. The accusative case is the form used as the direct object. A verb expressing a direct action is called a transitive verb.

† For a further difference see Lesson 7.

[25]

Ich sehe den Film. *I see the film.*
Trinken Sie den Kaffee? *Are you drinking the coffee?*

2.8 Word order. German and English differ in many ways in word order and this is one of the greatest sources of difficulty for the English-speaking student. As these various differences are mentioned the student should note them and *train his mind to the German pattern.*

The first and perhaps most important rule for German word order is: *The inflected verb* (the form with the personal ending) *is the second element in a statement.* If the subject is first it is followed by the verb, and we speak of "normal word order," as in the first example below. If any other element comes first it may be followed only by the verb and the subject comes *after* the verb; we then speak of "inverted word order."

The first element may consist of a word, a phrase, or even of a subordinate clause.

If any other element but the subject is placed first it is usually done for emphasis.

> Wir gehen heute ins Kino. *We are going to the movies today.*
> Heute gehen wir ins Kino. *Today we are going to the movies.*
> Ins Kino gehen wir heute. *It's the movies we're going to today.*
> Um den deutschen Film zu sehen, gehen wir heute ins Kino.
> *In order to see the German film, we are going to the movies today.*

2.9 Word order in commands and questions. A sentence begins with the verb when the imperative is used and when a question is asked which is to be answered by **Ja** or **Nein.**

> Warten Sie auf mich! *Wait for me.*
> Gehen Sie heute ins Kino? *Are you going to the movies today?*

GESPRÄCH

Professor Stuber: Guten Tag, Fräulein Schroeder. Wohin gehen Sie denn*?
Margarete: Guten Tag, Herr Professor. Ich gehe ins Kino*. Heute

[26]

spielt ein deutscher Film, und einen deutschen Film sehe ich
so oft wie möglich. 5
Stuber: Das ist sehr gescheit*. Da lernen Sie noch mehr Deutsch.
Aber genießen Sie das Stück! Vergessen Sie nicht, es ist keine
Deutschstunde!
Margarete: Vielen Dank*, Herr Professor. —Hier aber warte ich
auf Otto und Rudolf. Sie sehen deutsche Filme auch gern. 10
Stuber: Auf Wiedersehen, Fräulein Schroeder.
Margarete: Auf Wiedersehen, Herr Professor.
   (Otto und Rudolf kommen.)
Otto und Rudolf: Hallo, Margarete.
Margarete: Seid nicht so munter! Es ist schon ziemlich spät. 15
Glaubt ihr, wir haben den ganzen Nachmittag?
Rudolf: Sei nicht böse, Margarete! Das Stück beginnt erst um
drei. Wir haben noch Zeit, eine Tasse Kaffee zu trinken. Komm,
wir kaufen dir eine*.
Margarete: Schön*! Aber das nächste Mal . . . 20
Otto: Das nächste Mal läßt* du uns da stehen. Das wissen wir.
Diesmal aber—gehen wir* alle drei.

*denn *often inserted colloquially
   in direct questions, but not to
   be translated*
*ins Kino to the movies
*gescheit smart, clever
*Vielen Dank thank you very
   much

*wir kaufen dir eine we'll buy
   you one
°schön all right, O.K.
°läßt (*from* lassen) will let
°gehen wir let's go

LESESTÜCK

Josef Haydn ist in London zu Besuch*. Eines Tages erscheint
er im Orchester und setzt sich an das Pianoforte. Er will seine
Symphonie leiten. Die neugierigen Londoner verlassen die Sitze
und drängen sich an die Orchesterbrüstung*. Sie wollen den
berühmten Mann besser sehen. Dadurch* werden die Sitze in 5
der Mitte des Hauses* leer. Nun beginnt die Musik. Die Leute
sind enthusiastisch. Aber plötzlich fällt der große Kronleuchter*
herab und zerbricht* mit donnerndem Krach* in tausend Stücke.
Nach dem ersten Schreck erkennen die Leute an der Brüstung*,

[27]

10 welcher Gefahr sie entronnen sind*. Von Lippe zu Lippe geht
das Wort: Mirakel!

Haydn ist innig gerührt*. Er wirft* einen Blick zum Himmel*
und sagt zu den Herren im Orchester: „Sehen Sie, meine Musik
ist doch etwas wert—jetzt hat sie mindestens dreißig Menschen
15 das Leben gerettet*."

*zu Besuch for a visit
*die Orche'sterbrüstung, -en or-
  chestra railing
*dadurch through that
*des Hauses of the house
*der Kronleuchter, - chandelier
*zerbricht breaks to pieces, shat-
  ters
*der Krach, -e crash
*die Brüstung, -en railing

*welcher Gefahr sie entronnen
  sind what danger they have
  escaped
*innig gerührt deeply moved
*wirft throws
*zum Himmel to heaven
*hat . . . dreißig Menschen das
  Leben gerettet has saved the
  lives of thirty people

EXERCISES

I. Answer with complete German sentences: (1) Wohin geht
Margarete? (2) Was für ein Film spielt heute? (3) Sieht (*3rd
sing. of* sehen) Margarete deutsche Filme gern? (4) Wer geht
mit Margarete ins Kino. (5) Geht Professor Stuber auch ins
Kino? (6) Wann beginnt der Film? (7) Trinken die drei eine
Tasse Kaffee?

II. Conjugate in the present tense and give the three imperative forms of: sein, haben, werden, genießen, beginnen, warten.

III. Fill in the correct form of the definite article: (1) __ Tag
ist schön. (2) Ich sehe heute __ deutschen Film. (3) Er trinkt
__ Tasse Kaffee. (4) __ Kaffee ist gut. (5) Wir haben __ ganzen
Nachmittag.

IV. Rewrite, placing the underlined words or phrases first: (1)
Es ist schon ziemlich spät. (2) Später wird der Nachmittag
warm. (3) Josef Haydn ist in London zu Besuch. (4) Er setzt
sich an das Pianoforte. (5) Sie wollen den berühmten Mann
sehen. (6) Von Lippe zu Lippe geht das Wort. (7) Zum Himmel wirft er einen Blick.

[28]

V. Fill in the correct verb endings: (1) Die Studentin geh— ins Kino. (2) Sie wart— nicht auf Otto. (3) Du lern— Deutsch. (4) Wir seh— das Stück gern. (5) Ich lass— die Tasse hier. (6) Wir trink— gern Kaffee. (7) Trink— Sie den Kaffee nicht hier! (8) Geh— sie dann?

VI. Translate into German: (1) The afternoon is getting cool. (2) We are all as diligent as possible. (3) I like to drink a cup of coffee in the morning (am Morgen). (4) Where is Margaret going? (5) Are you learning German (*three forms*)? (6) Otto is getting angry. (7) Do you like to go to the movies? (8) The cinema is not a German class.

VOCABULARY

aber but, however
an to, at
beginnen begin
bei with
berühmt famous
besser better
der **Blick, -e** glance
böse angry
da then
der **Dank** thanks
diesmal this time
doch after all
donnernd thundering
drängen sich force their way
drei three
dreißig thirty
enthusia′stisch enthusiastic
erkennen recognize
erscheinen appear
etwas something
fallen fall
der **Film, -e** film, movie
fünf five
ganz whole
genießen enjoy
gern *with a verb gives the idea of "to like to." * **Sie sehen gern** They like to see

glauben believe, think
groß large
haben have
hallo hello (*This is not the equivalent of the American* hello *but an exclamation used only in calling out to people to attract their attention.*)
das **Haus, ⸗er** house
herab′ down
der **Herr, -en** gentleman
heute today
hier here
in (*with acc.*) into
jetzt now
der **Kaffee** coffee
kaufen buy
lassen leave, let
leer empty
leiten conduct, direct
lernen learn
die **Leute** (*pl.*) people
die **Lippe, -n** lip
der **Londoner, -** Londoner
das **Mal, -e** time
der **Mann, ⸗er** man
mehr more
mindestens at least

das **Mira'kel,** - miracle
mit with
die **Mitte** middle
möglich possible
munter cheerful
die **Musik'** music
nach after
der **Nachmittag,** -e afternoon
nächst next
neugierig curious
nun now
oft often
das **Orche'ster,** - orchestra
das **Pianoforte,** -s piano
plötzlich suddenly
retten save
sagen say
schon already
der **Schreck** fright
sehen see
sehr very
setzt sich sits down
der **Sitz,** -e seat

so so; ___ . . . **wie** as . . . as
spielen play
stehen stand
das **Stück,** -e piece, play, (moving) picture
die **Stunde,** -n lesson
die **Symphonie',** -n symphony
der **Tag,** -e day
die **Tasse,** -n cup
tausend thousand
trinken drink
vergessen forget
verlassen leave
warten (**auf**) wait (for)
werden become, get
wert worth
will wants
wissen know
wohin to what place, where
wollen want
das **Wort,** -e *and* =er word
die **Zeit,** -en time
ziemlich rather, fairly

LESSON 3

*Past tense of weak verbs; past tense of strong verbs; present
tense and imperative of strong verbs*

3.1 Strong and weak verbs. There are two types of verbs in
English and in German. One type indicates change to past tense
by a change of the stem vowel alone. We speak of these as
"strong" verbs. The other type, called "weak" verbs, forms its
past tense in English by adding *-t* or *-(e)d* to the present. The
same type in German adds *-(e)t-*. Examples of strong verbs are:

English		*German*	
find	found	finden	fand
drink	drank	trinken	trank

Examples of weak verbs are:

believe	believed	glauben	glaubte
answer	answered	antworten	antwortete

Just as there is no way of knowing that *write* and *freeze* are
strong verbs in English without learning the fact that they are,
so in German the strong verbs must be learned as such.

3.2 Past tense of weak verbs. The past tense of a weak verb
in German is formed by adding **-t** or **-et** (the latter after **d** or **t**

or after **m** or **n** when preceded by one or more consonants) to the present stem and then the personal endings:

-e	-en
-est	-et
-e	-en

The past tense forms of **glauben** and **antworten** are:

ich	glaubte	ich	antwortete
du	glaubtest	du	antwortetest
er	glaubte	er	antwortete
wir	glaubten	wir	antworteten
ihr	glaubtet	ihr	antwortetet
sie	glaubten	sie	antworteten
Sie	glaubten	Sie	antworteten

3.3 Past tense of strong verbs. The past tense of a strong verb is formed by adding the personal endings to the past stem. The past stem must be learned for each verb. The personal endings are:

—	-en
-(e)st	-(e)t
—	-en

After a sibilant the ending in the second singular is either -t or -est.

The past tense forms of **fallen, finden,** and **genießen** (*to enjoy*) are:

ich	fiel	ich	fand	ich	genoß
du	fielst	du	fandest	du	genoßt *or* genossest
er	fiel	er	fand	er	genoß
wir	fielen	wir	fanden	wir	genossen
ihr	fielt	ihr	fandet	ihr	genoßt
sie	fielen	sie	fanden	sie	genossen
Sie	fielen	Sie	fanden	Sie	genossen

Certain strong verbs have some form of irregularity in the stem consonant in changing from the present stem to the past. These again must be learned individually. Examples are:

kommen	kam (come)	treffen	traf (meet)
reiten	ritt (ride)	ziehen	zog (pull)

[32]

3.4 *Haben, sein, werden.* **Haben** is an irregular weak verb, **sein** and **werden** are irregular strong verbs. Their past tense forms are:

ich hatte	ich war	ich wurde
du hattest	du warst	du wurdest
er hatte	er war	er wurde
wir hatten	wir waren	wir wurden
ihr hattet	ihr wart	ihr wurdet
sie hatten	sie waren	sie wurden
Sie hatten	Sie waren	Sie wurden

3.5 Irregularities in the present. Strong verbs with **e** in the infinitive (except **gehen, heben,** and **stehen**) change the **e** to **ie** or **i** in the second and third person singular present. Short **e** always becomes short **i**; long **e** in general becomes **ie**, but not in **nehmen, geben,** and **treten,** in which it becomes **i**. Verbs with **a** add the umlaut in the second and third singular, and the umlaut is also added in these forms of **laufen** and **stoßen.** Examples are:

ich lese	ich helfe	ich nehme	ich fahre	ich laufe
du liest	du hilfst	du nimmst	du fährst	du läufst
er liest	er hilft	er nimmt	er fährt	er läuft
wir lesen	wir helfen	wir nehmen	wir fahren	wir laufen
ihr lest	ihr helft	ihr nehmt	ihr fahrt	ihr lauft
sie lesen	sie helfen	sie nehmen	sie fahren	sie laufen
Sie lesen	Sie helfen	Sie nehmen	Sie fahren	Sie laufen

3.6 Irregularities in the imperative. Those strong verbs which change **e** to **ie** or **i** according to § 3.5 also have this change in the first of the imperative forms; the other imperative forms have no vowel change. When the vowel **e** is changed there is no ending in the imperative form. Examples are:

lies	hilf	nimm	fahre	laufe
lest	helft	nehmt	fahrt	lauft
lesen Sie	helfen Sie	nehmen Sie	fahren Sie	laufen Sie

GESPRÄCH

Otto: Was machst du heute nachmittag*, Rudolf?
Rudolf: Ich fahre mit meinem Rad* in die Stadt. Meine Uhr geht nicht richtig, und ich bringe sie zum* Uhrmacher.

Otto: Warum fährst du? Ich würde* gern mitgehen*, aber nicht
5 mitfahren*.

Rudolf: Warum so viel Energie?

Otto: Der schöne Frühlingstag gefällt mir*.

Rudolf: Gut, ich gehe. Aber später hilfst du mir dann ein bißchen
mit der Schularbeit, nicht wahr*? Ich habe nämlich nicht zu
10 viel Zeit.

Otto: Ich kann dir* beim* Abendessen helfen. Wo ißt du heute
abend?

Rudolf: Das ist es eben. Ich esse mit Margarete. Aber das dauert
nicht lange. Wir treffen uns* nachher.

15 **Otto:** Dann triffst du mich zu Hause*. Komm', es ist schon zwei.

Rudolf: Aber laufe doch* nicht so schnell!

Otto: Na schön*. Aber höre mal*, ich muß um fünf zurück sein.

*heute nachmittag this afternoon
*das Rad = das Fahrrad, ⁼er bi-
cycle
*zum = zu dem to the
*würde would
*mitgehen walk along
*mitfahren ride along
*mir (*dative*) me
*nicht wahr? (*turns a statement
into a question*) won't you?

*dir (*dative*) you
*beim = bei dem at
*uns each other
*zu Hause at home
*doch *idiomatic, and to be
omitted in translation*
*Na schön Oh, all right
*mal *idiomatic, and to be omitted
in translation*

LESESTÜCK

In Deutschland war das Studentenleben* früher viel lustiger als
bei uns. So entstanden viele Anekdoten über Studentenstreiche*.
Folgende Anekdote ist solch eine.

Eines Tages ging ein Student in ein Kaffeehaus. Dort setzte
5 er sich an einen Tisch, bestellte ein Stück Kuchen und begann
in der Zeitung zu lesen. Das Mädchen brachte den Kuchen. Nach
einigen Minuten rief er das Mädchen wieder und sagte: „Bitte,
nehmen Sie diesen Kuchen und bringen Sie mir* eine Tasse
Kaffee dafür*!" Das Mädchen nahm den Kuchen fort und
10 brachte ihm* eine Tasse Kaffee.

Der Student las weiter* in der Zeitung und trank langsam den
Kaffee. Nach einer Weile stand er auf und wollte fortgehen. Da

[34]

kam das Mädchen von selbst*. „Mein Herr, Sie haben noch nicht bezahlt*!" „Bezahlt? Was noch nicht bezahlt?" „Den Kaffee!" „Aber ich habe Ihnen* doch* den Kuchen dafür gegeben*!" „Ja, aber d e n † haben Sie auch* nicht bezahlt!" „Aber meine Liebe*, d e n habe ich auch* nicht gegessen*!" Und damit* verließ er schnell das Lokal*. 15

*das Studentenleben, - student life
*der Studentenstreich, -e student prank
*mir (*dative*) to me
*dafür in place of it
*ihm (*dative*) to him
*las weiter went on reading
*von selbst by herself, i.e. without being called
*haben . . . bezahlt have paid
*Ihnen (*dative*) to you
*doch *idiomatic, do not translate*

*habe . . . gegeben gave
*auch (*Here used to mean*) either
*meine Liebe my dear girl
*auch *Here not to be translated; merely used for emphasis*
*habe . . . nicht gegessen didn't eat
*damit with that
*das Lokal', -e place (*used of a restaurant or beer hall particularly*)

EXERCISES

I. Answer with complete German sentences: (1) Wohin fährt Rudolf? (2) Geht seine Uhr richtig? (3) Wohin bringt er sie? (4) Warum hat Otto so viel Energie? (5) Warum muß Otto Rudolf mit der Schularbeit helfen? (6) Wann hilft er ihm? (7) Mit wem ißt Rudolf? (8) Wo ist Otto nach (after) dem Abendessen? (9) Warum läuft Otto so schnell? (10) Wohin ging ein Student eines Tages? (11) Was aß er da? (12) Was trank er da? (13) Rief er das Mädchen wieder? (14) Was machte er dann?

II. Conjugate in the past tense: bestellen, warten, hören; sehen, gehen, nehmen, verlassen; sein, haben, werden.

III. Conjugate in the present tense: essen, finden, gefallen, helfen, nehmen.

IV. Give the three imperative forms of: sehen, helfen, nehmen, fahren.

† German uses spaced type instead of italic.

V. Fill in the correct endings where needed: (1) Fräulein Schroeder ging—— in das Kaffeehaus. (2) Ihr sah—— einen neuen Film. (3) Da fand—— wir Otto und Rudolf. (4) Heute nachmittag fuhr—— ich zur Universität. (5) Was bestellt—— sie (*two forms*)? (6) Wartet—— er auf Otto? (7) Was nahm—— Sie fort?

VI. Translate into German: (1) The watch runs correctly. (2) He is bringing it to the jeweler. (3) Did you see (*three forms*) me? (4) Did you eat at home, Professor Stuber? (5) Otto is meeting his friend this afternoon. (6) Don't run so fast, Margaret. (7) He doesn't like to wait for me. (8) So he ordered a cup of coffee. (9) Rudolf didn't eat with Otto. (10) Take the watch! (*three forms*)

VOCABULARY

der **Abend, -e** evening; *see* **heute**
das **Abendessen, -** supper, evening meal
als than
die **Anekdo'te, -n** anecdote
bestellen order
ein bißchen a bit
bitte please
brachte brought
bringen bring
dauern last
den that
dort there
eben just
einige a few
die **Energie'** energy
entstehen, entstand arise
die **Erzählung, -en** narrative
essen, aß eat
fahren, fuhr ride
folgend following
fort away
fortgehen go away
früher formerly
der **Frühlingstag, -e** spring day
gehen, ging go; **richtig ——** be right (*timepiece*)

gut good; all right
helfen, half help (*with dative*)
mein Herr sir
heute abend this evening, tonight
hören listen
ja yes
das **Kaffeehaus, -er** café
kann can
der **Kuchen, -** cake
lange long, for a long time
langsam slowly
laufen, lief run
lesen, las read
lustiger gayer
das **Mädchen, -** girl, waitress
die **Minu'te, -n** minute
nachher afterward
nämlich you see
nehmen, nahm take
neu new
noch nicht not yet
richtig correctly
rufen, rief call
schnell fast
schön beautiful
die **Schularbeit** homework
sehen, sah see

[36]

solch such
die Stadt, ⸗e city
der Tisch, -e table
tragen, trug wear
treffen, traf meet
über about (*with acc.*)
die Uhr, -en watch
der Uhrmacher, - jeweler

verlassen, verließ leave
was what
die Weile, -n while
wo where
wollte was about to
die Zeitung, -en newspaper
zurück back
zwei two

LESSON 4

Dative case; prepositions with the dative, with the accusative, with both

4.1 Dative case. In the singular the dative case is chiefly recognizable by the form of the article:

dem Tag	der Nacht	dem Jahr
einem Tag	einer Nacht	einem Jahr
keinem Tag	keiner Nacht	keinem Jahr

Masculine and neuter nouns of one syllable may add an **-e** to the noun. This is not, however, a requirement.

dem Tage   dem Jahre

The dative plural always ends in **-n**. If the nominative plural of a noun ends in **-n** already, nothing is added; if it does **not**, then **-n** is added for the dative: †

den Tagen den Nächten den Jahren

4.2 Personal pronoun forms in the dative. The dative forms of the personal pronouns are:

mir	dir	Ihnen	ihm	ihr	ihm
uns	euch	Ihnen		ihnen	

† This **-n** is, of course, not added if the nominative plural ends in **-s.**

[38]

4.3 Prepositions with the dative. The dative case is always used after these prepositions:

> aus *out of, from*
> außer *outside of, beside, in addition to*
> bei *in the case of, by, at, near, with, at the house of*
> mit *with*
> nach *after, toward, according to*
> seit *since* (temporal)
> von *from, of, by, about*
> zu *to, at, toward*

4.4 Prepositions with the accusative. The accusative case is always used after these prepositions:

> durch *through, by means of* ohne *without*
> für *for* um *around; at* (expressions of time)
> gegen *against* wider *against, in opposition to*

4.5 Prepositions with either the dative or accusative. The following prepositions are followed by the accusative case when the word they govern indicates **the point at which a motion comes to an end.** They are followed by the dative case when the word they govern indicates the **place where or time when** something is or happens.

> an *at, at the side of, on* über *over, above, concerning*
> auf *on, upon* unter *under, among*
> hinter *behind* vor *in front of, before, of, ago*
> in *in, into* zwischen *between*
> neben *beside*

Er geht in das Laboratorium. *but* Er ist in dem Laboratorium.
Er legt das Buch auf den Tisch. *but* Das Buch liegt auf dem Tisch.

4.6 Contractions. Many prepositions are contracted with certain forms of the definite article. The spoken language uses these contractions to a much greater extent than the literary language (compare spoken English *isn't* and the written *is not*). Some common ones are:

[39]

am = an dem	beim = bei dem	vom = von dem
ans = an das	im = in dem	zum = zu dem
aufs = auf das	ins = in das	zur = zu der

GESPRÄCH

Franz: Guten Tag, Lisl! Was hast du da in der Tüte*?

Lisl: Das ist mein Mittagessen. Heute bleibe ich im Laboratorium.

Franz: Wie lange bleibst du da?

5 Lisl: Das weiß ich* nicht. In meinem Experiment müssen alle Tiere durch einen Tunnel in den anderen Käfig* gehen. Aber sie laufen alle zur Öffnung und dann wieder von der Öffnung weg.

Franz: Warum tun sie das? Liegt etwas Futter* auf dem Boden in dem anderen Käfig?

10 Lisl: Nein, natürlich nicht. Sonst würde das erste Tier alles auffressen*. Sie sollen es aus Neugierde* tun. Von dem anderen Käfig können sie nicht wieder in den ersten zurückkommen.

Franz: Ich bleibe lieber bei* der Physik. Da brauche ich auf keine dumme Ratte zu warten.

15 Lisl: Ja, aber da habt ihr zu viel mit der Elektrizität zu tun. Vor einer Ratte habe ich keine Furcht, aber gegen die Elektrizität bin ich ganz wehrlos*.

Franz: Hier muß ich um die Ecke biegen. Ich gehe zur Bibliothek. Auf Wiedersehn, Lisl.

20 Lisl: Auf Wiedersehn, Franz. Denke heute nachmittag an mich. Ich weiß bestimmt, du bleibst nicht in der Bibliothek, sondern gehst auf den Tennisplatz.

*die Tüte, -n paper bag
*Das weiß ich I know that
*der Käfig, -e cage
*das Futter (animal) food

*würde . . . auffressen would eat up
*die Neugierde curiosity
*Ich bleibe lieber bei I'll stick to
*wehrlos defenseless

LESESTÜCK

Auf einer topographischen Karte sieht man, Deutschland hat drei Teile. I Süddeutschland* oder Oberdeutschland*. Da gibt es hohe Berge. II Mitteldeutschland*. Hier findet man auch Berge,

aber sie sind nicht so hoch wie die Berge Süddeutschlands.
III Norddeutschland*. Hier finden wir keine Berge. Dies ist 5
Tiefland*. Man nennt einen Teil von diesem Tiefland auch
Niederdeutschland*.

In dem deutschen Tiefland ist der Ackerbau* wichtig. Die
Leute sind nicht arm, aber das Leben ist hart, denn der Boden
ist schwer, besonders in dem reklamierten Land an der Nord- 10
seeküste*. So sind die Bauern hier meistens stille, ernste Menschen. Dann und wann* aber wird ein Bauer von dem harten
einsamen Leben doch schwermütig*. Er glaubt, seine Sorgen*
sind zu schwer für ihn. Er glaubt, er muß sich* das Leben durch
Alkohol erleichtern*—ein altes deutsches Sprichwort* sagt: „Wer 15
Sorgen hat, hat auch Likör*"—und er beginnt zu trinken. Die
deutsche Literatur hat viele Geschichten und Anekdoten über
solch problematische Menschen. Folgende ist solch eine Anekdote.

Klaus Martens war ein guter Mensch, aber er trank zu viel. 20
Benebelt* sah er dann doppelt. So kam er an einem Abend nach
Hause und sah seine Frau bei einem Lichte spinnen. Er wurde
böse. „Warum hast du zwei Lichter? Glaubst du, das Geld
wächst auf Bäumen? E i n Licht ist genug. Oder noch besser,
spinn' am Tage!" Ein andermal ging er am Abend ins Schlaf- 25
zimmer. Da sah er ein zweites Kind neben seinem Söhnchen*
liegen. Er wurde wild und schrie: „Wie kommt dies fremde Kind
in mein Haus?" Endlich kam er an einem Sonntag aus dem Wirtshaus und ging in die Küche. Seine Frau stand am Ofen. Sie hatte
einen Topf auf dem Feuer und kochte. „Was hast du in den zwei 30
Töpfen?" fragte er. „Ich habe zwei Hühnchen*, eins für dich
und eins für mich. Nimm du das eine* und ich nehme das andere." Damit zog sie den Topf schnell vom Feuer. Der hungrige
und benebelte Bauer, indem er nach dem vermutlichen zweiten
Topf griff*, steckte die Hand in die Flamme und verbrannte 35
sich*. Seit der Zeit trank er nicht mehr und sah auch nicht mehr
doppelt.

*(das) **Süddeutschland** South
  Germany
*(das) **Oberdeutschland** Upper
  Germany

*(das) **Mitteldeutschland** Middle
  Germany
*(das) **Norddeutschland** North
  Germany

Essentials of German

*das **Tiefland** lowland
*(das) **Niederdeutschland** Low Germany
*der **Ackerbau** agriculture
*die **Nordseeküste** North Sea coast
*dann und wann now and then
*wird doch schwermütig does succumb to depression
*die **Sorge, -n** worry
*sich for himself

*erleichtern brighten, make easier
*das **Sprichwort, -ër** proverb
*der **Likör', -e** liquor, strong drink
*benebelt foggy, tipsy
*das **Söhnchen, -** little son
*das **Hühnchen, -** little chicken
*das eine the one
*indem . . . griff by reaching for the imagined pot
*verbrannte sich burned himself

EXERCISES

I. Answer with complete German sentences: (1) Wo bleibt Lisl heute? (2) Wie können die Tiere in den anderen Käfig kommen? (3) Kommen sie schnell dahin? (4) Was tun sie? (5) Finden sie Futter im anderen Käfig? (6) Wie kommen sie in den ersten Käfig zurück? (7) Warum bleibt Lisl lieber bei den Ratten? (8) Warum bleibt Franz lieber bei der Physik? (9) Wie viele Teile hat Deutschland? (10) Wo findet man hohe Berge? (11) Wo liegt das Tiefland? (12) Wie ist das Leben an der Nordseeküste? (13) Was für Menschen findet man hier? (14) Wer war Klaus Martens? (15) Inwiefern (in what way) war er problematisch? (16) Wer kurierte (cured) ihn?

II. Give the dative singular and dative plural, with the definite article, of: Berg, Baum, Hand, Teil, Licht, Küche, Feuer, Haus, Frau, Schlafzimmer.

III. Fill in the correct endings where required: (1) D__ Tier läuft in ein__ Käfig. (2) Der Käfig ist in d__ Laboratorium. (3) Der Topf ist auf d__ Ofen. (4) Der Mann steht zwischen d__ Frau und d__ Kind. (5) Lisl geht in d__ Haus. (6) Die Ratte geht an d__ Öffnung. (7) Die Frau legt das Kind auf d__ Boden. (8) Dann spinnt sie unter d__ Licht.

IV. Translate into German: (1) Today Lisl is staying home. (2) Yesterday she went to the laboratory. (3) Franz was not in the laboratory. (4) He was at home and was reading a story about Klaus Martens. (5) Klaus Martens was a farmer near the North Sea coast. (6) Many farmers find life difficult in the low-

[42]

land. (7) Most have nothing against the life, however, for they are not poor. (8) Franz tells Lisl about the story. (9) Lisl says, "I am glad I am a student in America and not a farmer's wife in North Germany."

VOCABULARY

der **Alkohol'**, -e alcohol
alt old
an on
ein **andermal** another time
arm poor
auf on
aus out of, from
der **Bauer,** -n farmer, peasant
der **Baum,** -e tree
bei by
der **Berg,** -e mountain
bestimmt definitely
biegen, **bog** turn
bleiben, **blieb** stay
der **Boden,** = bottom, floor, soil
brauchen need, use
damit with that
dann then
denken (an) think (of)
doppelt double
dumm stupid
durch through, by means of
die **Ecke,** -n corner
einsam lonely
die **Elektrizität,** -en electricity
endlich finally
ernst serious
etwas some
das **Experiment'**, -e experiment
das **Feuer,** - fire
die **Flamme,** -n flame
die **Frau,** -en wife
fremd strange
die **Furcht** (vor) fear (of)
ganz completely
gegen against
das **Geld** money
die **Geschichte,** -n story, history

die **Hand,** =e hand
hart hard
hoch high
hohe (*from* hoch) high
hungrig hungry
die **Karte,** -n map
kochen cook
können can
die **Küche,** -n kitchen
das **Land,** =er land
das **Leben,** - life
liegen, **lag** lie, be situated
das **Licht,** -er light
die **Literatur'**, -en literature
man one
mehr more, longer; **nicht mehr no** longer
meistens mostly, for the most part
das **Mittagessen,** - lunch, **noon** meal
müssen must
nach Hause home
natürlich naturally
neben beside
nennen name, call
oder or
der **Ofen,** = stove
die **Öffnung,** -en opening
problematisch problematical
das **Schlafzimmer,** - bedroom
schnell quickly
schreien, **schrie** yell, scream
schwer difficult, heavy, hard **to** work
seit since
sollen be supposed to
sondern but
der **Sonntag,** -e Sunday

[43]

sonst otherwise
die Sorge, -n worry
spinnen, spann spin
stecken stick, put
still silent
der Teil, -e part
der Tennisplatz, ⸗e tennis court
das Tier, -e animal
der Topf, ⸗e pot
topogra′phisch topographical
tun, tat do
der Tunnel, - tunnel

um around
wachsen, wuchs grow
weg away
wer whoever
wichtig important
wie how
wild wild
das Wirtshaus, ⸗er inn, tavern
ziehen, zog pull
zurückkommen come back
zweit second

LESSON 5

Genitive case; prepositions with the genitive; other uses of the genitive; personal pronouns

5.1 Genitive endings. All neuter nouns and almost all masculine nouns add -s or -es in the genitive singular.† Nouns of one syllable usually add -es, although this may be contracted to -s. Nouns of more than one syllable add -s unless the connecting -e- is necessary.

Feminine nouns add no ending in the genitive singular.

The genitive plural adds no ending to the nominative plural form.

The genitive forms of **Tag, Nacht,** and **Jahr** are:

des Tages	der Nacht	des Jahres
eines Tages	einer Nacht	eines Jahres
keines Tages	keiner Nacht	keines Jahres
der Tage	der Nächte	der Jahre
keiner Tage	keiner Nächte	keiner Jahre

5.2 Uses of the genitive. The genitive case is used:

(a) After a large number of prepositions, the more common of which are:

† For an exception see Lesson 7.

anstatt *instead of*	**statt** *instead of*
außerhalb *outside of*	**trotz** *in spite of*
diesseits *this side of*	**um . . . willen** *for the sake*
innerhalb *within*	*of*
jenseits *that side of, the other*	**unterhalb** *below*
side of, beyond	**während** *during*
oberhalb *above*	**wegen** *on account of*

For example:

> **anstatt eines Gesprächs** *instead of a conversation*
> **während der ersten Jahre** *during the first years*

(b) To show possession.

> **den Dialekt seiner Eltern** *the dialect of his parents*

(c) As an adverbial construction to show indefinite time or time of customary action.

> **Eines Tages war er hier.** *One day he was here.*
> **Morgens fahre ich immer in die Stadt.** *Mornings I always go to town.*

(d) To express the whole, part of which is taken.

> **einige dieser Dialekte** *a few of these dialects*

(e) After a number of adjectives, as

bewußt *conscious of*	**wert** *worth*
fähig *capable of*	**würdig** *worthy of*
müde *tired of*	

(f) After a few verbs.

> **Ich erinnere mich des Mannes nicht.** *I do not remember the man.*

5.3 Genitive forms of the personal pronouns. The genitive forms of the personal pronouns are infrequently found and then only in the uses described in §§ 5.2 (a), (e), and (f). The forms are:

meiner	deiner	Ihrer	seiner	ihrer	seiner
unser	eurer	Ihrer		ihrer	

With **um . . . willen** and **wegen** the final **-er** becomes **-et**. Notice how the words are joined to form a compound.

> **um meinetwillen** *for my sake*   **um deinetwillen** *for your sake*
> **seinetwegen** *on his account*

5.4 Review of personal pronoun forms. The complete declension of the personal pronoun is:

ich	du	Sie	er	sie	es
meiner	deiner	Ihrer	seiner	ihrer	seiner
mir	dir	Ihnen	ihm	ihr	ihm
mich	dich	Sie	ihn	sie	es

wir	ihr	Sie	sie
unser	eurer	Ihrer	ihrer
uns	euch	Ihnen	ihnen
uns	euch	Sie	sie

5.5 Compounds with da-. When referring to a thing **da-** (before a consonant) or **dar-** (before a vowel) is used with prepositions, instead of a pronoun.

> **Die Frau hatte zwei Mark und kaufte Milch damit.** *The woman had two marks and bought milk with them.*
> **Er ging an den Tisch und legte das Buch darauf.** *He went to the table and laid the book on it.*

GESPRÄCH

Frau Röhl: Guten Tag, Frau Schneider. Wohin gehen Sie so früh?

Frau Schneider: Ich gehe zum Onkel von meinem Mann. Er ist krank.

Frau Röhl: Was fehlt ihm denn*? 5

Frau Schneider: Er hat nur die Grippe*. Aber etwas Schlimmes kann daraus werden.

Fraul Röhl: Jawohl. Zwei von meinen Kindern haben beinahe Lungenentzündung* gekriegt*.

Frau Schneider: Nun, einmal werden die Ärzte doch noch ein 10 Mittel dagegen finden*.

Frau Röhl: Hoffentlich.

Frau Schneider: Und Sie, Frau Röhl, was machen Sie in diesem Viertel* der Stadt?

Frau Röhl: Ich gehe nur spazieren. Die ersten zwanzig Jahre 15 meines Lebens habe ich hier gewohnt*, und ein paar von meinen alten Freunden wohnen noch hier.

Frau Schneider: Hier bin ich schon bei dem Onkel. Also, auf Wiedersehen, Frau Röhl.

20 **Frau Röhl:** Auf Wiedersehen, Frau Schneider.

*Was fehlt ihm denn? What's the matter with him?	*haben . . . gekriegt got, caught
*die **Grippe** flu, grippe	*werden . . . finden will find
*die **Lungenentzündung** pneumonia	*das **Viertel** quarter
	*habe . . . gewohnt lived

LESESTÜCK

Hier in der Klasse lernen wir die deutsche Schriftsprache*, d. h.* wir lernen die offizielle* Sprache der deutschsprechenden Teile Europas: Deutschlands, Österreichs* und eines Teils der Schweiz*. Außer dieser Schriftsprache gibt es aber auch viele 5 Dialekte. Während der ersten Jahre seines Lebens spricht ein Kind gewöhnlich den Dialekt seiner Eltern. Dann geht es aber eines Tages in die Schule und hier lernt es die Schriftsprache. Von da an* spricht das Kind zwei Sprachen: innerhalb der Familie und unter Freunden meistens den väterlichen* Dialekt, 10 in der Schule und im formellen Umgang* die Schriftsprache.

Diese Schriftsprache ist schon etliche hundert Jahre alt–sie ruht auf* Luthers Bibelübersetzung*–aber die Dialekte sind viel älter*, und so haben sie einen fortwährenden* Einfluß auf die Schriftsprache. Das sieht man besonders bei den formelleren* 15 Formen der Sprache, z. B. bei dem Genitiv. Trotz der Lehren der Schriftsprache kann sich der Genitiv in der Umgangssprache des Volkes nur schwer behaupten*. So lehrt das Textbuch: „Ich erinnere mich seiner* nicht." Der Deutsche in der täglichen Rede sagt aber: „Ich erinnere mich nicht an ihn*." Statt „meines 20 Vaters Haus" hört man „das Haus von meinem Vater." Manchmal findet man sogar ganz inkorrekte* Formen. So z. B. anstatt „meines Freundes wegen" findet man häufig „wegen meinem Freund."

Daraus sehen wir natürlich wieder: Sprachen sind dynamisch*. 25 Sie haben trotz Schule und Regeln ein eigenes Leben und sind einer fortwährender Entwicklung fähig. Das gilt* sowohl für die deutsche Schriftsprache als für die deutschen Dialekte. Glauben

Sie aber deshalb nicht, Sie brauchen Regeln und Formen nicht
zu lernen. So schnell verändert sich* die Sprache nicht.

*die **Schriftsprache, -n** literary
  language, standard language
*d. h. = das heißt that is, that
  means
*offiziell' official
* (das) **Österreich** Austria
*die **Schweiz** Switzerland
*von da an from then on
*väterlich (paternal) parental
*der **Umgang** association
*ruht auf is based on
*Luthers **Bibelübersetzung** Luther's translation of the Bible
*älter older

*fortwährend continuous
*formel'leren more formal
*kann sich . . . behaupten the
  genitive has difficulty in main-
  taining itself in the everyday
  language of the people
*ich erinnere mich seiner *and* ich
  erinnere mich an ihn I remember him
*inkorrekt incorrect
*dynamisch dynamic
*gilt holds, holds true
*verändert sich changes

EXERCISES

I. Answer with complete German sentences: (1) Wohin geht
Frau Schneider? (2) Was fehlt dem Onkel? (3) Warum ist Frau
Schneider besorgt (worried)? (4) Was macht Frau Röhl in
diesem Teil der Stadt? (5) Wie lange hat Frau Röhl hier gewohnt? (6) Wohnt sie noch hier? (7) Was ist die deutsche
Schriftsprache? (8) Wann lernt das Kind die Schriftsprache?
(9) Wo lernt das Kind den Dialekt? (10) Wann spricht es gewöhnlich den Dialekt? (11) Wann spricht es die Schriftsprache?
(12) Warum verändern sich Sprachen?

II. Give the genitive singular and plural with the definite article
of: Kind, Arzt, Mittel, Stadt, Freund, Onkel, Klasse, Leben,
Schule, Buch.

III. Translate into German: (1) The child learns Standard German in school. (2) However, in spite of the rules and forms of
Standard German he also speaks his dialect. (3) We are studying
Standard German instead of a dialect. (4) There is a considerable difference (ein ziemlicher Unterschied) between the dialects
of North Germany and of South Germany. (5) Languages are
dynamic and capable of development. (6) One afternoon a week
ago I did not go to school. (7) He always worked at home dur-

ing the day. (8) My parents had the flu. (9) But nothing serious developed out of it. (10) The man was tired of life.

VOCABULARY

also well, so
anstatt instead of
der **Arzt,** ⁼e doctor
außer beside
bei in, in the case of, at, at the home of
beinahe almost
deshalb therefore
deutschsprechend German-speaking
der **Dialekt',** -e dialect
doch; ___ **noch** still
der **Einfluß,** -flüsse influence
einmal some day
die **Eltern** (*pl.*) parents
die **Entwicklung,** -en development
etliche several
(das) **Euro'pa** Europe
fähig capable (of)
die **Fami'lie,** -n family
die **Form,** -en form
formell' formal
der **Freund,** -e friend
der **Genitiv** genitive
häufig frequently
hoffentlich I hope so
hören hear
hundert hundred
innerhalb within
das **Jahr,** -e year
jawohl yes indeed
krank sick

die **Lehre,** -n teaching, rule
lehren teach
machen do, make
manchmal often
der **Mann,** ⁼er husband
das **Mittel,** - (**gegen**) remedy (for)
nun well
der **Onkel,** - uncle
ein paar a couple of
die **Rede,** -n speech
die **Regel,** -n rule
schlimm bad, serious
die **Schule,** -n school; **in die** ___ to school
sogar even
sowohl . . . als both . . . and, as well as
spazieren-gehen go for a walk
die **Sprache,** -n language
sprechen, sprach speak
statt instead of
täglich daily
das **Textbuch,** ⁼er textbook
trotz in spite of
unter among
der **Vater,** ⁼ father
das **Volk,** ⁼er people
während during
wegen on account of
wohnen live, reside
zwanzig twenty

LESSON 6

Other uses of the accusative, of the dative

6.1 **Additional uses of the accusative.** Besides the uses indicated in Lessons 2 and 4 the accusative is used:

(a) to denote definite time.

> **Diese Woche geht er weg.** *This week he is going away.*
> **Jeden Tag lernen wir etwas.** *Every day we learn something.*

(b) to denote extent of time or space.

> **Er blieb zwei Wochen.** *He stayed two weeks.*
> **eine lange Strecke gehen** *to go a long distance*

6.2 **Additional uses of the dative.** Besides the uses indicated in Lesson 4 the dative is used:

(a) to denote the indirect receiver (indirect object) of the action of the verb.

> **Ich bringe ihm das Essen.** *I am bringing him his food.*
> **Sie zeigt mir das Buch.** *She shows me the book.*

(b) to denote the person or thing interested in the situation involved (dative of interest).

Er kauft mir eine Tasse Kaffee. *He is buying me a cup of coffee.*
Ich besorge dem armen Mann allerlei. *I provide all sorts of things for the poor man.*

(c) to denote that from which something is taken or removed.

Der Mann nahm ihr das Geld weg. *The man took the money away from her.*

(d) after a number of verbs, such as:

antworten *to answer*	**gefallen** *to please*
begegnen *to meet*	**gehorchen** *to obey*
danken *to thank*	**gehören** *to belong to*
dienen *to serve*	**gelingen** *to succeed*
folgen *to follow*	**helfen** *to help*

Er hilft meinem Mann. *He helps my husband.*
Warum antworten Sie mir nicht? *Why don't you answer me?*

(e) after many adjectives, such as:

ähnlich *similar*	**fremd** *strange, foreign*
angenehm *agreeable, pleasant*	**gleich** *equal*
bekannt *known*	**verwandt** *related*

Das ist mir nicht bekannt. *That is not known to me.*

6.3 Order of objects. The indirect object precedes the direct object if the latter is a noun. If the direct object is a pronoun it precedes the indirect.

Ich bringe meinem Onkel sein Essen. *I bring my uncle his food.*
Ich bringe ihm sein Essen.
Ich bringe es meinem Onkel.
Ich bringe es ihm.

6.4 Uses of the article.

(a) In German the definite article is regularly used with a noun denoting a part of the body or part of the clothing, where in English a possessive adjective is used.

Legt die Hände auf den Tisch. *Put your hands on the table.*
Er kann die Schuhe nicht anziehen. *He can't put on his shoes.*

Lesson 6

Frequently, to show the possessor, the dative of interest is used. It is often referred to as the "dative of possession."

Ich lasse mir die Haare schneiden. *I am having my hair cut.*

(b) A predicate noun that denotes the occupation, profession, or nationality of the subject is used in German without any article.

Er war Arzt. *He was a doctor.*
Mein Mann ist Lehrer. *My husband is a teacher.*

When the predicate noun is modified by an adjective, however, the indefinite article is expressed.

Er war ein guter Arzt. *He was a good doctor.*

(c) The definite article is used with abstract nouns and with nouns denoting material, substance, etc. It is also used with the days of the week, months, and seasons.

Wir suchen nach der Wahrheit. *We are searching for truth.*
Das Wasser ist schwerer als die Luft. *Water is heavier than air.*
Er war am Montag hier. *He was here on Monday.*

GESPRÄCH

Frau Röhl: Guten Abend, Frau Schneider. Ein schöner Abend, nicht wahr?
Frau Schneider: Ja, und das ist mir besonders angenehm. Ich muß wieder zum Onkel von meinem Mann.
Frau Röhl: Geht's* ihm immer noch schlecht?   5
Frau Schneider: Es geht ihm schon viel besser. Aber er lebt da allein, und ich muß dem armen Mann in vielem helfen. Zum Beispiel kann er die Schuhe nicht anziehen, die Füße tun ihm weh. Da kann er nicht aus dem Hause gehen. Ich muß ihm jeden Tag das Essen bringen.   10
Frau Röhl: Wie lange kann das dauern?
Frau Schneider: Es kann noch zwei oder drei Wochen dauern. Aber das macht mir nichts aus*. Ich tue es gern, denn er hilft meinem Mann so oft mit seinem Geld.
Frau Röhl: Ja, aber müssen Sie nicht eine lange Strecke gehen?   15

[53]

Frau Schneider: Ach, es ist ja nur eine Viertelstunde*. Bei schönem Wetter ist mir das eigentlich* ein Genuß.

Frau Röhl: Ist Ihr Onkel ziemlich reich?

Frau Schneider: Reich nicht, aber er war früher Arzt und hat
20 sein Geld gespart*. Wenn man Lehrer ist*, wie mein Mann, ist das nicht so leicht. Aber jetzt muß ich gehen. Auf Wiedersehen, Frau Röhl.

Frau Röhl: Auf Wiedersehen.

*Geht's = Geht es
*das macht mir nichts aus That doesn't bother me
*die Viertelstunde, -n quarter of an hour

*eigentlich really
*hat . . . gespart saved
*Wenn man Lehrer ist When you are a teacher

LESESTÜCK

London ist die Hauptstadt von England, Paris ist die Hauptstadt von Frankreich, Rom ist die Hauptstadt Italiens, und Wien ist die Hauptstadt von Österreich.

In dieser Stadt lebte Beethoven und hier starb er im Jahre 1827
5 (achtzehnhundertsiebenundzwanzig). Schon während seines Lebens wurde er wegen seiner Musik sehr berühmt. Aber nicht nur wegen seiner Musik! Denn er war auch sehr exzentrisch. Zum Beispiel, er war oft tief in Gedanken. Dann vergaß er sich zu waschen. Sein Anzug war auch oft ganz vernachlässigt*.
10 Eines Tages sah ein junger Student Beethoven elegant gekleidet ins Kaffeehaus gehen. Das erstaunte ihn und er sprach den nächsten Abend davon zu seinem Lehrer, einem alten Freunde Beethovens.

Der Lehrer lachte. „Ach," sagte er, „du siehst Beethoven in
15 einem neuen Anzug und bist erstaunt. Ja, Beethoven ist ein großer Komponist*, aber leider hält er nichts auf sein Äußeres*, so müssen die Freunde ihm helfen. Wir sahen, zum Beispiel, Beethoven brauchte einen neuen Anzug. Also kauften wir einen und gingen damit am Abend zu ihm. Der Meister saß im
20 Schlafrock* am Pianoforte und spielte. Er sah uns gar nicht. Da nahmen wir ihm den alten, vernachlässigten Anzug vom Stuhl und ließen den neuen. Beethoven merkte nichts. Am nächsten Morgen zog er dann ganz einfach den neuen an*, wieder ohne

[54]

etwas zu merken*. So kommt er von Zeit zu Zeit an einen neuen Anzug."

*vernachlässigt neglected
*der Komponist', -en composer
*leider hält er nichts auf sein Äußeres unfortunately he doesn't care about his appearance

*der Schlafrock, =e dressing gown
*zog . . . an *past tense of* anziehen
*ohne etwas zu merken without noticing anything

EXERCISES

I. Answer with complete German sentences: (1) Wie geht's dem Onkel von Herrn Schneider? (2) Warum muß Frau Schneider ihm noch helfen? (3) Wie oft geht sie zu ihm? (4) Was bringt sie ihm? (5) Wie weit wohnt sie vom Onkel? (6) Warum hilft sie ihm gern? (7) Was ist die Hauptstadt von Österreich? (8) Was erstaunte einen jungen Studenten? (9) Warum erstaunte es ihn? (10) Wie kam Beethoven an einen neuen Anzug?

II. Replace each noun in the dative with the correct pronoun: (1) Die Frau bringt der Studentin das Essen. (2) Die Studentin dankt der Frau. (3) Otto antwortet seinem Onkel nicht. (4) Der Mann gibt Lisl den Käfig. (5) Die Freunde bringen Beethoven neue Anzüge.

III. Replace each accusative in sentences 1, 4, and 5 in exercise II with the correct pronoun.

IV. Replace both objects in sentences 1, 4, and 5 in exercise II with the correct pronouns.

V. Fill in the correct endings when necessary: (1) Er bleibt ein__ Woche auf d__ Lande. (2) Alle Leute müssen d__ Meister gehorchen. (3) Der Abend war d__ Frau sehr angenehm. (4) Die Karte ist nur ein__ Fuß lang. (5) Dieser Dialekt war m__ (for me) sehr schwer. (6) Diese Formen sind d__ Professor fremd. (7) Frau Schroeder half d__ Lehrer gar nicht.

VI. Translate into German: (1) Father helps me with the work. (2) The doctor gave the woman a cup of coffee. (3) The experiment lasts two hours. (4) That is very interesting to me, but not to her. (5) Every day the children play in school. (6) Franz met

the lady at home. (7) My foot hurts. (8) That doesn't please
me. (9) The students always answer the teacher. (10) The men
are staying a year in Germany.

VOCABULARY

ach oh
allein' alone
angenehm pleasant
anziehen put on
der Anzug, ⸗e suit
einfach simply
elegant' elegantly
(das) England England
erstaunen astonish; erstaunt astonished
das Essen, - meal, food
exzen'trisch eccentric
(das) Frankreich France
der Fuß, ⸗e foot
gar nicht not at all
der Gedanke, -n thought
gekleidet dressed
der Genuß, Genüsse pleasure, enjoyment
groß great
die Hauptstadt, ⸗e capital
(das) Ita'lien Italy
ja indeed
jeder every, each
lachen laugh
lang long

lassen, ließ leave
leben live
der Lehrer, - teacher
leicht easy
(das) London London
der Meister, - master
merken notice
nichts nothing
(das) Paris' Paris
reich rich
(das) Rom Rome
saß *past tense of* sitzen sit
schlecht badly
der Schuh, -e shoe
sich himself
sterben, starb die
die Strecke, -n distance
der Stuhl, ⸗e chair
tief deeply
waschen, wusch wash
weh tun, tat weh hurt
wenn when
das Wetter weather
wie like
(das) Wien Vienna
die Woche, -n week

LESSON 7

Declension of nouns

7.1 Nominative plural. There are four different ways in which the nominative plural of German nouns is formed. To the nominative singular is added:

(a) no ending   (c) **-er**
(b) **-e**   (d) **-(e)n**

Furthermore, in classes a and b the umlaut may be added, as in **der Vater, die Väter** and **die Nacht, die Nächte**, or not added, as in **der Onkel, die Onkel** and **der Tag, die Tage.** Class c always adds umlaut if possible and class d never.

Since there is in general no way of knowing in which class a German noun falls, the student must learn the plural of each noun as it enters his vocabulary (but see § 7.6).

7.2 Principal parts. The eight forms of a given noun are readily derived from three, called the "principal parts." They are: nominative singular, genitive singular, and nominative plural. In vocabularies and dictionaries these are indicated as follows:

der Tag, -es, -e   die Nacht, -, ⸚e

These mean that the genitive singular of **der Tag** is **des Tages**, of die Nacht it is **der Nacht**; the nominative plural of **der Tag** is **die Tage**, of **die Nacht** it is **die Nächte**. Frequently, as in this book, the genitive singular is not indicated except for those nouns discussed in §§ 7.4 (a) and (b).

7.3 Sample declensions. Most German nouns are declined (the eight forms given) on the basis of what has been presented up to this point. Here are a few sample declensions:

der	Vater	die	Mutter	das	Mädchen
des	Vaters	der	Mutter	des	Mädchens
dem	Vater	der	Mutter	dem	Mädchen
den	Vater	die	Mutter	das	Mädchen
die	Väter	die	Mütter	die	Mädchen
der	Väter	der	Mütter	der	Mädchen
den	Vätern	den	Müttern	den	Mädchen
die	Väter	die	Mütter	die	Mädchen
der	Tag	die	Nacht	das	Buch
des	Tages	der	Nacht	des	Buches
dem	Tag(e)	der	Nacht	dem	Buch(e)
den	Tag	die	Nacht	das	Buch
die	Tage	die	Nächte	die	Bücher
der	Tage	der	Nächte	der	Bücher
den	Tagen	den	Nächten	den	Büchern
die	Tage	die	Nächte	die	Bücher

der	Staat	der	Doktor †	die	Frau	das	Auge
des	Staates	des	Doktors	der	Frau	des	Auges
dem	Staat(e)	dem	Doktor	der	Frau	dem	Auge
den	Staat	den	Doktor	die	Frau	das	Auge
die	Staaten	die	Doktoren	die	Frauen	die	Augen
der	Staaten	der	Doktoren	der	Frauen	der	Augen
den	Staaten	den	Doktoren	den	Frauen	den	Augen
die	Staaten	die	Doktoren	die	Frauen	die	Augen

7.4 Exceptions.

(a) A small group of masculine nouns add **-n** or **-en** to every form but the nominative singular. The vocabulary or dictionary

† Other nouns ending in **-or** are declined like **Doktor**. The accent on these words is always on the next to the last syllable, e.g. **Dok′tor—Dokto′ren**.

indicates this in the principal parts thus: **der Student, -en, -en.**
The noun **der Herr** adds **-n** in the singular and **-en** in the plural.

der Student	der Knabe (boy)	der Herr
des Studenten	des Knaben	des Herrn
dem Studenten	dem Knaben	dem Herrn
den Studenten	den Knaben	den Herrn
die Studenten	die Knaben	die Herren
der Studenten	der Knaben	der Herren
den Studenten	den Knaben	den Herren
die Studenten	die Knaben	die Herren

(b) A very small group of masculine nouns add **-ns** in the
genitive singular and **-n** to the remaining forms. The principal
parts of one of these, **der Name**, are **der Name, -ns, -n.** Similar
to these is the important noun **das Herz**, which is declined:

das Herz	die Herzen
des Herzens	der Herzen
dem Herzen	den Herzen
das Herz	die Herzen

(c) Nouns derived from Latin sometimes have a plural in
-ien, as **das Mineral', -s, -ien.** In some Latin and Greek words
the final syllable of the singular becomes **-en** in the plural, as
das Muse'um, -s, -en, which stands for **das Museum, des Mu-
seums, die Museen;** or **das Drama, -s, -en,** in which **-en** indicates
die Dramen. A few nouns from English and French have a plural
in **-s.** These add no **-n** in the dative plural, as **den Radios.**

7.5 Proper names. Proper names add an **-s** to show possession,
unless the name ends in a sibilant. In the latter case the **-s** ending is omitted and in writing is indicated by an apostrophe. If
the article precedes the name, no **-s** is added.

Heinrichs   Klaus'   des alten Johann

7.6 Recognition aids. It was stated in § 7.1 that there is in general
no way of knowing in which class a German noun will fall without knowing the plural. However, the following statements, if
learned completely and correctly, will give the student the grammatical knowledge about many German nouns:

(a) All nouns formed with the suffixes **-chen** and **-lein** are neuter and add no ending in the plural. The umlaut is always present if possible in all forms of the noun. These nouns are diminutives; with a few important exceptions they are used either to denote a small version of what is represented by the simple word, or to indicate affection. The two suffixes are generally interchangeable when awkwardness of pronunciation is not involved.

das Kindchen or **das Kindlein,** but only **das Büchlein.**

(b) The infinitive of a verb may be capitalized and used as a noun. Such a noun is neuter, and the few that have a plural add no ending. Practically all these nouns denote the action of the verb.

das Trinken *drinking* **das Lernen** *learning*

(c) All nouns formed with the suffixes **-heit, -keit, -in,** and **-ung** are feminine and add **-en** to form the plural. Nouns ending in **-in** double the **n** before the plural ending to retain the correct pronunciation, just as the *t* is doubled in the English word *sitting*.

die Wahrheit, -en *truth* **die Geschwindigkeit, -en** *velocity*
die Wohnung, -en *residence* **die Lehrerin, -nen** *woman teacher*

GESPRÄCH

Margarete: Guten Morgen, Rudolf. Schon so früh auf?
Rudolf: Morgen, Grete! Ja, leider habe ich heute eine Prüfung in Geschichte.
Margarete: Aber doch nicht um acht Uhr!
5 **Rudolf:** Nein, erst heute nachmittag. Aber wir müssen uns doch vorbereiten. So treffen sich* einige von uns heute morgen bei Otto. Wir wollen das Material der Vorlesungen nochmal wiederholen und die Fragen von einigen alten Prüfungen besprechen.
Margarete: Ja, das ist bei solchen Kursen immer ein Problem.
10 Da gibt es so viele Details: Daten, Namen, Ereignisse.
Rudolf: Und das Dumme* ist, übermorgen ist die Biologieprüfung. Da haben wir wieder dasselbe in Grün*.
Margarete: Das ist aber doch deine letzte Prüfung dieses Semester, nicht wahr?

Rudolf: Ja, Gott sei Dank*.   15

Margarete: Na, ich muß gehen. Hals- und Beinbruch*!

Rudolf: Vielen Dank! Auf Wiedersehn!

*treffen sich meet
*das Dumme the stupid thing
*dasselbe in Grün the same prob-
lem
*Gott sei Dank thank God

*Hals- und Beinbruch I hope you
break your neck and leg (*traditional student remark to another who is about to take his
examinations*)

LESESTÜCK

Johann Wolfgang von Goethe ist der berühmteste Dichter der
deutschen Literatur. Er lebte von 1749 (siebzehnhundertneun-
undvierzig) bis 1832 (achtzehnhundertzweiunddreißig) und hat
während dieser Zeit viele Werke geschrieben*. Das bedeutendste
dieser Werke ist *Faust*.   5

Faust ist Professor an einer mittelalterlichen* Universität. Er ist
berühmt und viele Studenten kommen zu ihm. Aber er ist sehr
unglücklich, denn er ist ein äußerst* dynamischer Mensch, und
das begrenzte Leben eines Professors befriedigt ihn nicht. Also
macht er endlich einen Pakt mit dem Teufel. Der größte Teil 10
dieses langen Werkes zeigt uns dann Fausts weiteres Leben und
Streben.

Das Motiv eines unbefriedigten Menschen, der* einen Pakt
mit einem bösen Geist macht, ist uralt. Es ist natürlich nicht ein
ursprünglich deutsches Motiv, sondern gehört der Weltliteratur 15
an*. Das erste Werk mit diesem Motiv in der deutschen Literatur
war aber nicht das Drama *Faust* von Goethe, sondern die
Legende *Theophilus* von einer Nonne* aus dem zehnten Jahrhundert, Roswitha von Gandersheim.

*hat . . . geschrieben wrote
*mittelalterlich medieval
*äußerst extremely
*der who

*gehört der Weltliteratur an be-
longs to world literature
*die Nonne, -n nun

EXERCISES

I. Answer with complete German sentences: (1) Wann trifft
Margarete Otto? (2) Wohin geht er? (3) Was wollen die Stu-

[*61*]

denten machen? (4) Warum wollen sie das? (5) Was ist das Problem bei Kursen wie Geschichte oder Biologie? (6) Wer war Goethe? (7) Was ist das bedeutendste seiner Werke? (8) Was ist das Motiv dieses Werkes? (9) Ist das ein deutsches Motiv? (10) Wer schrieb das erste Werk in der deutschen Literatur mit diesem Motiv?

II. Decline in the singular and plural: das Leben, kein Professor, der Student, die Studentin, das Werk, kein Licht, die Literatur, keine Stadt.

III. Give the principal parts with the definite article of: Frau, Land, Feuer, Hand, Haus, Teil, Dichter, Prüfung, Semester, Problem.

IV. Translate into German: (1) Today Rudolf has a test in history. (2) It is not until this afternoon, however. (3) The students are reviewing the material of the lectures. (4) In such courses there are always problems. (5) Have you a test tomorrow or the day after? (6) Do you have many tests during the semester? (7) *Faust* is the work of the poet Goethe. (8) The motif is not, however, originally German. (9) The first work in German literature with this motif was not a drama. (10) Roswitha lived a long time ago.

VOCABULARY

bedeutendst most significant
befriedigen satisfy
begrenzt limited
berühmtest most famous
besprechen, besprach discuss
die **Biologie′prüfung, -en** examination in biology
bis until
böse evil
das **Datum, -en** date
das **Detail′** (*pronounced* **detaij′**), **-s** detail
der **Dichter, -** poet
das **Drama, -en** drama
das **Ereignis, -se** event
Faust *proper name*

die **Frage, -n** question
der **Geist, -er** spirit
größt largest
das **Jahrhundert, -e** century
der **Kursus, -se** course
die **Legen′de, -n** legend
letzt last
das **Material′, -ien** material
das **Motiv′, -e** motif
na well
nochmal once again
der **Pakt, -e** pact
das **Problem′, -e** problem
die **Prüfung, -en** examination, test
Roswitha von Gandersheim *proper name*

[62]

das **Streben** striving
der **Teufel, -** devil
Theophilus *proper name*
übermorgen day after tomorrow
acht Uhr eight o'clock
unbefriedigt dissatisfied
unglücklich unhappy
uralt ancient
ursprünglich originally

von by
vorbereiten prepare
die **Vorlesung, -en** lecture
weiter further
das **Werk, -e** work
wiederholen review
zehnt tenth
zeigen show

LESSON 8

Der-words and ein-words; interrogative pronouns

8.1 Limiting adjectives. There are two groups of words which in some way limit the nouns they modify and are therefore referred to as "limiting adjectives." These two groups are called "**der**-words" and "**ein**-words" after the definite and indefinite articles.

8.2 The *der*-words. The **der**-words are **der** itself and:

dieser *this*	**mancher** *many a, many, some*
jeder *each, every*	**solcher** *such a, such*
jener *that (particular one)*	**welcher** *which, what (a)*

Aside from **der** they are all declined like **dieser**, which is given as an example:

dieser Tag	diese Nacht	dieses Jahr
dieses Tages	dieser Nacht	dieses Jahres
diesem Tag	dieser Nacht	diesem Jahr
diesen Tag	diese Nacht	dieses Jahr
diese Tage	diese Nächte	diese Jahre
dieser Tage	dieser Nächte	dieser Jahre
diesen Tagen	diesen Nächten	diesen Jahren
diese Tage	diese Nächte	diese Jahre

[64]

Mancher, solcher, and **welcher** are sometimes used before the indefinite article. In this situation the stem forms **manch, solch,** and **welch** remain unchanged and the article is declined.

manch einem Mann   solch eines Staates

Dieser and **jener** are frequently used in the meanings *the latter* and *the former.*

Rudolf und Otto gehen in die Stadt, dieser geht zur Post und jener will nur seinen Freund begleiten. *Rudolf and Otto are going to town; the latter is going to the post office and the former only wants to keep his friend company.*

8.3 The *ein*-words. The **ein**-words consist of **ein, kein,** and the possessive adjectives. The last named modify a noun and are used to show the possessor of what the noun refers to. Since they are adjectives it is important to remember that the endings must agree in gender, number, and case with the noun modified. They are:

mein *my*	**unser** *our*
dein *your*	**euer** *your*
Ihr *your*	**Ihr** *your*
sein *his, its*	
ihr *her, its*	**ihr** *their*
sein *its*	

Like English *a, an,* German **ein** does not exist in the plural. **Kein** will serve as a model for the singular and plural.

kein Tag	keine Nacht	kein Jahr
keines Tages	keiner Nacht	keines Jahres
keinem Tag	keiner Nacht	keinem Jahr
keinen Tag	keine Nacht	kein Jahr
keine Tage	keine Nächte	keine Jahre
keiner Tage	keiner Nächte	keiner Jahre
keinen Tagen	keinen Nächten	keinen Jahren
keine Tage	keine Nächte	keine Jahre

It will be noticed that the **ein**-words have no endings in the masculine nominative singular and the neuter nominative and accusative singular.

In the inflected forms of **unser** and **euer** the **e** before the **r** may be dropped, or the **e** after the **r** if it is not final.

unsres *or* unsers   eurem *or* euerm

8.4 *Der*-words and *ein*-words as pronouns. Both the der-words and the ein-words may be used as pronouns. For the use of **der** as a pronoun see §§ 16.1 and 16.5. The other der-words have the same endings that they have as adjectives. When used as pronouns the ein-words have the endings of **dieser** (except that the neut. nom. and acc. sing. may be contracted, as meins, seins).

> **Kein Mensch war da. Es war keiner da.** *Nobody was there. There was nobody there.*
> **Sie hatte kein Buch und ich hatte auch keins.** *She had no book and I didn't have one, either.*

8.5 The interrogative pronoun. The interrogative pronoun is declined as follows:

wer *who*		was *what*	
wessen *whose*		wessen *of what* (rare)	
wem *(to) whom*		——	
wen *whom*		was *what*	

8.6 Interrogative compounds and expressions. When referring to a thing, **wo-** or **wor-** is used with prepositions instead of the forms of the interrogative pronoun. Compare § 5.6.

wofür *for what*   womit *with what*   worin *in what*

Was für ein, *what kind of (a),* and **was für,** *what kind of,* are indeclinable except for the word **ein** itself. The noun following has the case called for by its use in the sentence. **Was** and **für** may be separated by other words of the sentence.

> **Was für einen Anzug kaufen Sie?** *What kind of a suit are you buying?*
> **Was für ein Mann ist das?** *What kind of a man is that?*
> **Was hast du für Sachen drin?** *What sort of things have you in it?*

8.7 Special constructions with *dies, das,* and *es.* Dies ist and **dies sind** mean *this is* and *these are* and are followed by a noun in the singular and one in the plural respectively.

Das ist and das sind mean *that is* and *those are* and are followed by a singular and plural noun respectively.

Es ist and es sind mean *it is* and *they are* and are also followed
by a singular and plural noun respectively.

> **Dies ist mein Teil.** *This is my part.*
> **Welche Titel sind das?** *What titles are those?*
> **Es sind Detektivromane.** *They are detective stories.*

Es gibt, which takes a direct object in the accusative case,
means *there is* or *there are*, depending whether the object is singular or plural. It is used in making a general statement, not a
specific one. The idiom is also used in other tenses besides the
present.

> **Es gibt allerlei Menschen in dieser Welt.** *There are all kinds of
> people in this world.*
> **Aber es gab nur einen Alexander den Großen.** *But there was only
> one Alexander the Great.*

GESPRÄCH

Rudolf: Otto, was hast du heute vor*?
Otto: Ich habe allerlei zu tun, aber nichts Wichtiges*. Diese
Pakete muß ich zur Post tragen. Dann ist meine Füllfeder* ka-
putt*. Das muß ich auch besorgen.
Rudolf: Laß mich dir mit den Paketen helfen. Ich trage eins. 5
Kannst du solche großen Pakete mit der Post schicken?
Otto: Ich glaube schon. Diese habe ich schon gemessen* und
sie sind gerade klein genug.
Rudolf: Aber schwer sind sie. Was hast du für Sachen drin,
Backsteine*? 10
Otto: Nein, dies sind Bücher und das ist meine Wäsche*.
Rudolf: Ja, aber deine Wäsche wiegt so schwer. Warum schickst
du deine Wäsche nicht jede Woche nach Hause?
Otto: Ich vergesse das immer.
Rudolf: Wem schickst du die Bücher? 15
Otto: Meinem Bruder. Es sind Detektivromane*. Mit seinen drei
Kindern hat er wenig Geld für so etwas und solche Romane liest
er gern.

Rudolf: Welche Titel* sind das? Vielleicht kann ich dir auch ein
20 paar für ihn geben.

Otto: Das wäre* freundlich von dir. Aber hier sind wir schon.
Vielen Dank, Rudolf.

Rudolf: Wofür? Es ist gern geschehen*. Das nächste Mal hilfst
du mir. Also, grüß Gott.

25 **Otto:** Grüß Gott, Rudolf.

*hast . . . vor plan, have in mind
*nichts Wichtiges nothing impor-
tant
*die Füllfeder, -n fountain pen
*kaputt' broken, out of order
*habe . . . gemessen measured
*der Backstein, -e brick

*die Wäsche laundry
*der Detektiv'roman, -e detective
story
*der Titel, - title
*wäre would be
*Es ist gern geschehen I was glad
to do it

LESESTÜCK

Es* kam eines Abends ein hungriger und müder Wanderer in
ein kleines Gasthaus in Tirol*. Er aß und trank und ging dann
hinauf in die Schlafstube*, wo er sich in eines der Betten legte*.
Nach einer Weile kam ein anderer Gast, ein junger Bauer. Dieser
5 zog sich aus*, zog ein Nachthemd an*, und ging dann auch zu
Bett. Plötzlich stand er aber wieder auf*, holte ein Paar Pantoffel*
aus seinem Bündel*, band die Pantoffel an die Füße und legte
sich dann wieder ins Bett. Der Wanderer wurde hierüber neugierig und fragte den Bauer: „Was machst du denn da? Warum
10 ziehst du Pantoffel an*, wenn du schlafen gehst? Noch nie habe
ich so etwas gesehen*, einen Menschen mit Pantoffeln an ins Bett
gehen." „Ja, lieber Freund," sagte der Bauer, „die Sache ist
nämlich die. Einmal trat ich im Traum in eine Glasscherbe*. Ich
hatte solch große Schmerzen im Traume, daß ich nie wieder
15 barfuß schlief."

*Es There
*(das) Tirol *a province of west-
ern Austria*
*die Schlafstube, -n bedroom
*sich . . . legte lay down
*zog sich aus undressed
*zog ein Nachthemd an put on a
nightshirt

*stand . . . auf got up
*der Pantof'fel, - slipper
*das Bündel, - bundle
*ziehst . . . an put on
*habe . . . gesehen have seen,
saw
*die Glasscherbe, -n piece of
broken glass

[68]

Lesson 8

EXERCISES

I. Answer with complete German sentences: (1) Was hat Otto heute vor? (2) Wohin geht er mit seinen Paketen? (3) Warum ist eins davon so schwer? (4) Wieviele Pakete nimmt Rudolf? (5) Wohin schickt Otto seine Wäsche? (6) Was für Bücher liest Ottos Bruder gern? (7) In was für ein Gasthaus kam eines Abends ein Wanderer? (8) Hatte der Gast sein eigenes Schlafzimmer? (9) Wer kam später in dieses Zimmer? (10) Warum schlief dieser nie barfuß?

II. Decline in the singular and plural: dieses Paket, kein Gast, jener Bauer, manches Buch, unser Professor, ihr Bett, sein Bruder.

III. Fill in the correct endings wherever necessary: (1) Mit solch__ Paketen geht man nicht zur Post. (2) Dies__ Studentin bringt ihr__ Bruder kein__ Bücher. (3) Ich sehe Ihr__ Haus aber nicht unser__. (4) In was für ein__ Haus wohnen solch__ Leute? (5) An jed__ Tisch stehen Stühle. (6) Deutsch ist für manch__ Studenten (*singular*) nicht leicht. (7) Frau Schneider geht zum Onkel ihr__ Mannes. (8) Der Mann stand zwischen dies__ Frauen. (9) Grete blieb ein__ ganzen Nachmittag in dem Laboratorium.

IV. Translate into German: (1) These are our packages and that is his laundry. (2) Whose package is this on the table? (3) What kind of books do you like to read? (4) His uncle lives in the city, mine lives in (auf) the country. (5) Where is your brother now? (6) In our class we have ten male students and five co-eds. (7) Such a man never goes to bed early. (8) What kind of a girl is she? (9) Who is that professor? (10) Why is he opposed to her husband?

VOCABULARY

allerlei all sorts of things
ander other
barfuß barefoot
besorgen take care of
das Bett, -en bed

binden, band tie
der Bruder, = brother
das Buch, =er book
daß that
einmal once

[*69*]

etwas; so ___ such a thing, such things
fragen ask
freundlich kind, friendly
der Gast, ⸗e guest
das Gasthaus, ⸗er inn
genug enough
gerade exactly
hierüber about this
hinauf up
holen get, fetch
jung young
klein small
müde tired
nämlich namely, for
nie never; noch ___ never yet

das Paar, -e pair
das Paket', -e package
die Post mail, post office
der Roman', -e novel
die Sache, -n thing
schicken send
schlafen, schlief sleep
der Schmerz, -en pain
tragen, trug carry
der Traum, ⸗e dream
treten, trat step
vielleicht perhaps
der Wanderer, - wanderer, traveler
wenig little
wiegen, wog weigh

LESSON 9

Declension of adjectives

9.1 Descriptive adjectives. The vast majority of adjectives are of the type that describe and hence are called "descriptive" adjectives. A descriptive adjective may be used in two ways:

(a) as a **predicate** adjective (§ 1.6). The stem form of the adjective is used in German, no matter what the gender or number of the subject.

> **Der Mann ist reich.** *The man is rich.*
> **Die Tante ist reich.** *The aunt is rich.*
> **Die Mädchen sind reich.** *The girls are rich.*

(b) as an **attributive** adjective. This means that it stands before the noun it modifies. *An attributive adjective in German always has a case ending* in agreement with the noun it modifies.

> **Der reiche Onkel lebt in Deutschland.** *The rich uncle lives in Germany.*

9.2 Adjective endings. There are two sets of endings for the attributive adjective. One set, called the "strong" endings, is like the endings of **dieser** except for the masculine and neuter genitive singular.

	singular		plural
-er	-e	-es	-e
-en	-er	-en	-er
-em	-er	-em	-en
-en	-e	-es	-e

The other set is called the "weak" endings.

-e	-e	-e	-en
-en	-en	-en	-en
-en	-en	-en	-en
-en	-e	-e	-en

9.3 If one or more adjectives of any type stand before a noun the attributive adjective has the strong ending if no strong ending precedes it; it has the weak ending if a strong ending does precede it. *Two or more attributive adjectives always have the same ending.* In practice there are three possibilities: (1) that a **der** word precedes the attributive adjective, (2) that an **ein** word precedes it, (3) that no limiting adjective precedes it.

9.4 Adjectives after *der* words. If a **der** word precedes it, the attributive adjective has the weak ending.

dieser	gute	Mann	diese	schöne	Frau
dieses	guten	Mannes	dieser	schönen	Frau
diesem	guten	Mann	dieser	schönen	Frau
diesen	guten	Mann	diese	schöne	Frau

diese	guten	Männer	diese	schönen	Frauen
dieser	guten	Männer	dieser	schönen	Frauen
diesen	guten	Männern	diesen	schönen	Frauen
diese	guten	Männer	diese	schönen	Frauen

dieses	kleine	Kind
dieses	kleinen	Kindes
diesem	kleinen	Kind
dieses	kleine	Kind

diese	kleinen	Kinder
dieser	kleinen	Kinder
diesen	kleinen	Kindern
diese	kleinen	Kinder

9.5 Adjectives after *ein* words. If an **ein** word precedes it, the attributive adjective has the strong ending when the **ein** word has none (see § 8.3), the weak ending when the **ein** word has an ending.

kein	guter	Mann	keine	schöne	Frau
keines	guten	Mannes	keiner	schönen	Frau
keinem	guten	Mann	keiner	schönen	Frau
keinen	guten	Mann	keine	schöne	Frau
keine	guten	Männer	keine	schönen	Frauen
keiner	guten	Männer	keiner	schönen	Frauen
keinen	guten	Männern	keinen	schönen	Frauen
keine	guten	Männer	keine	schönen	Frauen

kein	kleines	Kind
keines	kleinen	Kindes
keinem	kleinen	Kind
kein	kleines	Kind
keine	kleinen	Kinder
keiner	kleinen	Kinder
keinen	kleinen	Kindern
keine	kleinen	Kinder

9.6 Adjectives not preceded by a *der* or *ein* word. If no limiting adjective precedes it, the attributive adjective has the strong ending.

guter	Mann	schöne	Frau	kleines	Kind
guten	Mannes	schöner	Frau	kleinen	Kindes
gutem	Mann	schöner	Frau	kleinem	Kind
guten	Mann	schöne	Frau	kleines	Kind
gute	Männer	schöne	Frauen	kleine	Kinder
guter	Männer	schöner	Frauen	kleiner	Kinder
guten	Männern	schönen	Frauen	kleinen	Kindern
gute	Männer	schöne	Frauen	kleine	Kinder

9.7 Adjectives after other limiting adjectives. In the plural the strong declension of the attributive adjective is used after certain limiting words, like **andere, einige, viele.** After **alle** the weak forms are used.

> **einige reiche Tanten** *some rich aunts*
> **alle reichen Tanten** *all rich aunts*

9.8 Adjectives used as nouns. If an adjective is capitalized and used as a noun, it is still declined as an adjective.

> Alte und Junge *old and young*
> Der Alte ging weg. *The old man went away.*

Certain words that we think of as nouns are adjectival in German. An example is the word for *relative*. It is based on the adjective **verwandt.**

> Hat sie Verwandte dort? *Has she relatives there?*
> Er ist ein Verwandter von mir. *He is a relative of mine.*

After **nichts, etwas, viel,** and a few other such indefinite pronouns, the adjective is capitalized and used with the neuter strong ending.

> nichts Neues *nothing new*   viel Gutes *much that is good*

After **alles** the weak ending is used.

> alles Schöne *everything beautiful*

9.9 Irregularities. The adjective **hoch** changes the **ch** to silent **h** before an ending beginning with a vowel.

> Das Fenster liegt hoch. *The window is situated high up.*
> ein hohes Fenster *a high window*

Adjectives ending in -el, -en, and -er may drop the **e** before an ending beginning with a vowel.

> ein edler Mann (edel) *a noble man*
> der goldne Ring (golden) *the golden ring*

9.10 Adverbs. The stem form of the adjective, without further ending, is used as the adverb.

> Der Mann läuft schnell. *The man runs fast.*

An uninflected adjectival-type word standing somewhere before a noun is therefore an adverb and does not modify the noun.

> Das ist ein ziemlich reicher Mann. *That is a fairly rich man.*

9.11 Word order of predicate adjectives. The predicate adjective is placed as near the end of the clause as it can come, following adverbs and adverbial phrases, but not verb forms. The predicate adjective is an important element and this position tends to emphasize it.

Mein Büro ist am Tage heiß. *My office is hot during the day.*
Der Professor bleibt seinen Studenten immer freundlich gesinnt.
The professor always remains kindly disposed toward his students.

GESPRÄCH

Herr Schmidt: Guten Morgen, Herr Pfeiffer. Ein herrlicher Tag, nicht wahr?
Herr Pfeiffer: Das kann man wohl sagen. An so einem schönen Morgen habe ich keine Lust, im Büro zu sitzen.
Schmidt: Ich muß nicht nur im Büro sitzen, sondern auch die ganze Arbeit zu Hause machen. Meine Frau macht nämlich eine Reise nach Kalifornien.
Pfeiffer: Hat sie Verwandte dort?
Schmidt: Nur eine alte Tante. Aber die ist ziemlich reich und hat ihr das Reisegeld* geschickt*, denn sie will noch einmal ihre liebe Nichte sehen. Ich wünsche, mein reicher Onkel in Deutschland würde mir auch das Reisegeld schicken*, ihn zu besuchen.
Pfeiffer: Sie haben also einen Onkel da drüben*?
Schmidt: Ja, er ist der einzige von meinen Verwandten, der noch da lebt. Er hat eine ganze Menge Geld, aber er scheint kein großes Interesse daran zu haben, seinen lieben Neffen zu sehen*.
Pfeiffer: Das ist wirklich schade. Aber Gott sei Dank, daß es noch einige reiche Tanten gibt, die auch gute Herzen haben. Glücklicherweise* habe ich auch eine. Sie lebt hier ganz in der Nähe und schickt mir also kein Reisegeld. Dafür hilft sie mir mit meinem neuen Haus.
Schmidt: Ja, so geht's im Leben*. Meine Frau reist nach Kalifornien, Sie kriegen* ein neues Haus. Und ich, ich kann hier sitzen und fleißig arbeiten und mir einmal in der Woche ein kleines Glas Bier leisten*.
Pfeiffer: Nun, so schlimm ist es nun doch nicht.
Schmidt: Sie haben recht. Das eigentlich Unangenehme ist, daß

ich nicht gern allein lebe. Aber hier kommt die Elektrische*.
Also, bis morgen, Herr Pfeiffer!

30 **Pfeiffer:** Auf Wiedersehn, Herr Schmidt!

*das **Reisegeld** fare
*hat . . . geschickt sent
*würde . . . schicken would send
*da drüben over there
*daran . . . zu sehen in seeing
*glücklicherweise fortunately

*so geht's im **Leben** that's life
*kriegen get
*leisten afford
*die **Elektrische** (electric) street-
car

LESESTÜCK

Robert Schumann und Richard Wagner waren zwei deutsche
Komponisten* des neunzehnten Jahrhunderts. Schumann wurde
1819 (achtzehnhundertundneunzehn) geboren* and starb 1856
(achtzehnhundertsechsundfünfzig). Wagner wurde 1813 (acht-
5 zehnhundertunddreizehn) geboren und starb 1883 (achtzehn-
hundertdreiundachtzig). Sie lebten also ungefähr zur gleichen
Zeit. Aber ihre Musik war grundverschieden*, und so grundverschieden wie ihre Musik waren auch sie selbst. So erzählt der
Wiener Musikkritiker* Eduard Hanslick* folgendes:
10 Als junger Mensch besuchte ich Robert Schumann in Dresden.
Wir sprachen über dieses und jenes und endlich kamen wir auf
Richard Wagner. „Verkehren Sie mit Wagner?" fragte ich Schumann. „Nein," erwiderte dieser, „für mich ist Wagner unmöglich; er ist gewiß ein begabter Mensch, aber er redet in einem
15 fort. Man kann doch nicht immer reden!" Am nächsten Tage
besuchte ich Richard Wagner. Der junge Meister kam nach einer
Weile auf Schumann zu sprechen. „Wir stehen äußerlich gut miteinander*, aber mit Schumann kann man nicht verkehren, denn
er redet gar nicht. Nach meiner Ankunft aus Paris besuchte ich
20 ihn, erzählte ihm viel Interessantes über die Pariser Oper, die
Konzerte, die Komponisten—Schumann sah mich unbeweglich
an* oder schaute in die Luft, aber er sagte kein Wort. Da sprang
ich auf* und lief fort. Ein unmöglicher Mensch!"

*der **Komponist'**, -en, -en composer
*wurde . . . geboren was born

*grundverschieden fundamentally
different
*der **Musikkritiker**, - music critic

[76]

*Hanslick (1825-1904) *and Wag-*
ner later became bitter enemies.
*Wir . . . miteinander We are
on good terms superficially

*sah . . . an looked at
*sprang . . . auf jumped up

EXERCISES

I. Answer with complete German sentences: (1) Was für ein Tag war es? (2) Wann saß Herr Pfeiffer nicht gern in seinem Büro? (3) Was mußte Herr Schmidt zu Hause machen? (4) Warum mußte er das? (5) Wo wohnte Frau Schmidts reiche Tante? (6) Hatte Herr Schmidt reiche Verwandte? (7) Was kriegte Herr Schmidt von seinem reichen Onkel? (8) Haben alle reichen Tanten gute Herzen? (9) Was kriegte Herr Pfeiffer? (10) Wie arbeitete Herr Schmidt? (11) Wer waren Robert Schumann und Richard Wagner? (12) Wer besuchte sie? (13) Wo lebten die beiden zu dieser Zeit? (14) Was erzählte Wagner Schumann über Paris? (15) Was sagte Schumann dazu? (16) Was für ein Mensch war Schumann in Wagners Augen?

II. Decline in the singular and plural: kein schöner Morgen, ihre liebe Nichte, gutes Herz, unser neues Haus, das letzte Jahr, der westliche Teil, jene große Universität, dieser müde Wanderer, dieses hohe Zimmer, der Verwandte, kein Verwandter, ihr alter Onkel.

III. Fill in the correct endings: (1) Sein___ jung___ Frau macht mit ihr___ klein___ Kindern eine Reise nach Deutschland. (2) Sie will ihr___ alt___ Vater und ihr___ alt___ Mutter sehen. (3) Aber klein___ Kinder werden von ein___ so lang___ Reise müde. (4) Viel___ alt___ Leute reisen auch nicht gern über den Ozean. (5) Wir wünschen ihm alles Gut___ und nichts Schlimm___. (6) Er hat groß___ Interesse daran, ein___ gut___ Anzug zu wählen. (7) Deutsch und Englisch sind verwandt___ Sprachen. (8) Das machen wir nur bei schön___ Wetter.

IV. Translate into German: (1) Now I must work the whole day in my hot office. (2) Americans are usually friendly people. (3) My relatives are traveling to the western part of the country. (4) Not all students find great difficulties in the German language. (5) There is nothing heavy in this package. (6) He sat there a long time and said not a word. (7) Dresden is a beautiful city. (8) The southern part of Germany is very beautiful. (9) Some people speak rather slowly. (10) Is that really bad?

VOCABULARY

die **Ankunft, ⁼e** arrival
die **Arbeit, -en** work, labor
arbeiten work
begabt talented
besuchen visit
das **Büro', -s** office
(das) **Dresden** *German city*
noch einmal once more
einzig only
erwidern reply
erzählen narrate, tell
fort; in einem ___ constantly
ganz all
gewiß certain
das **Glas, ⁼er** glass
gleich same
gut kind
herrlich splendid, glorious
das **Herz, -ens, -en** heart
interessant' interesting
das **Interes'se, -n (an)** interest (in)
(das) **Kalifornien** California
das **Konzert', -e** concert
lieb dear
die **Luft** air
die **Lust, ⁼e** desire
die **Menge, -n** amount
morgen tomorrow

nach to
die **Nähe** vicinity; **in der ___**
  nearby
der **Neffe, -n, -n** nephew
neunzehn nineteenth
die **Nichte, -n** niece
die **Oper, -n** opera
Pari'ser (of) Paris
recht right; **___ haben** be right
reden talk
die **Reise, -n** trip
reisen travel
schade too bad
schauen look
scheinen, schien seem
selbst themselves
so such
die **Tante, -n** aunt
unangenehm unpleasant
unbeweglich immovable
ungefähr about, approximately
unmöglich impossible
verkehren associate
verwandt relative
Wiener (of) Vienna
wirklich real
wohl indeed
wünschen wish

LESSON 10

Present and past perfect tenses of weak verbs

10.1 Formation of present and past perfect. The present perfect tense is formed by using the past participle of the verb in question with the present tense of the auxiliary verb; the past perfect (or pluperfect) tense is formed by using the past participle of the verb in question with the past tense of the auxiliary verb. This produces such forms as:

Er hat das Buch gekauft. *He has bought the book.*
Er hatte das Buch gekauft. *He had bought the book.*

10.2 Formation of the past participle. The past participle of a weak verb (see § 3.1) is formed by prefixing **ge-** to the stem and adding **-(e)t** to the stem.

sagen—gesagt   arbeiten—gearbeitet

One exception to this is the class of verbs ending in **-ieren** (see § 0.5) which forms the past participle without **ge-**, as **studieren—studiert**. The other exception consists of verbs with the prefixes **be-**, **emp-**, **ent-**, **er-**, **ge-**, **ver-**, and **zer-**, which also do not add **ge-** to the past participle. These verbs are discussed in Lesson 17.

10.3 Use of *sein* and *haben* as auxiliaries. In German all transitive verbs (see § 2.7) and most intransitive verbs take **haben** as the auxiliary of the perfect tenses.

hat gesagt   hat geregnet

If an intransitive verb shows change of position or change of condition, the auxiliary is **sein**.

Er ist weit gewandert. *He has wandered far.*

10.4 Principal parts of a verb. The infinitive, the third singular of the past tense, the third singular of the present perfect, and the third singular of the present tense are called the principal parts of a verb. From these four forms the whole set of forms of a given verb can be derived, just as in English the whole conjugal system of the verbs *talk* and *go* can be derived from the forms *talk, talked, talked,* and *go, went, gone.*

sagen	sagte	hat gesagt	sagt
studieren	studierte	hat studiert	studiert
wandern	wanderte	ist gewandert	wandert

From now on the vocabulary will show when **sein** is the auxiliary by including (**ist**) with the principal parts.

10.5 Model conjugations of the present and past perfect tenses. The present perfect and past perfect tenses of **sagen** and **wandern** are:

ich habe gesagt	ich bin gewandert
du hast gesagt	du bist gewandert
er hat gesagt	er ist gewandert
wir haben gesagt	wir sind gewandert
ihr habt gesagt	ihr seid gewandert
sie haben gesagt	sie sind gewandert
ich hatte gesagt	ich war gewandert
du hattest gesagt	du warst gewandert
er hatte gesagt	er war gewandert
wir hatten gesagt	wir waren gewandert
ihr hattet gesagt	ihr wart gewandert
sie hatten gesagt	sie waren gewandert

10.6   Word order. As seen from the above, the auxiliary is the inflected part of the verb. It is therefore the second element in statements, and the first in questions that are not introduced by an interrogative word.

> **Ich habe das Bild überall gezeigt.** *I have been showing the picture everywhere.*
> **Das hatten wir eigentlich nicht geplant.** *We really hadn't planned that.*
> **Haben Sie gestern die Vorlesung gehört?** *Did you hear the lecture yesterday?*

10.7   The present participle. The present participle is formed by adding **-end** to the stem of the verb. If the stem ends in **-er** or **-el** the participial ending is **-nd.** In German the present participle is most frequently used as an adjective.

> **die folgende Anekdote** *the following anecdote*
> **der wandernde Student** *the wandering student*

GESPRÄCH

Robert: Nun sage mir, Paul, was hast du gestern gemacht? Ich habe dich überall gesucht.

Paul: Wir sind nach Wilmannsdorf gewandert.

Robert: Ja, was hat euch denn bewogen, so einen gottverlassenen* Ort zu besuchen?   5

Paul: Das hatten wir eigentlich nicht geplant. Ich hatte nur meiner Frau gesagt, wir sollten* ein bißchen in die frische Luft hinauswandern, wir bleiben zu viel im Hause. Das war am vorigen Freitag. Am Samstag hat's geregnet und am Sonntag war es so fürchterlich kalt. Also mußten wir bis gestern warten.   10

Robert: Da habt ihr euch einen wirklich schönen Tag gewählt. Ich wollte mit dir Tennis spielen, aber dann habe ich den ganzen Nachmittag im Garten gearbeitet. Habt ihr euch wenigstens in Wilmannsdorf gut amüsiert*?

Paul: Ja, das haben wir. Wir haben ein ganz kleines Wirtshaus   15 gefunden*, wo man im Freien sitzen kann und wo das Bier sehr gut ist. Da haben wir auch gespeist. Im ganzen hat unser Ausflug* acht Stunden gedauert.

[*81*]

Robert: Das erklärt mir immer noch nicht, weshalb ihr Wilmanns-
20 dorf gewählt habt.

Paul: Ich habe dir schon gesagt, wir hatten es nicht geplant. Wir
haben uns einfach auf den Weg gemacht* und sind dann der
Nasenspitze* gefolgt. Die hat uns dahin geführt.

*gottverlassen godforsaken	*der **Ausflug**, ⁼e excursion, jaunt
*sollten ought to	*uns auf den Weg gemacht
*Habt ihr euch gut amüsiert?	started out
Did you have a good time?	*die **Nasenspitze**, -n tip of the
*gefunden found	nose

LESESTÜCK

Heutzutage sehen wir in der Welt einen intensiven Glaubenskampf*. Es ist der Kampf des neuen „Glaubens," des Kommu-
nismus, gegen die traditionellen Religionen im Osten sowie im
Westen. Zu Zeiten ist er offen und blutig, zu Zeiten ist er weniger
5 offen, aber immer ist er intensiv und konsequent*.

Diesen Kampf sieht man natürlich besonders in den Ländern
oder Länderteilen* unter kommunistischer Domination, so wie
z. B. in der Ostzone Deutschlands. Und da kommt dann die
Frage: Was ist eigentlich die Situation in Deutschland über-
10 haupt? Und welchen Einfluß, welchen Erfolg kann der Kom-
munismus gegen die traditionellen Konfessionen in Deutschland
haben?

Diese Frage ist keine eitle, denn die soziale und politische
Entwicklung nicht nur Deutschlands, sondern des ganzen
15 Westens hängt von der Beantwortung dieser Frage ab*. Daher
ist ein Vergleich der konfessionellen Situation vor dem Krieg
und jetzt nicht nur interessant, sondern äußerst wichtig.

1939 (neunzehnhundertneununddreißig) waren 60,6% (sechzig
Komma sechs Prozent) der Bevölkerung evangelisch*, 33,3%
20 (dreiunddreißig Komma drei Prozent) katholisch, 6,1% (sechs
Komma eins Prozent) anderer Konfessionen und Konfessionslose*. Vorwiegend* protestantisch waren der Norden und Osten,
katholisch der Süden und Westen. Heutzutage ist das Bild folgendes: Westdeutschland: Protestanten 51,2 (einundfünfzig
25 Komma zwei), Katholiken 45,2 (fünfundvierzig Komma zwei),

andere Gemeinschaften und Konfessionslose 3,6 (drei Komma sechs); Ostzone: Protestanten 80,2 (achtzig Komma zwei), Katholiken 12,7 (zwölf Komma sieben), andere Konfessionen und Konfessionslose 7,1 (sieben Komma eins).

Geographisch gesehen* ist die Verteilung der Konfessionen 30 also noch so ziemlich dieselbe wie vor dem Krieg. Aber durch den Zuwachs an* Katholiken—ein großer Teil der Flüchtlinge und Vertriebenen* sind katholisch—sowie infolge der Konzentrierung* des katholischen Teils der Bevölkerung in der Bundesrepublik* hat dieser Teil erheblich an Bedeutung gewonnen*. 35 Dieses wird nicht nur großen Einfluß auf die Stabilität der traditionellen Konfessionen haben*, sondern auch auf die gesamte Weiterentwicklung* Deutschlands.

Zum Schluß können wir noch sagen, in Deutschland, gerade wie in den Vereinigten Staaten, gibt es keine Staatskirche*. Aber 40 eines ist doch anders. In den Vereinigten Staaten liegt die Finanzierung* der Religionsgemeinschaften* in privaten Händen. In Deutschland kommt das Geld zur Finanzierung der Kirchen nicht von privater Seite, sondern von einer allgemeinen Kirchensteuer*.
45

*der **Glaubenskampf** religious war, struggle
*konsequent consistent, logical
*die **Länderteile** sections of countries
*hängt . . . ab depends
*evange'lisch protestant
*konfessionslos without denomination, non-churchgoer
*vorwiegend predominant
*gesehen seen
*der **Zuwachs an** increase in
*der **Vertriebene** displaced person

*die **Konzentrierung**, -en concentration
*die **Bundesrepublik** Federal Republic
*hat . . . gewonnen an gained in
*wird . . . haben will have
*die **Weiterentwicklung**, -en further development
*die **Staatskirche** state church
*die **Finanzierung**, -en financing
*die **Religionsgemeinschaft**, -en church group
*die **Kirchensteuer**, -n church tax

EXERCISES

I. Answer with complete German sentences: (1) Wo war Paul gestern? (2) Mit wem war er da? (3) Was hatte Robert gestern gemacht? (4) Hatte Paul auch am Samstag einen Spaziergang

[83]

gemacht? (5) Warum nicht? (6) Was für einen Kamp finden wir heute in der Welt? (7) Was ist das Charakteristische an diesem Kampf? (8) Wo sieht man den Kampf besonders? (9) Warum ist die Stabilität der traditionellen Konfessionen besonders wichtig in Deutschland? (10) Wie bekommen (get) die Kirchen in Deutschland ihr Geld?

II. Conjugate the following in the present and past perfect tenses: (1) Ich plane eine Reise. (2) Ich wandere nach Wilmannsdorf. (3) Ich arbeite den ganzen Tag. (4) Ich folge meiner Nasenspitze.

III. Give the principal parts of: glauben, haben, spielen, warten, hören, setzen, reisen, lieben.

IV. Translate into German, using the present perfect tense for each English past tense: (1) It rained the whole afternoon. (2) The students had planned their work well. (3) Robert followed his wife into the garden. (4) His aunt has often sent him money. (5) Yesterday he worked for his uncle all day. (6) The northern part of Germany is predominantly protestant, the southern part is predominantly catholic. (7) There is no state church in Germany, but there is a general church tax. (8) He traveled to Germany last year. (9) I played tennis with him three days ago. (10) Goethe selected the Faust theme (das Faustmotiv).

VOCABULARY

allgemein general
anders different
die **Bedeutung, -en** significance
die **Bevölkerung, -en** population
bewegen, bewog move, induce
das **Bild, -er** picture
blutig bloody
daher therefore
dahin to that place, there
die **Domination'** domination
eitel vain
der **Erfolg, -e** success
erheblich considerable
erklären explain

der **Flüchtling, -e** fugitive
frei free; ___ **haben** be off, have off; **im Freien** in the open, out of doors
der **Freitag, -e** Friday
frisch fresh
führen lead
fürchterlich frightful, fearful
im ganzen on the whole
der **Garten, =** garden
die **Gemeinschaft, -en** congregation
geographisch geographic
gesamt total

gestern yesterday
der **Glaube**, -ns, -n belief
heutzutage in these days
hinauswandern (ist) wander out
infolge as a result of
intensiv' intensive
kalt cold
der **Kampf**, ⸗e fight, struggle
der **Katholik'**, -en, -en Catholic
katho'lisch catholic
die **Kirche**, -n church
der **Kommunis'mus** communism
kommuni'stisch communistic
die **Konfession'**, -en creed
konfessionell' pertaining to creed
der **Krieg**, -e war
das **Land**, ⸗er country
liegen, lag be situated
der **Mittwoch**, -e Wednesday
mußten had to
der **Norden** north
offen open
der **Ort**, -e *or* ⸗er place, village
der **Osten** east
die **Ostzone** east zone
planen plan
poli'tisch political
privat' private
der **Protestant'**, -en, -en Protestant
protestan'tisch protestant
das **Prozent'**, -e per cent
regnen rain

die **Religion'**, -en religion
der **Samstag**, -e Saturday
der **Schluß**, ⸗sse conclusion
die **Seite**, -n side
die **Situation'**, -en situation
sowie as well as
sozial' social
speisen eat
die **Stabilität'** stability
die **Stunde**, -n hour
suchen look for
der **Süden** south
das **Tennis** tennis
traditionell' traditional
überall everywhere
überhaupt in general
der **Vergleich**, -e comparison
die **Verteilung**, -en distribution
vor before
vorig last, previous
wandern (ist) wander, hike
der **Weg**, -e way; **uns auf den __**
machen start out
weniger less
wenigstens at least
weshalb why
(das) **Westdeutschland** West
Germany
der **Westen** west
wollte wanted to
so ziemlich pretty much
zu at, for

LESSON 11

Present and past perfect tenses of strong verbs

11.1 Formation of present and past perfect. Everything said in Lesson 10 about the formation of the perfect tenses of weak verbs applies to the formation of the same tenses of strong verbs, once the difference in the past participle forms has been learned.

11.2 Past participles of strong verbs. The past participle of a strong verb is formed by prefixing **ge-** to the stem (but see § 10.2), and adding **-en.** Furthermore the stem syllable will have a vowel that depends on the class to which the verb belongs. There are several classes of strong verbs, and within each class the verbs exhibit the same vowel change, called **Ablaut** in German, just as in English *write, ride, stride, smite, strive,* and *drive* all exhibit the same vowel change, *i–o–i.* In Appendix D the most important strong verbs with their principal parts are listed according to classes. The student, however, should learn the vowel change of each new strong verb that he encounters. From now on the lesson vocabulary will list the vowel changes that a strong verb undergoes in the past tense, the past participle,

[86]

and (if it occurs) in the third singular of the present tense. The general vocabulary will also list them thus.

11.3 Consonant irregularities in strong verbs. A number of strong verbs have slight irregularity in that the stem consonant may be doubled, or if double may become single, and in a few instances may change to another consonant (cf. § 3.3). A few examples are:

bitten	bat	hat gebeten	bittet
kommen	kam	ist gekommen	kommt
reiten	ritt	hat *or* ist geritten	reitet
schneiden	schnitt	hat geschnitten	schneidet
sitzen	saß	hat gesessen	sitzt
stehen	stand	hat. gestanden	steht
tun	tat	hat getan	tut
ziehen	zog	hat *or* ist gezogen	zieht

11.4 Additional verbs with *sein*. In addition to intransitive verbs showing change of place and condition, **sein, bleiben, gelingen,** and **geschehen** also are conjugated with **sein.**

sein	war	ist gewesen	ist
bleiben	blieb	ist geblieben	bleibt
gelingen	gelang	ist gelungen	gelingt
geschehen	geschah	ist geschehen	geschieht

11.5 The past participle as adjective. Like the present participle, the past participle of a verb, strong or weak, can be used as an adjective.

die geplante Reise *the planned trip*
die verschriebene Medizin *the prescribed medicine*

GESPRÄCH

Frl*. Hammer: Guten Morgen, Fräulein Bonner, ich habe Sie schon lange nicht gesehen.
Frl. Bonner: Guten Tag, Fräulein Hammer. Ich war acht Wochen fort und erst seit vorgestern bin ich* wieder zu Hause. Ich habe eine Reise gemacht.
Hammer: Sind Sie mit der Eisenbahn gefahren, oder wie?

5

[87]

Bonner: Meine Kusine und ich sind mit ihrem Auto gefahren.

Hammer: Das ist wohl die beste Weise, das Land zu sehen, es kann aber ermüdend werden.

10 **Bonner:** Ja, deshalb haben wir uns genügend Zeit gelassen. Unsere tägliche Strecke war nie mehr als zweihundert (200) Meilen und oft weniger. Wir sind nie müde geworden. Dazu haben wir miteinander am Steuerrad abgewechselt*.

Hammer: Sind Sie denn die ganzen acht Wochen gereist? Ich

15 bleibe immer gern eine Weile an einem schönen oder interessanten Ort.

Bonner: Dazu sind wir nicht oft gekommen. Unser längster Aufenthalt hat nur zwei Tage gedauert. Wir hatten so viel von New Orleans gehört und gelesen und wir haben es wirklich so inte-

20 ressant gefunden, daß wir zwei Tage da geblieben sind. Meistenteils* aber haben wir in vier oder fünf Stunden genug gesehen.

Hammer: Haben Sie keine Schwierigkeiten gehabt?

Bonner: Zweimal haben wir eine Reifenpanne* gehabt, aber der Motor ist die ganze Zeit tadellos* gelaufen. Wir haben nicht ein-

25 mal mit dem Wetter Pech gehabt*. Einmal ist meine Kusine ein bißchen krank geworden, denn sie hatte zu viel Gefrorenes* gegessen, aber das war alles. Wir werden wohl etwas Ähnliches im nächsten Sommer machen*.

*Frl. = Fräulein Miss	*die **Reifenpanne, -n** flat tire
*bin ich I have been	*tadellos faultless
*am Steuerrad abwechseln alter-	*Pech haben have trouble
nate at the steering wheel	*Gefrorenes ice cream
*meistenteils usually, generally	*werden . . . machen will do

LESESTÜCK

Ein Apotheker stand eines Tages vor seiner Apotheke. Da kam ein Mann, der hatte eine Tür auf seinem Wagen. Der Mann hielt vor der Apotheke, nahm die Tür vom Wagen und trug sie in den Laden.

5 Der Apotheker war erstaunt, denn er hatte keine Tür bestellt. „Was wollen Sie da mit der Tür?" fragte er den Mann.

„Ach," sagte dieser, „meine Frau ist krank. Da ist der Doktor da gewesen und hat Medizin verschrieben*. Aber ich hatte keine

Feder, keine Tinte, keinen Bleistift und kein Papier, sondern nur
Kreide. Da hat er das Rezept* an die Tür geschrieben. Also, hier 10
ist das Rezept. Bitte, präparieren Sie es."
  Der Apotheker lachte und gab dem Mann die verschriebene
Medizin. Darauf ist der Mann mit der Medizin und der Tür
glücklich fortgefahren*.

*verschreiben, ie, ie prescribe   *fortfahren, u, a, ä (ist) ride
*das Rezept', -e prescription   away

EXERCISES

I. Answer with complete German sentences: (1) Wie lange war
Frl. Bonner auf Reisen? (2) Wie lange ist sie schon wieder zu
Hause? (3) Mit wem ist sie gefahren? (4) Was tut Frl. Ham-
mer gern, wenn sie reist? (5) Haben Frl. Bonner und ihre
Kusine das auch gemacht? (6) Was wollen sie im nächsten
Sommer machen? (7) Wo hat ein Apotheker eines Tages ge-
standen? (8) Wer ist da mit einem Wagen gekommen? (9)
Was hat der Mann in den Laden getragen? (10) Was hat der
Mann gewollt?

II. Conjugate in the present perfect and the past perfect tenses:
fahren, singen, schneiden, werden, sein.

III. Give the principal parts of: sein, lassen, liegen, sehen, stehen,
trinken, bitten, essen, finden, gehen, helfen, nehmen, tragen,
bleiben, scheinen, sitzen, tun, kommen, schreiben, sprechen,
geben, lesen.

IV. Change the following sentences into the present perfect and
the past perfect: (1) Wir nehmen uns ziemlich viel Zeit. (2) Das
Fräulein bleibt gern an einem schönen Ort. (3) Die Studenten
finden ihren Professor sehr interessant. (4) Der Mann geht in
den Laden. (5) Das Kind läuft in den Park. (6) Er hilft seinem
Freund mit der Schularbeit. (7) Das Wetter wird warm. (8)
Es gibt immer solche Leute. (9) Sein Freund steht an der Tür.
(10) Ihre Kusine sitzt auf dem Sofa.

V. Translate into German using the present perfect tense for
each English past tense: (1) Last summer we went by train

(mit der Eisenbahn) to New Orleans. (2) The trip finally became fatiguing. (3) Which book did the student give his brother? (4) The teacher was not right this time. (5) His uncle went into a café and drank a cup of coffee. (6) They didn't stay there more than two days. (7) Where did you see that? (8) The children ate their ice cream much too fast. (9) He had often helped me. (10) He hadn't carried anything the whole day.

VOCABULARY

ähnlich similar
die Apothe′ke, -n drugstore
der Apothe′ker, - druggist
der Aufenthalt stay
das Auto, -s auto
best best
der Bleistift, -e pencil
darauf thereupon
dazu in addition
der Doktor, -en doctor
die Eisenbahn, -en railroad
ermüdend fatiguing
die Feder, -n pen
genügend sufficient
glücklich happy
halten, ie, a, ä stop
die Kreide, -n chalk
die Kusi′ne, -n (female) cousin

der Laden, ⸗ store
längst longest
lassen, ie, a, ä allow
die Medizin′, -en medicine
die Meile, -n mile
der Motor, -en motor
das Papier′, -e paper
die Schwierigkeit, -en difficulty
der Sommer, - summer
die Tinte, -n ink
die Tür, -en door
vor in front of
vorgestern day before yesterday
der Wagen, - wagon
die Weise, -n way
wohl probably
zweimal twice

LESSON 12

Future tenses; use of tenses

12.1 The future tense. The future tense of any verb is formed in German on the same principle that it is in English: the infinitive of the verb is used in conjunction with the present tense of the auxiliary verb.

In German the auxiliary verb is **werden.**

ich	werde machen		ich	werde gehen
du	wirst machen		du	wirst gehen
er	wird machen		er	wird gehen
wir	werden machen		wir	werden gehen
ihr	werdet machen		ihr	werdet gehen
sie	werden machen		sie	werden gehen

12.2 The future perfect tense. The future perfect tense is formed by using the present tense of **werden** in conjunction with the perfect infinitive. (The past participle plus **haben** or **sein**, the auxiliary of the perfect tense, constitutes the perfect infinitive.)

ich	werde gemacht haben		ich	werde gegangen sein
du	wirst gemacht haben		du	wirst gegangen sein
er	wird gemacht haben		er	wird gegangen sein
wir	werden gemacht haben		wir	werden gegangen sein
ihr	werdet gemacht haben		ihr	werdet gegangen sein
sie	werden gemacht haben		sie	werden gegangen sein

12.3   Position of *werden*. In the future tenses the form of **werden** is the inflected verb and stands first or second. The infinitive in the future tense and the perfect infinitive in the future perfect tense come last in the clause, following everything else.

> **Sie wird auch in Buffalo übernachten.** *She will also spend the night in Buffalo.*
> **Sie wird wohl da übernachtet haben.** *She probably spent the night there.*

12.4   Synopsis. If a form of every tense of a verb is given with the same subject, we have a synopsis. For exercise in word order a synopsis is usually given with the verb in a complete sentence. Below are two synopses, one of a weak verb with **haben,** one of a strong verb with **sein.**

> Ich sage es ihm nicht.
> Ich sagte es ihm nicht.
> Ich habe es ihm nicht gesagt.
> Ich hatte es ihm nicht gesagt.
> Ich werde es ihm nicht sagen.
> Ich werde es ihm nicht gesagt haben.

> Er kommt in die Stadt.
> Er kam in die Stadt.
> Er ist in die Stadt gekommen.
> Er war in die Stadt gekommen.
> Er wird in die Stadt kommen.
> Er wird in die Stadt gekommen sein.

12.5   Use of tenses. On the whole, German agrees with English in the use of tenses. Certain differences exist.

(a) The present tense is used frequently for future time, especially when some other part of the sentence denotes future time.

> **Kommen Sie morgen?** *Will you come tomorrow?*

(b) The present tense is used to denote something that started in the past and is still going on. English uses the present perfect tense. In such a sentence in German the adverb **schon** will be used, or a phrase beginning with **seit,** or both.

Schon seit anderthalb Wochen besucht sie eine Schulfreundin.
For a week and a half she has been visiting a school friend.
Schon zwei Tage (or seit zwei Tagen) ist er hier. *He has been
here for two days.*

(c) The present perfect tense is frequently used in the spoken
language to state a happening in past time. Compare the
GESPRÄCHE of Lessons 10 and 11.

(d) The past tense is the tense of literary narrative.

(e) The past tense is used to denote something that started in
the past and was still going on at a later time. See b above.
Schon or **seit** or both will also be found in such a sentence.

Wir wohnten schon ein halbes Jahr in unserem Haus. *We had
been living a half a year in our house.*

(f) The future tense, especially with **wohl,** is often used to
denote probability.†

Sie werden sich wohl viel zu sagen haben. *They probably have
a lot to say to each other.*

GESPRÄCH

Herr Pfeiffer (im Autobus): 'n Abend*, Herr Schmidt. Wie
geht's Ihnen heute?
Herr Schmidt: So ziemlich. Und Ihnen?
Pfeiffer: Auch so ziemlich. Aber was ist los*? Ist Ihre Frau noch
nicht zurück?   5
Schmidt: Nein, sie kommt erst in der nächsten Woche.
Pfeiffer: Ist sie immer noch in Kalifornien?
Schmidt: Nein, schon seit anderthalb* Wochen besucht sie eine
alte Schulfreundin in Chicago. Die hat sie lange nicht gesehen,
und sie werden sich* wohl viel zu sagen haben. Und wenn sie   10
noch Zeit hat, wird sie auch in Buffalo übernachten*, um den
Niagara-Wasserfall zu sehen.
Pfeiffer: Und Sie bleiben inzwischen zu Hause und tun die ganze
Hausarbeit.

† The future perfect with **wohl** expresses probability about past time.

Damals wird man wohl daran geglaubt haben. At that time people
probably believed it.

[93]

15 **Schmidt:** Neulich hat die Hausarbeit etwas gelitten. Aber ehe sie kommt, werde ich mich anstrengen* und das Haus und alles darin blitzblank* putzen.

Pfeiffer: Warum haben Sie keine Arbeitsfrau?

Schmidt: Erstens kann ich keine finden, und zweitens werde ich 20 wohl gut tun, das Geld zu sparen. Wenn die Tante ihr auch das Reisegeld geschickt hat, wird es mich doch ziemlich viel kosten. Sagen Sie, sind Sie schon in das neue Haus eingezogen*?

Pfeiffer: Ist es wirklich so lange her, daß wir miteinander gesprochen haben? Wir wohnen schon drei Wochen drin. Meine 25 Frau weiß beinahe schon, wo sie die Sachen hinstellen* will.

Schmidt: Wir wohnten schon ein halbes Jahr in unserem Haus, ehe meine Frau die richtige Anordnung* getroffen hat, denn die Sachen haben nicht zum Haus gepaßt. So geht's aber immer, wenn man in ein neues Haus zieht.

30 **Pfeiffer:** Ja, das ist ein Problem. Na, hier steige ich aus*. Auf Wiedersehen, Herr Schmidt.

Schmidt: Auf Wiedersehen!

---

*'**n Abend** = **Guten Abend** good evening
***was ist los?** what's the matter?
***anderthalb** one and a half
***sich** to each other
***übernachten** spend the night
***mich anstrengen** exert myself

***blitzblank** clean and shining, spick-and-span
***eingezogen** moved in
***hinstellen** put, place
***die Anordnung, -en** arrangement
***steige aus** get out

LESESTÜCK

Jedes Volk hat seine eigene Mythologie. Reste von der Mythologie der germanischen* Völker finden wir in den altnordischen Eddaliedern*. Diese sind Geschichten von den germanischen Göttern, und unter diesen Geschichten ist die der Götterdäm- 5 merung* nicht nur die interessanteste*, sondern auch die berühmteste*.

Dieser Geschichte nach wird einst eine Zeit kommen, die* drei Jahre dauert und die mit Kriegen erfüllt ist. Bruder wird Bruder emorden, und Vater den Sohn. Darauf werden drei Jahre ohne 10 Sommer folgen. Wölfe* werden die Sonne und den Mond ver-

[94]

schlingen*. Selbst die Götter, Odin, Thor und andere, werden
den Tod im Kampf gegen die Mächte der Finsternis finden.
Zuletzt wird die ganze Erde in Flammen aufgehen.

Aber dann wird eine neue, bessere Welt entstehen. Ein neues
Geschlecht der Götter wird über die Menschen herrschen, und 15
die Menschen werden in Frieden und Unschuld leben.

Diese Geschichte erzählte man vor mehr als tausend Jahren.
Damals wird man wohl daran geglaubt haben.

*germanisch Germanic
*das **altnordische Eddalied, -er**
  song from the Old Norse Edda
*die **Götterdämmerung** twilight
  of the gods
*interessanteste most interesting
*berühmteste most famous
*die which
*der **Wolf,** ⸗e wolf
*verschlingen, a, u devour

EXERCISES

I. Answer with compete German sentences: (1) Wann kommt
Frau Schmidt nach Hause? (2) Wo ist sie jetzt? (3) Wie lange
ist sie schon da? (4) Hatte sie ihre Schulfreundin neulich vor
dem Besuch in Chicago gesehen? (5) Warum wird sie in Buffalo
übernachten? (6) Ist Herrn Schmidts Haus jetzt blitzblank?
(7) Warum hat Herr Schmidt keine Arbeitsfrau? (8) Wie lange
wohnt Herr Pfeiffer schon in seinem neuen Haus? (9) Welches
Problem hat man immer mit einem neuen Haus? (10) Wo finden
wir die Geschichte der Götterdämmerung? (11) Wie lange wird
die Zeit dauern, die mit Kriegen erfüllt ist? (12) Was wird auf
diese Zeit folgen? (13) Was wird aus der Sonne und dem Mond
werden? (14) Wer wird den Göttern den Tod geben? (15)
Wird es Menschen in der neuen, besseren Welt geben? (16) Wie
werden sie leben?

II. Conjugate in the future and future perfect tenses: folgen,
glauben, hoffen, treffen, passen.

III. Give synopses of the following sentences: (1) Es geht mir
gut. (2) Seine Frau kommt in der nächsten Woche. (3) Sie sieht
ihre Schulfreundin in Chicago. (4) Herr Schmidt bleibt inzwischen zu Hause. (5) Die Hausarbeit leidet etwas. (6) Ich tue
das nicht. (7) Die Tante schickt seiner Frau das Reisegeld.

(8) Wir sprechen miteinander. (9) Du triffst die richtige Anordnung. (10) Drei Jahre ohne Sommer folgen darauf.

IV. Translate into German: (1) The cleaning woman will do the housework. (2) The people have been hoping for peace for three years. (3) At that time he had been cleaning the house for a whole hour. (4) We will also find the story of the Twilight of the Gods in Wagner's opera. (5) The sun will probably shine tomorrow. (6) Many people today do not believe in this story. (7) The powers of darkness will not win the last battle. (8) How long have you been waiting? (9) Are your friends going tomorrow? (10) When did she see her new house?

VOCABULARY

die **Arbeitsfrau, -en** cleaning woman
aufgehen go up
der **Autobus, -se** bus
damals at that time
ehe before
einst at one time
die **Erde, -n** earth
erfüllen fill
ermorden murder
erstens in the first place
die **Finsternis** darkness
folgen (ist) auf follow on
der **Friede, -ns, -n** peace
das **Geschlecht, -er** race
halb half
die **Hausarbeit** housework
her ago
herrschen rule
inzwischen meanwhile
kosten cost
leiden, litt, gelitten suffer
die **Macht, ⸗e** power
der **Mond, -e** moon
die **Mythologie'** mythology
nach according to

neulich recently
Odin *proper name*
passen fit
putzen clean, polish
der **Rest, -e** remainder
die **Schulfreundin, -nen** school friend
selbst even
der **Sohn, ⸗e** son
die **Sonne, -n** sun
Thor *proper name*
der **Tod** death
treffen, traf, getroffen, trifft hit upon
über over
um . . . zu *with infinitive* in order to
die **Unschuld** innocence
der **Wasserfall, ⸗e** waterfall
weiß knows
wenn (. . .) auch even if
ziehen, zog, gezogen (ist) move
so ziemlich so so
zuletzt at the last
zweitens in the second place

LESSON 13

Conjunctions; word order

13.1 Co-ordinating conjunctions. Co-ordinating conjunctions are words that connect two words, phrases, or clauses of equal value. There are six simple ones in German, five in common use. They are:

aber *but, however*	**sondern** *but* (see § 13.2)
denn *for*	**und** *and*
oder *or*	**allein** *however* (literary and more rarely used)

These conjunctions have no effect on the word order of a clause, which is the same whether or not the conjunction is present. In other words, a co-ordinating conjunction does not count as a sentence element.

> **Das ist mir unangenehm, denn es blendet mir die Augen.** *That is unpleasant for me, for it dazzles my eyes.*

13.2 *Aber* and *sondern*. Aber may stand first in the clause or it may follow one or more words. In the latter case it means *however*.

> **Aber was ist los?** *But what is the matter?*
> **Ich kann aber keine Arbeitsfrau finden.** *However, I cannot find a cleaning woman.*

Sondern is used only after a negative to introduce the other alternative. The two alternatives must be mutually exclusive. It conveys the idea of "but on the contrary."

> Ich nehme keine Erbsensuppe, sondern die Hühnerbrühe. *I won't take pea soup, but the chicken broth.*

13.3 Correlative conjunctions. A correlative conjunction consists of more than one word. The three most important in German are **entweder . . . oder,** *either . . . or,* **weder . . . noch,** *neither . . . nor,* and **sowohl . . . als auch,** *as well as.*

> Wir haben weder zu viel Licht noch zu wenig. *We have neither too much light nor too little.*
> Ich nehme sowohl die Suppe als auch Fleisch. *I'll take the soup as well as meat.*

13.4 Subordinate clauses. A subordinate clause is one that is not a complete statement in itself, but is connected in some way to a part of the main statement. It is also called a "dependent" clause. Examples in English (the italicized part of each sentence) are:

> We read that *when we were young.*
> He asked *if I had read that.*
> I am the one *who read it.*

It can be seen from these examples that a subordinate clause will be an indirect question or be a clause introduced either by a conjunction or a relative pronoun. The latter construction is discussed in Lesson 16.

13.5 Word order in a subordinate clause. In a subordinate clause in German the inflected part of the verb is normally the last word of the clause. All the other elements remain in their usual positions. If the main clause follows the subordinate clause, the subject is placed after the verb, as the subordinate clause is one element of the main clause and the verb of the latter must be the second element. In other words, if a sentence begins with a subordinate clause the main clause has inverted word order.

A subordinate clause in German is always set off by a comma or commas.

Wenn man mit einem Schiff nach Europa fährt, dauert die Reise mehrere Tage. *When you travel to Europe by boat the trip lasts several days.*
Ich will, da ich müde bin, eine Tasse Kaffee trinken. *I want, since I am tired, to drink a cup of coffee.*

Note. The conjunction **wenn,** meaning *if, when,* or *whenever,* may be omitted. In this situation the inflected verb is placed *first* in the clause instead of last.

Kommt er morgen, so gehe ich mit ihm. *If he comes tomorrow, I'll go with him.*

13.6 Subordinating conjunctions. The more common subordinating conjunctions in German are:

als *when*	ob *if, whether*
bevor *before*	obgleich *although*
bis *until*	seitdem *since* (temporal)
da *since* (causal)	während *while*
damit *in order that*	wann *when*
daß *that*	weil *because*
ehe *before*	wenn *if, when, whenever*
nachdem *after*	

Als is used with a past tense in referring to a single event in past time; **wenn** with the present or future tenses expresses *when* or *whenever;* **wenn** with a past tense means only *whenever;* **wann** is used only in direct and indirect questions.

Als Frau Schmidt in Chicago war, besuchte sie eine Freundin. *When Mrs. Schmidt was in Chicago* (one time) *she visited a friend.*
Wenn Frau Schmidt nach Chicago fuhr, nahm sie ihre Tochter mit. *Whenever Mrs. Schmidt rode to Chicago she took her daughter along.*
Herr Schmidt weiß nicht, wann sie zurückkommt. *Mr. Schmidt doesn't know when she is coming back.*

GESPRÄCH

Robert (im Restaurant): Na, wo wollen wir sitzen?
Heinrich: Es ist mir eigentlich gleich. Vielleicht da beim Fenster?
Robert: Dann sitzt einer von uns der weißen Mauer drüben*

gegenüber. Das ist mir wenigstens unangenehm, denn das
5 blendet* mir die Augen.
Heinrich: Schön! Setzen wir uns* an diesen Tisch. Hier haben
wir weder zu viel Licht noch zu wenig.
Robert: Herr Ober*, die Speisekarte, bitte!
(Der Kellner bringt sie.)
10 **Kellner:** Was möchten* die Herrschaften trinken?
Robert: Ich trinke ein Helles*.
Heinrich: Bringen Sie mir ein Dunkles, bitte.
Kellner: Jawohl. (Geht zum Ausschank* und bringt das Bier.)
Robert und Heinrich (heben die Gläser): Prost*!
15 **Heinrich:** Nun, was gibt's heute zu essen. Ich habe keinen sehr
großen Appetit, da ich ziemlich spät gefrühstückt habe.
Robert: Ich habe nur eine Tasse Kaffee gehabt. Ich habe mich
nämlich heute morgen verschlafen*, weil ich sehr spät zu Bett
gegangen bin. (Zum Kellner) Ich nehme eine Vorspeise* und
20 auch eine Suppe*.
Heinrich: Hier kann man gewöhnlich eine ausgezeichnete
Linsensuppe* bekommen, ich finde sie aber heute nicht auf der
Karte*.
Kellner: Nein, mein Herr, heute ist die Wahl entweder Erbsen-
25 suppe* oder Hühnerbrühe*.
Robert: Die Erbsensuppe hier ist beinahe so gut wie die Linsen-
suppe. Also, die nehme ich, aber zuvor möchte ich* eine Portion
marinierten Hering*. Dann Sauerbraten* mit Kartoffelklößen*
und Salat*.
30 **Heinrich:** Ich will keine Vorspeise und auch keine Erbsensuppe.
Ich nehme lieber* die Hühnerbrühe. Ich weiß noch nicht, ob ich
Fleisch will. Das kann ich ja später bestellen.
(Während die beiden Freunde miteinander plaudern und ihr
Bier trinken, bringt der Kellner jedem eine Serviette*, ein Messer,
35 eine Gabel und einen Suppenlöffel, nachher das Essen.)

*drüben over there
*blenden blind
*Setzen wir uns let's sit down
*Herr Ober (Ober = Oberkell-
ner) headwaiter (*the way to
address any waiter*)
*die Speisekarte, -n menu

*möchten would like
*Helles (Bier) a glass of light
beer
*der Ausschank, =e *place where
drinks are served, usually for
waiters only*
*Prost (*or* Prosit) To your health

*mich . . . verschlafen overslept
*die Vorspeise, -n appetizer
*die Suppe, -n soup
*die Linsensuppe lentil soup
*Karte = die Speisekarte menu
*die Erbsensuppe pea soup
*die Hühnerbrühe chicken broth
*ich möchte I'd like

*marinierten Hering marinated
  herring
*der Sauerbraten beef soaked in
  vinegar (*use the German term*)
*der Kartoffelkloß, =e potato
  dumpling
*der Salat' salad
*nehme lieber prefer (to take)
*die Serviet'te, -n napkin

LESESTÜCK

Jedes Kulturvolk* hat seine klassischen Dichter. Die bekanntesten* Klassiker* der Deutschen sind Lessing, Schiller und Goethe, die* die meisten ihrer Werke in der klassischen Periode der deutschen Literatur geschrieben haben, also in der zweiten Hälfte des achtzehnten Jahrhunderts. Es gab aber noch ein 5 anderes klassisches Zeitalter in der deutschen Literatur. Das war im dreizehnten Jahrhundert und da hatte man auch berühmte Namen. Die berühmtesten unter ihnen waren die Epiker* Hartmann von Aue, Wolfram von Eschenbach und Gottfried von Straßburg und der Lyriker* Walther von der Vogelweide. Diese 10 nennt man die „Mittelhochdeutschen* Klassiker," weil sie in der mittelhochdeutschen und nicht in der neuhochdeutschen* Sprache dichteten.

Vergleicht man die folgenden Zeilen Hartmanns mit der neuhochdeutschen Übertragung, so sieht man etwas von dem Unterschied 15 zwischen dem Mittelhochdeutschen und dem Neuhochdeutschen.

Mittelhochdeutsch: Ein ritter sô gelêret was
                    daz er an den buochen las
                    swaz er dar an geschriben vant   20
                    der was Hartman genant

Übertragung: Ein Ritter so gelehret war,
                    Daß er in den Büchern las,
                    Was er darin geschrieben fand;
                    Der war Hartmann genannt*.   25

*das **Kulturvolk,** ⸗er highly civilized people
*bekanntesten best known
*der **Klassiker,** - classical writer
*die who
*der **Epiker,** - epic poet
*der **Lyriker,** - lyric poet

*mittelhochdeutsch Middle High
German
*neuhochdeutsch New High Ger-
man
*genannt *past participle of* **nennen**

EXERCISES

I. Answer with complete German sentences: (1) Warum wollten
die Freunde nicht am Fenster sitzen? (2) Wer wählte endlich
den Tisch? (3) Was brachte der Kellner zuerst? (4) Was wollte
Heinrich trinken? (5) Was sagt ein Deutscher, wenn er mit
einem Freund trinkt? (6) Warum hatte Heinrich keinen großen
Appetit? (7) Was hatte Robert zum Frühstück gehabt? (8)
Warum hatte er sich verschlafen? (9) Was taten die beiden
Freunde, während sie ihr Bier tranken? (10) Wer waren Lessing,
Schiller und Goethe? (11) Wann haben sie gedichtet? (12)
Nennen Sie noch andere berühmte deutsche Dichter. (13) Wann
haben die gedichtet? (14) Warum nennt man sie „Mittelhoch-
deutsche Klassiker"? (15) Nennen Sie einige Klassiker der an-
deren Kulturvölker.

II. Make one sentence out of each of the following pairs of sentences, using the conjunction indicated: (1) Robert wollte nicht
am Fenster sitzen. Da sah man gerade auf eine Mauer.(weil)
(2) Robert hatte großen Hunger. Er hatte kein Frühstück gehabt.(denn) (3) Das Mittagessen schmeckt sehr gut. Man hat
Hunger.(wenn) (4) Er kam nach Hause. Der Krieg war schon
ein Jahr zu Ende.(als) (5) Wir fahren nächstes Jahr nach Kalifornien. Wir fliegen nach Europa.(oder) (6) Man reist nach
Europa. Man muß einen Paß (passport) haben. (bevor) (7) Der
Mann ging nach Hause. Er nahm seine Tür und das Rezept.(ehe)
(8) Schumann sprach wenig. Er war für Wagner unmöglich.(da)

III. In the following sentences fill in the blank with **aber** or
sondern as required by meaning: (1) Der Mann hatte keinen
großen Hunger, __ er aß ziemlich viel. (2) Heinrich wollte beim
Fenster sitzen, Robert __ wollte es nicht. (3) Frau Schneider

war jetzt nicht in Kalifornien, __ sie besuchte ihre Tante in Chicago. (4) Es kostet nicht viel, __ etwas Geld muß man haben. (5) Die Sachen sind für das Haus nicht zu groß, __ sie sind in Wirklichkeit (reality) zu klein.

IV. Translate into German: (1) Since Robert didn't like to sit by the window, they took a table near the door. (2) Whenever the two friends were together, they liked to drink a glass of beer. (3) The waiter brings the menu before they ask for it. (4) The (je) more one travels the (desto) more one sees (*use inverted word order*). (5) We have no opera, but only the movies. (6) It rained while the students were working in the library. (7) Since the doctor had no paper, he wrote the prescription on the door. (8) Before the druggist saw the man the latter had taken his door from the wagon. (9) Nowadays it is always either too hot or too cold. (10) The Eskimos (Eskimos) have no classic writers, for they are not a highly civilized people.

VOCABULARY

achtzehnt eighteenth
also that is
der **Appetit'** appetite
das **Auge, -n** eye
ausgezeichnet excellent
die **beiden** the two
bekommen, bekam, bekommen get
das **Bier, -e** beer
da since
dichten write poetry
dreizehnt thirteenth
dunkel dark
entweder . . . oder either . . . or
das **Fenster, -** window
das **Fleisch** meat
frühstücken eat breakfast
die **Gabel, -n** fork
gegenüber facing
gelehret learned (*poetic form not used in everyday German*)

gleich same; **es ist mir __** it makes no difference to me
Gottfried von Straßburg proper name
die **Hälfte, -n** half
Hartmann von Aue proper name
heben, o, o lift
hell light
die **Herrschaften** (*pl.*) gentlemen
der **Kellner, -** waiter
klassisch classic(al)
die **Mauer, -n** wall
das **Messer, -** knife
der **Name, -ns, -n** name
die **Perio'de, -n** period
plaudern chat
die **Portion', -en** portion
das **Restaurant', -s** restaurant
der **Ritter, -** knight
der **Suppenlöffel, -** soup spoon
die **Übertragung, -en** translation
der **Unterschied, -e** difference

vergleichen, i, i compare
die Wahl, -en choice
während while
Walther von der Vogelweide
  proper name
weder . . . noch neither . . . nor
weil because

weiß white
Wolfram von Eschenbach *proper
  name*
die Zeile, -n line
das Zeitalter, - age
zuvor before, first

LESSON 14

Impersonal and reflexive verbs; expletive **es**

14.1 Impersonal verbs. An impersonal verb is one that is used in the third singular and has as its subject the neuter pronoun, which, however, does not refer to an antecedent. In English such verbs are used in connection with the weather and in a few other situations.

It is raining. *It seems to me.*

There are many more impersonal verbs in German. They refer to the weather, to states of the mind, and to states of the body; and there are others not readily classified. The most common are:

es regnet *it is raining*	**es gelingt ihm** *he succeeds*
es schneit *it is snowing*	**es freut mich** *I am glad*
es scheint mir *it seems to me*	**es gefällt mir** *it pleases me,*
es tut mir leid *I am sorry*	*I am glad*
es geht mir gut *I am well*	

14.2 Reflexive pronouns. A reflexive pronoun is one that refers back to the subject of discussion. In English the reflexive pronouns are formed by adding *-self* or *-selves* to the personal pronoun or possessive adjective: *myself, himself,* etc.

In German the reflexive pronouns occur only in the dative and the accusative. The forms are:

mir	dir	sich	sich *is both the dative and accusa-*
mich	dich	sich	*tive of the reflexive pronoun for*
uns	euch	sich	**Sie** *and for all pronouns of the*
uns	euch	sich	*third person, singular and plural.*

14.3 Reflexive verbs. A reflexive verb is one formed by using the reflexive pronoun in conjunction with the simple verb. It then has a meaning which is not a literal addition of the two. For example, the English verb *to enjoy oneself* is practically synonymous with *to have a good time*, and *to betake oneself* is practically synonymous with *to go*.

There are many of these reflexive verbs in German. Among the most commonly used are:

sich **ärgern** *be annoyed*	sich **freuen** *be glad*
sich **aufhalten** *stay*	sich **irren** *be mistaken*
sich **befinden** *be, be located*	sich **legen** *lie down*
sich **beeilen** *hurry*	sich **setzen** *sit down*
sich **erholen** *recover*	sich **verlassen auf** *depend on*
sich **erinnern** *remember*	

14.4 Conjugation and synopses of reflexive and impersonal verbs. As examples for the forms of reflexive and impersonal verbs there are given below the present tense and then a synopsis of **freuen** used as an impersonal verb and then the same forms of it used as a reflexive verb. The principal parts of the reflexive verb **freuen** are given last.

es freut mich	ich freue mich
es freut dich	du freust dich
es freut ihn *or* sie	er *or* sie freut sich
es freut uns	wir freuen uns
es freut euch	ihr freut euch
es freut sie	sie freuen sich

Es freut mich sehr.	Ich freue mich darauf.
Es freute mich sehr.	Ich freute mich darauf.
Es hat mich sehr gefreut.	Ich habe mich darauf gefreut.
Es hatte mich sehr gefreut.	Ich hatte mich darauf gefreut.
Es wird mich sehr freuen.	Ich werde mich darauf freuen.
Es wird mich sehr gefreut haben.	Ich werde mich darauf gefreut haben.

sich freuen	freute sich	hat sich gefreut	freut sich

14.5 Special uses of reflexive verbs.

(a) In English many verbs are used both transitively and intransitively, for example, *we move the auto* and *the auto moves.* In German **bewegen** means *to move something;* the second English usage is rendered in German with the reflexive verb, and the two sentences in German are **Wir bewegen das Auto** and **Das Auto bewegt sich.** There are many more such verbs in German but it would not be feasible to try to list them.

(b) When **lassen** is followed by the reflexive infinitive the whole has the meaning of *can be done.*

> **Das Experiment läßt sich nur mit reinem Wasser durchführen.** *The experiment can only be carried out with pure water.*
> **Diese Unregelmäßigkeiten lassen sich leicht erklären.** *These irregularities can easily be explained.*

(c) The reflexive verb is frequently used in German to express an idea that is expressed with the passive voice in English.

> **In der folgenden Tabelle finden sich die wichtigsten Elemente.** *In the following table are found the most important elements.*
> **Diese Änderungen wiederholen sich von Zeit zu Zeit.** *These changes are repeated from time to time.*

14.6 Expletive es. It often happens that a speaker or writer wants for some reason to put all of the sentence, including the subject, after the verb. To avoid starting the sentence with the verb, which would form a question, a colorless word called the "expletive" is placed first. In English it is *there.* That this has no reference to place is clear from such a sentence as *There are three books there.* In German the expletive is **es,** and the English sentence would be rendered **Es sind drei Bücher da.** The expletive occurs more frequently in German than in English and must therefore be omitted sometimes in translating German.

> **Es sind dies ganz neue Begriffe.** *These are completely new concepts.*

GESPRÄCH

Otto: Spielst du heute nachmittag Tennis?
Rudolf: Ich glaube kaum. Wenn ich mich nicht irre, wird's regnen. Und außerdem fühle ich mich nicht besonders wohl.

Otto: Was hast du denn?

5 Rudolf: Ich habe mich noch nicht völlig von der Grippe erholt.

Otto: Das tut mir leid! Na, ich habe keine Zeit krank zu sein. Ich muß gehörig* büffeln*. Ich hoffe nämlich auf ein Stipendium* für nächstes Jahr.

Rudolf: Um welches hast du dich denn beworben*?

10 Otto: Um das beste, natürlich, und deshalb ist mir bange. Denn wenn ich das Geld nicht bekomme, kann ich nicht weiterstudieren*.

Rudolf: Na, hoffentlich gelingt's dir! Besonders da du dich so anstrengst. Ich werde für dich den Daumen drücken*.

15 Otto: Danke! Aber es tut mir leid, daß du noch immer Beschwerden* hast. Und auch tut's mir leid, daß wir nicht spielen können, denn ich freue mich immer auf ein Tennisspiel mit dir.

Rudolf: Mir macht es auch Spaß. Leider haben wir im vorigen Frühling nur zweimal gespielt. Erinnerst du dich?

20 Otto: Ja! Immer die alte Geschichte! Entweder regnete es oder ich konnte mich nicht entschließen, die Bücher liegen zu lassen.

Rudolf: Nun, vielleicht geht's mir morgen besser. Und wenn es dann klar ist, und w e n n du dich von deinen Büchern auf einige Stunden trennen kannst, dann können wir ja spielen.

25 Otto: Gut, ich freue mich darauf.

*gehörig proper, suitable
*büffeln work hard, grind
*das Stipen'dium, -dien scholarship
*sich bewerben, a, o, i (um) apply (for)
*weiterstudieren continue with one's studies

*den Daumen drücken squeeze one's thumb (*the equivalent of crossing one's fingers to bring luck*)
*die Beschwerde, -n difficulty

LESESTÜCK

Klara Schumanns Name verbreitete sich schneller als der ihres Mannes. Er freute sich natürlich über den Erfolg seiner Frau, aber dann und wann—wie man sich denken kann—hat er sich doch im Stillen geärgert, besonders über Vorfälle wie der fol-
5 gende.

Klara war in einem Wiener Hofkonzert* mit glänzendem

[*108*]

Lesson 14

Erfolg aufgetreten*. Nachher wurde sie dem König der Nieder-
lande* vorgestellt*. Es zog Seine Majestät die Künstlerin in ein
längeres* Gespräch. Endlich wendete er sich auch an den da-
beistehenden Robert: „Nun, und Sie? Sind Sie auch musikalisch?" 10

*das **Hofkonzert, -e** court concert
***war . . . aufgetreten** had ap-
   peared
*die **Niederlande** the Netherlands

***wurde . . . vorgestellt** was pre-
   sented
***längeres** rather long

EXERCISES

I. Answer with complete German sentences: (1) Warum glaubt
Robert kaum, daß sie am Nachmittag Tennis spielen werden?
(2) Warum studiert Otto die ganze Zeit? (3) Weshalb ist es
ihm bange? (4) Was wird Robert morgen tun, wenn es ihm
besser geht? (5) Worauf freut sich Otto immer? (6) Wer war
Klara Schumann? (7) Wo trat sie einmal auf? (8) Freute sich
ihr Mann über ihren Erfolg?

II. Conjugate in the present tense: sich irren, sich verlassen, sich
erholen, sich ärgern.

III. Give synopses of: (1) Es geht mir gut. (2) Es gibt so viele
Dinge. (3) Es tut seinem Freund leid. (4) Es regnet stark.
(5) Solche Geschichten finden sich nicht leicht. (6) Ich wasche
mir die Hände.

IV. Translate into German: (1) The girls were looking forward
to an afternoon at the movies. (2) There were three students in
the room at that time. (3) It pleased him that we spoke to him
this morning. (4) There are more poor people in the world than
rich ones. (5) Don't rely on me! (*three forms*) (6) Three years
ago when I traveled to Panama it rained (*pres. perf.*) the whole
summer. (7) Hydrogen (der Wasserstoff) combines with oxygen
and in this process (der Prozeß) the individual gases change.
(8) How are you? (*three forms*) (9) Where are you going when
you have recovered? (10) Why don't you sit down? (*three
forms*)

[*109*]

VOCABULARY

sich **ärgern** be annoyed
auf for (*a period of time*)
außerdem furthermore
bange worried
dabeistehend standing nearby
danke thanks
sich **denken** imagine
sich **entschließen, o, o** decide
sich **erholen** recover
sich **freuen;** __ **auf** look forward
to; __ **über** be glad about
der **Frühling, -e** spring
sich **fühlen** feel
gelingen, a, u (ist) succeed
glänzend brilliant
sich **irren** be mistaken
kaum hardly, scarcely
klar clear

der **König, -e** king
die **Künstlerin, -nen** artist
leid; das tut mir __ I'm sorry
about that
die **Majestät', -en** majesty
musika'lisch musical
der **Spaß;** __ **machen** give pleasure
sure
studieren study
das **Tennisspiel, -e** game of tennis
nis
trennen separate
verbreiten spread
völlig complete, full
der **Vorfall, ⸚e** incident
sich **wenden (an)** turn (to)
wohl well

LESSON 15

Passive voice; substitutes for the passive; **lassen**

15.1 The passive voice. The passive voice indicates that the subject of the clause is the receiver of the action, not the doer of the action.

The formation of the passive voice is the same in principle for both English and German. The past participle of the verb in question is used with the various tense forms of the auxiliary. In English the auxiliary is *to be*.

> *The gas is compressed by the piston.*
> *This engine had been invented by Lenoir.*

Each of these sentences indicates that an action is performed and that the subject is the receiver of the action. By comparison, notice these same statements with the subject the doer and the verb in the active voice.

> *The piston compresses the gas.*
> *Lenoir had invented this engine.*

15.2 Formation of the passive. To form the passive voice in German we take the past participle of the verb in question and use **werden** as the auxiliary. The only irregularity in the conjugation of **werden** is that **worden** is used instead of **geworden**

for the past participle. The following synopsis will show not only
the forms but also the position of the verbal elements.

Der Mann wird öfters hier gesehen. *The man is frequently
seen here.*

"	"	wurde	"	"	gesehen.
"	"	ist	"	"	gesehen worden.
"	"	war	"	"	gesehen worden.
"	"	wird	"	"	gesehen werden.
"	"	wird	"	"	gesehen worden sein.

15.3 Agency and means. Agency with the passive voice is expressed by **von** with the dative case. Means or instrument is
expressed by **durch** with the accusative case. Sometimes the distinction between the two seems very fine. The agent is the *doer*
of the action—and becomes the subject if the sentence is put into
the active voice. The means or instrument is what the agent *uses*
—and in the active voice it remains unchanged as a phrase with
durch.

> **Die Maschine wurde von einem Franzosen gebaut.** *The engine
> was built by a Frenchman.*
> **Das Gemisch wird von einem Chemiker durch eine Flamme
> erhitzt.** *The mixture is heated by a chemist by means of a
> flame.* (In the active voice this sentence reads: **Der Chemiker
> erhitzt das Gemisch durch eine Flamme.**)

15.4 Impersonal passive. In German only the direct receiver of
the action can be the subject of the passive verb. However, a
fairly frequent construction in German is the impersonal passive.
This denotes only that an action is performed; the subject is
always **es.** If **es** is not the first word it is omitted.

> **Dann wurde an dem Problem gearbeitet.** *Then work was done
> on the problem.*
> **Hier wird nicht geraucht.** *There is no smoking here.*

15.5 Verbs with the dative. The impersonal passive construction
is also used for those verbs which govern the dative, the dative
case remaining and the doer of the action being expressed by
von with the dative.

> **Ihm wurde nur von seinen Freunden geholfen.** *He was helped
> only by his friends.*

15.6 False passive. English has a type of statement, identical in form with the passive, that denotes a state of being.

The engine was already built when I saw it.

This type of statement is made in German with **sein** and the past participle used as a predicate adjective.

Die Maschine war schon gebaut, als ich sie sah.

The passive voice in German always denotes an action and the auxiliary is **werden**.

15.7 Substitutes for the passive. There are various constructions in German which parallel passive constructions in English.

(a) The use of **man** with the active.

Man baute letztes Jahr viele Häuser. *Many houses were built last year.*
Man findet diese Ausnahmen überall. *These exceptions are found everywhere.*

(b) The use of a reflexive verb. See § 14.5.
(c) The infinitive of a transitive verb used with **zu** after a form of **sein**.

Kein Mensch war zu sehen. *Nobody was to be seen.*
Die Medizin ist alle drei Stunden zu nehmen. *The medicine is to be taken every three hours.*

(d) The use of **lassen** with the infinitive of a transitive verb. The latter may have passive force and the whole may mean *to have something done.*

Er ließ sein Buch in Europa drucken. *He had his book printed in Europe.*
Der König läßt seine Minister rufen. (*The king is having his ministers called.*) *The king sends for his ministers.*

(e) The use of **lassen** with a reflexive infinitive. See § 14.5.

15.8 Uses of *lassen*. It can be seen from §§ 15.7 (d) and 14.5 (b) that **lassen** is an important verb. It must in addition be stressed here that it is also used in the meaning *to let* or *to leave* and as such can have a direct object.

Er ließ das Buch auf dem Tisch. *He left the book on the table.*
Der Chemiker läßt das Gemisch lange kochen. *The chemist lets the mixture boil a long time.*

GESPRÄCH

(Hans und Georg begegnen sich auf der Straße.)
Hans: Wo gehen Sie hin*?
Georg: In die Stadt. Ich habe allerlei zu besorgen. Und Sie?
Hans: Ich gehe auch in die Stadt. Vielleicht können wir einander
5 Gesellschaft leisten.
Georg: Das wäre* schön. Und wenn wir zur selben Zeit fertig
sind, können wir auch zusammen einen Kaffee trinken. Oder
möchten Sie lieber* ins Kino? Im Phöbus-Palast* wird ein be-
sonders guter Film gezeigt.
10 **Hans:** Nein, ich bleibe an so einem Tag lieber* im Freien. Wir
können unsren Kaffee da im Garten vor Werners Café trinken.
Georg: Gut! Ich gehe jetzt in die städtische Bibliothek, um diese
Bücher zurückzubringen*.
Hans: Warum haben Sie sich die nicht aus der Universitäts-
15 bibliothek geliehen?
Georg: Weil mir jemand zuvorgekommen* ist. So war ich froh,
daß ich sie wenigstens in der städtischen auftreiben* konnte.
Hans: Nun, in d e r Richtung gehe ich nicht, denn ich muß
zum Zahnarzt. Ich schlage also vor*, wir trennen uns jetzt und
20 treffen uns dann später in Werners Garten. Wie lange werden
Sie beschäftigt sein?
Georg: Ungefähr anderthalb Stunden.
Hans: Gut! Dann treff' ich Sie um drei Uhr. Auf Wiedersehn.
Georg: Auf Wiedersehn.

*wo . . . hin = **wohin** to what place, where
*wäre would be
*möchten Sie lieber would you rather go (gehen *is understood*)
*der **Phöbus-Palast** *name of a movie theater*
*bleibe . . . lieber would rather stay
*zurückbringen bring back
*zuvorkommen (ist) get in ahead of
*auftreiben "dig up"
*schlage . . . vor suggest

LESESTÜCK

Wenn ein Behälter mit Wasserstoff* und Sauerstoff* bei Zimmertemperatur gefüllt wird, haben wir ein Gasgemisch. Wenn aber das Gemisch durch eine Flamme oder einen elektrischen Funken erhitzt wird, erfolgt eine starke Explosion. Wir haben nicht mehr ein Gemisch, sondern eine chemische Verbindung. 5 Das gilt auch von anderen Gasen. Durch solche Explosionen werden alle Gasmaschinen getrieben.

Das Gasgemisch wird in einen Zylinder* geleitet, von dem Kolben* stark komprimiert* und durch einen Funken erhitzt. Der Kolben wird dann von der Kraft der Explosion wieder nach 10 auswärts* getrieben und dadurch wird die Maschine in Gang gesetzt.

Die ersten Versuche, eine Maschine durch explodierende Gase zu betreiben*, waren schon im siebzehnten Jahrhundert gemacht worden, aber erst im Jahre 1860 (achtzehnhundertundsechzig) 15 wurde eine wirklich brauchbare Maschine von dem Franzosen Lenoir gebaut. Dann wurde fleißig an dem Problem gearbeitet, bis eine deutsche Firma* achtzehn Jahre später die heutige Maschine erfand. Diese ist noch in unseren Autos zu finden.

*der **Wasserstoff** hydrogen	*komprimieren compress
*der **Sauerstoff** oxygen	*nach auswärts out, outward
*der **Zylin'der**, - cylinder	*betreiben operate
*der **Kolben**, - piston	*die **Firma**, -men firm

EXERCISES

I. Answer with complete German sentences: (1) Warum ging Georg in die Stadt? (2) Wo ging Hans hin? (3) Was tat Hans gern an einem schönen Tag? (4) Was wird im Phöbus-Palast gezeigt? (5) Wie lange wird Georg beschäftigt sein? (6) Wann werden sie sich wieder treffen? (7) Wann sind die ersten Versuche gemacht worden, eine Maschine durch explodierende Gase zu betreiben? (8) Von wem wurde die erste brauchbare Gasmaschine gebaut? (9) Von wem ist die heutige Maschine erfunden worden? (10) Wodurch werden alle Gasmaschinen getrieben?

[115]

II. Give synopses of: (1) Das Gasgemisch wird in einen Zylinder geleitet. (2) Alle Gasmaschinen werden durch Explosionen getrieben.

III. Translate into German: (1) An attempt to build a gas engine was made by a Frenchman. (2) The wall had already been built by the students. (3) The heavy packages are being raised by means of an engine. (4) The house has been cleaned by the cleaning woman. (5) The library was closed at five o'clock. (*Give this sentence two ways, to show a state and also an action.*) (6) The waiter let the man eat. (7) The professor sent for the students. (8) He wasn't helped by that (dadurch). (9) Beethoven's friends had a suit made for him (ihm). (10) Is German spoken here?

IV. Translate into English: (1) Frau Schmidt wird ihren Mann allein lassen. (2) Natürlich hat er die Sachen da gelassen, wo seine Frau sie hingestellt hatte. (2) Ohne Geld kann man das Haus nicht putzen lassen. (4) Später lassen wir das Essen bringen. (5) Das Gasgemisch läßt sich auf das halbe Volumen komprimieren. (6) Solche Geschichten lassen sich kaum vergessen. (7) Man braucht mehr Lehrer an dieser Schule. (8) Der Begriff des chemischen Elements entwickelte sich erst viel später. (9) Organische Stoffe haben sich immer in der Natur gefunden, aber sie lassen sich auch im Laboratorium herstellen. (10) Diesen Krieg nannte man den Zweiten Weltkrieg. (11) Eine passende Wohnung ist in dieser Stadt kaum zu finden. (12) Das läßt sich nicht so leicht sagen. (13) Die Frau ließ das beste Zimmer für ihren Bruder fertig machen. (14) Da es schon warm war, ließ er seinen Mantel zu Hause. (15) Ein Schall läßt sich entweder physikalisch oder psychisch betrachten.

VOCABULARY

bauen build
begegnen (ist) meet
der Begriff, -e concept
der Behälter, - container
beschäftigt busy
betrachten consider

brauchbar usable
chemisch chemical
elek'trisch electric(al)
entwickeln develop
erfinden, a, u invent
erfolgen (ist) result

erhitzen heat
explodieren explode
die **Explosion'**, -en explosion
fertig finished, ready
der **Franzo'se**, -n, -n Frenchman
froh glad
füllen fill
der **Funken**, - spark
der **Gang** motion, operation
das **Gas**, -e gas
das **Gasgemisch**, -e gas mixture
die **Gasmaschine**, -n gas engine
das **Gemisch**, -e mixture
die **Gesellschaft**; ___ leisten keep
  company
herstellen produce
heutig present-day
jemand some one
die **Kraft**, ⸗e force
leihen, ie, ie borrow
Lenoir *proper name*
der **Mantel**, ⸗ topcoat

die **Maschi'ne**, -n engine, machine
die **Natur'** nature
physika'lisch physical
psychisch psychic
die **Richtung**, -en direction
der **Schall** sound
selb same
setzen set
siebzehnt seventeenth
städtisch (of the) city, municipal
stark strong
der **Stoff**, -e substance
die **Straße**, -n street
treiben, ie, ie drive
die **Universitätsbibliothek**, -en
  university library
die **Verbindung**, -en compound
der **Versuch**, -e attempt
das **Volu'men**, -mina volume
der **Zahnarzt**, ⸗e dentist
die **Zimmertemperatur** room temperature

LESSON 16

Relative pronouns; demonstrative pronouns

16.1 Relative pronouns. There are two relative pronouns in German, one of which, **der**, is used much more frequently than the other, **welcher**. **Der** is declined as follows:

	singular		*plural*
masc.	*fem.*	*neut.*	*all genders*
der	die	das	die
dessen	deren	dessen	deren
dem	der	dem	denen
den	die	das	die

Welcher as a relative pronoun does not exist in the genitive case; otherwise it is declined like **dieser**.

16.2 Use of the relative pronoun. A relative pronoun introduces a relative clause and agrees in gender and number with its antecedent, the word to which it is connected by meaning. Its case depends upon its use in the relative clause.

Das ist der Mann, **der** mir geholfen hat.	*Nom.*
" " " " , **dessen** Frau morgen singt.	*Gen.*
" " " " , mit **dem** du Tennis gespielt hast.	*Dat.*
" " " " , auf **den** du wartest.	*Acc.*
Das sind die Männer, **die** vorher hier waren.	*Nom.*

16.3 Compounds with *wo(r)-*. Similar to the use of **da(r)-** and **wo(r)-** with prepositions in place of personal and interrogative pronouns (see §§ 5.5 & 8.6) is the use of **wo(r)-** with a preposition to introduce a relative clause when an inanimate object is referred to. However, there is this difference: in a relative clause this construction does not have to be used—a relative pronoun may be used when referring to a thing.

> **Der Saal, worin** (or **in dem**) **das Konzert gegeben wird,** *The hall in which the concert is being given*

16.4 *Wer* and *was*. **Wer** is used in the meaning *whoever*, **was** in the meaning *whatever*, as in the following examples:

> **Wer einen guten Platz bekommen will,** *Whoever wants to get a good seat*
> **Was Frau Waag singt, ist mir recht.** *Whatever Mrs. Waag sings is all right with me.*

Was is used when the antecedent is the neuter singular form of one of several indefinite pronouns, such as **alles, viel, nichts;** it is used when the antecedent is the neuter singular superlative of an adjective; and it is used when the antecedent is a preceding statement.

> **Alles, was er sagt,** *Everything that he says*
> **Nichts, was mir helfen kann,** *Nothing that can help me*
> **Das Beste, was er tun kann,** *The best that he can do*
> **Er ist wieder zu Hause, was uns freut.** *He is at home again, (a fact) which pleases us.*

16.5 The demonstrative pronoun *der*. A demonstrative pronoun is used to *demonstrate*, i.e. point out, but **der** is also frequently used instead of a personal pronoun for extra emphasis. Thus, **Ich weiß nicht, wer der ist** could mean either *I don't know who that person is* or *I don't know who he is*.

Even though the demonstrative pronoun **der** and the relative pronoun **der** have, with one exception, the same forms, they need not be confused because the demonstrative pronoun does not cause dependent word order.

> **Kann ich mit Hans sprechen? Nein, der ist nicht hier.** *Can I speak with Hans? No, he is not here.*

The demonstrative pronoun **der** is declined:

der	die	das	die
dessen	deren	dessen	deren, derer †
dem	der	dem	denen
den	die	das	die

16.6 *Derselbe* and *derjenige.* Derselbe, *the same,* is used both as a pronoun and to modify a noun. In either case the first part, the definite article, is declined as usual and the second part has the weak adjective endings to be expected after the article. If the article is contracted with a preposition, the second part is written as a separate word: **zur selben Zeit.**

Except that contraction with a preposition does not occur, the same statements hold true for **derjenige,** *that,* a literary word used as an antecedent of a relative pronoun or to modify the antecedent.

derselbe	dieselbe	dasselbe	dieselben
desselben	derselben	desselben	derselben
demselben	derselben	demselben	denselben
denselben	dieselbe	dasselbe	dieselben
derjenige	diejenige	dasjenige	diejenigen
desjenigen	derjenigen	desjenigen	derjenigen
etc.	etc.	etc.	etc.

All the limiting adjectives can be used pronominally (see § 8.4).

16.7 *Selber* and *selbst.* Selber and selbst are used, with no difference, as intensifying pronouns after nouns and pronouns. Intensifying pronouns are formed in English by adding *-self* or *-selves* to the personal pronouns.

> **der Mann selber** (or **selbst**) *the man himself*
> **die Leute selber** (or **selbst**) *the people themselves*

Selbst may precede a word or a phrase and then means *even.*

> **selbst dieser Mann** *even this man*
> **selbst diese Leute** *even these people*

† This second form is used only as the antecedent of a relative pronoun.

Therefore, distinction must be noted between such pairs as:

Ich selbst werde es tun. *I'll do it myself.*
Selbst ich werde es tun. *Even I will do it.*

GESPRÄCH

Karl: Gehst du heute abend ins Konzert?
Elsa: Konzert? Ich weiß nichts davon. Was gibt's denn?
Karl: Einen Liederabend*. Frau Waag, die voriges Jahr schon mal hier war, singt. Und auch ein Tenor. Ich glaube, der ist ihr Mann. 5
Elsa: Weißt du, was sie singen? Singen sie auch Duette?
Karl: Ich habe das Programm irgendwo gesehen. Es ist das Gewöhnliche, glaube ich, Schubert, Brahms, Schumann, usw*. Aber was Frau Waag singt, ist mir immer recht. Die ist ja fabelhaft*. Aber Duette gibt's nicht, so weit ich mich erinnern kann. 10
Elsa: Wann beginnt das Konzert?
Karl: Um acht Uhr. Aber der Saal ist ziemlich klein, und ich werde eine halbe Stunde früher hingehen*, um einen anständigen Platz zu bekommen. Einige von den Plätzen sind nämlich sehr schlecht. Man kann da weder hören noch sehen, was auf der 15 Bühne geschieht. Wer also einen anständigen Platz will, muß mindestens zwanzig Minuten früher hingehen.
Elsa: Ich glaube, ich komme auch, obgleich ich ziemlich viel zu Hause zu tun habe.
Karl: Gut. Ich komme um halb acht* bei dir vorbei*, wenn's dir 20 recht ist, und dann können wir beieinander sitzen.
Elsa: Das wäre* sehr nett. Ich gehe nämlich nicht gern allein ins Konzert. Was nicht sagen will*, daß ich die ganze Zeit rede, wenn ich da bin. O nein, ich sage fast kein Wort. Es ist nur, wenn man mit jemand geht—na, du weißt ja—„Geteilte Freude ist dop- 25 pelte Freude!"
Karl: Wunderbar! Eine Studentin, mit der ich neulich im Konzert war, hat die ganze Zeit geschwätzt. Es war zum Davonlaufen*! Alle Leute haben uns angeguckt*, und ich habe mir gedacht*: „Mit der gehe ich nie wieder!" Also, auf Wiedersehn bis heute 30 abend!
Elsa: Auf Wiedersehn!

*der **Liederabend**, -e evening of songs
*usw. = **undsoweiter** and so forth, etc.
*fabelhaft marvelous
*hingehen go there
*halb acht half past seven

*vorbei past
*wäre would be
*sagen will means
*zum Davonlaufen enough to make you run away
*angeguckt peered
*gedacht thought

LESESTÜCK

Wenige Leute, die das Wort „Kindergarten" hören, denken sich dabei, daß es ein deutsches Wort ist. Und noch wenigere werden wohl wissen, was das Wort eigentlich pädagogisch bedeutet.

Das Wort „Kindergarten" kommt von einem deutschen Pädago-
5 gen Friedrich Fröbel (1782-1852), der, angeregt* durch die deutsche Romantik* und einen Schweizer* Pädagogen Johann Heinrich Pestalozzi (1746-1827), eine neue Pädagogik in Deutschland einführen wollte. Seine Grundgedanken* waren die folgenden.

10 Die Natur, der Charakter, die Bedeutung eines Volkes wird zum großen Teil bestimmt durch seine Erziehung, und besonders durch die Erziehung des Kindes. Denn was aus einem Menschen, einem Volk, einer Nation wird, wird hauptsächlich davon ab-hängen, wie* das Kind zu Hause, in der Schule, in der Gemein-
15 schaft behandelt wird. Nun ist das Kind eine schöpferische Ein-heit, die sich organisch entwickeln will und muß. Daher darf* die Schule keine Anstalt sein, in der der Lehrer wie ein Diktator das Kind von außen formen und regieren will, sondern ein Garten, wo der Lehrer das Kind pflegt wie ein Gärtner die
20 Pflanze, und wo er durch Liebe und Verstand sein organisches Wachstum fördert. Ferner*, da der Einfluß des Elternhauses* von großer Bedeutung ist, sollen junge Mütter in die Schule kom-men, so daß auch sie lernen, wie man das Kind richtig behandelt.

Fröbels Schulen wurden weltberühmt*, aber seine Ideen
25 waren für seine Zeit zu radikal, und so wurden seine Kinder-gärten noch vor seinem Tode in Preußen* verboten. Heutzutage finden seine Ideen und seine Pädagogik die größte Anerkennung* und Verbreitung weder in Deutschland noch in Europa, sondern in den Vereinigten Staaten.

[*122*]

Lesson 16

*angeregt stimulated
*die Roman'tik romanticism
*Schweizer (*indecl. adj.*) Swiss
*der Grundgedanke, -ns, -n basic
  thought
*davon . . . wie on how
*darf (*with a negative*) must
  (not)

*ferner furthermore
*das Elternhaus, ⁼er parental
  house
*weltberühmt world-famous
*(das) Preußen Prussia
*die Anerkennung recognition

EXERCISES

I. Answer with complete German sentences: (1) Hatte Elsa von dem Konzert gehört? (2) Wer sagte ihr davon? (3) Wieviele Leute singen in dem Konzert? (4) Singen sie in einem großen Saal? (5) Sind alle Plätze in dem Saal gut? (6) Gehen Karl und Elsa zusammen ins Konzert? (7) Schwätzt Elsa die ganze Zeit während eines Konzerts? (8) Mit wem geht Karl nie wieder ins Konzert? (9) Woher kommt das Wort „Kindergarten"? (10) Wer war Pestalozzi? (11) Warum ist die Erziehung eines Kindes so wichtig? (12) Womit vergleicht Fröbel die Schule für Kinder? (13) Warum sollen junge Mütter auch in die Schule kommen? (14) Warum wurden Fröbels Schulen in Preußen verboten? (15) Wo fanden Fröbels Ideen die größte Verbreitung?

II. Fill in the correct form of the relative pronoun: (1) Den Tenor, (who) ⸺ mit Frau Waag singt, habe ich nie gehört. (2) Der Saal, in (which) ⸺ das Konzert gegeben wurde, war klein. (3) (Whatever) ⸺ Sie da sehen, wird interessant sein. (4) Die Leute, (to whom) ⸺ wir das erzählten, wollten es nicht glauben. (5) Ich tue alles, (that) ⸺ Sie wollen. (6) Fröbel, (whose) ⸺ Ideen berühmt wurden, war ein deutscher Lehrer. (7) (Whoever) ⸺ das Buch liest, wird viel daraus lernen. (8) Es war dasselbe Mädchen, (who) ⸺ letzte Woche hier war. (9) Grillparzer, (whose) ⸺ Namen Sie noch nicht gehört haben, war ein österreichischer Dichter.

III. Translate into German: (1) Haydn and Mozart are two composers whose music I like to hear. (2) Mrs. Waag was a woman about whom we had heard good reports (viel Gutes). (3) I have heard nothing that will help you. (4) Is that the same man with whom you went to Germany last year? (5) This is the century in which everything is done by means of machines. (6) Give me the names of those whom you are going to visit. (7) Who was the man with whom you were talking yesterday? (8) The problem on which I am working consists of three parts. (9) A school in which the teacher is only a dictator is a bad one. (10) There are many people who don't believe that.

VOCABULARY

die **Anstalt, -en** institution
anständig good, respectable
von **außen** from the outside
behandeln treat
beieinander next to one another
bestimmen determine
die **Bühne, -n** stage
der **Charak'ter, -e** character
der **Dikta'tor, -en** dictator
das **Duett', -e** duet
einführen introduce
die **Einheit, -en** unit
die **Erziehung** education
fast almost
fördern further, help
formen form, shape
die **Freude, -n** pleasure
der **Gärtner, -** gardener
die **Gemeinschaft, -en** community
hauptsächlich chief, main
die **Idee', -n** idea
irgendwo somewhere (or other)
der **Kindergarten, =** garden of children
die **Liebe** love
mal = einmal once
die **Mutter, =** mother

die **Nation', -en** nation
nett nice
obgleich although
der **Pädagog', -en, -en** pedagog
die **Pädago'gik** pedagogy
pädago'gisch pedagogic(al)
die **Pflanze, -n** plant
pflegen take care of
der **Platz, =e** seat
das **Programm', -e** program
radikal' radical
recht all right
regieren rule
der **Saal, Säle** hall
schöpferisch creative
schwätzen chatter
sollen are to
zum **Teil** in part
teilen share
der **Tenor', =e** *or* -e tenor
verbieten, o, o forbid
die **Verbreitung** dissemination
der **Verstand** understanding
das **Wachstum** growth
so **weit** as far as
wenige few; **wenigere** less, fewer
wunderbar wonderful

LESSON 17

Verbal prefixes

17.1 Verbal prefixes. There are two types of verbal prefixes in German. One, called "inseparable," corresponds to the English prefixes *be-*, *for-*, and *under-* in *become*, *forget*, and *understand*. The other, called "separable," corresponds to the adverbial element in such English phrases as *stand up*, *sit down*, and *carry on*.

17.2 Inseparable prefixes. The inseparable prefixes are **be-, emp-, ent-, er-, ge-, ver-,** and **zer-.†** With the exception of **zer-**, a verb with one of these prefixes should be considered a new verb and the meaning should be obtained from the vocabulary or dictionary. **Zer-** has the idea of *to pieces*: **brechen,** *break*—**zerbrechen,** *break to pieces, shatter.*

An inseparable prefix:

(a) is never separated,
(b) never has the accent,
(c) causes the past participle to be formed without adding **ge-.**

---

† **Miß-**, meaning *mis-*, **voll-**, meaning *full-*, **hinter-**, meaning *behind* or *back*, and **wider-**, meaning *against*, are almost always inseparable.

A sample synopsis with the imperative forms is:

Ich besuche meinen Onkel auf dem Land. *I visit my uncle in the country.*
Ich besuchte meinen Onkel auf dem Land.
Ich habe meinen Onkel auf dem Land besucht.
Ich hatte meinen Onkel auf dem Land besucht.
Ich werde meinen Onkel auf dem Land besuchen.
Ich werde meinen Onkel auf dem Land besucht haben.

Besuche deinen Onkel auf dem Land.
Besucht eueren Onkel auf dem Land.
Besuchen Sie Ihren Onkel auf dem Land.

17.3 Separable prefixes. With the exception of the prefixes already mentioned and those discussed in § 17.4, all other prefixes are separable. In general, the meaning of a verb with a separable prefix is the meaning of the verb plus the meaning of the prefix. When this is not the cause, as for example with **aufhören,** *cease, stop,* the student must simply learn the meaning of the compound.

A separable prefix:

(a) always has the main accent,

(b) is either the final element or part of the final element of the clause. If the stem syllable of the verb is part of the first or the second element of the clause separation must occur, but if the stem is part of the last element of the clause the prefix is written together with it. Hence, separation occurs in an independent clause in the present and past tenses, in an imperative sentence, and in a subordinate clause if, as when **wenn** is omitted, the verb is not last. Separation does not occur in the compound tenses and in a subordinate clause, except as just stated.

(c) is followed by ge- in the past participle and the whole is written as one word,

(d) is followed by the **zu** used with the infinitive and the whole is written as one word.

Below are two synopses, the three imperatives and the infinitive with **zu** of a verb having a separable prefix.

Er geht aufs Land hinaus. *He goes out into the country.*
Er ging aufs Land hinaus.

Er ist aufs Land hinausgegangen.
Er war aufs Land hinausgegangen.
Er wird aufs Land hinausgehen.
Er wird aufs Land hinausgegangen sein.

Es ist wahr, daß er aufs Land hinausgeht. *It is true that he goes out into the country.*
Es ist wahr, daß er aufs Land hinausging.
Es ist wahr, daß er aufs Land hinausgegangen ist.
Es ist wahr, daß er aufs Land hinausgegangen war.
Es ist wahr, daß er aufs Land hinausgehen wird.
Es ist wahr, daß er aufs Land hinausgegangen sein wird.

Gehe aufs Land hinaus.
Geht aufs Land hinaus.
Gehen Sie aufs Land hinaus.

Es ist schön, im Sommer aufs Land hinauszugehen.

17.4 Variable prefixes. Five prefixes are used both separably and inseparably: **durch-, über-, um-, unter-,** and **wieder-.**

When used separably they have all the features mentioned in § 17.3 and the meaning of the verb so formed is that of the simple verb plus that of the prefix.

> **wie'derholen** (wieder, *again* or *back;* holen *fetch* or *bring*)
> **holte wieder   hat wiedergeholt   holt wieder** *bring back*

When used inseparably they have all the features mentioned in § 17.2 and the meaning of the verb is a derived one which must be looked up in the dictionary.

> **wiederho'len   wiederholte   hat wiederholt   wiederholt**
> *repeat*

17.5 *Hin* and *her*. Two very important and frequently used separable prefixes are **hin-** and **her-.** The former indicates motion away from the speaker or the center of interest, the latter motion toward the speaker or center of interest. Each may be compounded with another prefix.

> **Wo gehen Sie hin?** *Where are you going?*
> **Kommen Sie her!** *Come here.*
> **Sie ziehen in ein anderes Land hinaus.** *They are moving to a different country.*
> **Er holte Nadel und Zwirn heraus.** *He took out needle and thread.*

GESPRÄCH

Hermann: Was tust du diesen Sommer, Lotte?
Lotte: Ich weiß noch nicht bestimmt. Ich versuche, eine gute Stellung hier in der Stadt zu kriegen. Wenn das nicht geht*, kann ich immer zu meinem Onkel aufs Land hinausgehen. Ich tue es
5 aber lieber nicht.
Hermann: Warum? Findest du es langweilig da draußen?
Lotte: Nein, das ist es nicht. Man kann sich dort sehr gut amüsieren*. Es ist ein kleiner See in der Nähe, wo man schwimmen und segeln kann.
10 **Hermann:** Wenn du dich gut amüsierst, warum willst du denn nicht hinaus*?
Lotte: Weil mein Onkel und meine Tante so alt sind. Sie hören nicht mehr gut, und, wenn ich sie anrede*, muß ich immer schreien. Ferner kommt noch dazu, daß entweder meine Tante
15 oder ich zu viel Arbeit hat, wenn ich für den ganzen Sommer hinausziehe.
Hermann: Nun, vor ein paar Tagen hat mir der Semmler gesagt, daß er eine Verkäuferin in seiner Buchhandlung* brauchen wird.
Lotte: Ach, das ist aber fein. Ich gehe sofort und bewerbe mich
20 darum*. So etwas wäre* mir viel lieber als immer an einer Schreibmaschine zu sitzen.

*das geht that's possible
*sich amüsieren have fun
*hinaus = hinausgehen go out
*anreden speak to

*die Buchhandlung bookstore
*sich bewerben um apply for
*wäre would be

LESESTÜCK

Die Deutschen haben viele Märchen. Die berühmtesten sind die Märchen, die von den Brüdern Jakob (1785-1863) und Wilhelm (1786-1859) Grimm gesammelt wurden und die sie dann in ihrem Werk *Kinder- und Hausmärchen** herausgaben*. Eines der
5 bekanntesten dieser Märchen ist *Schneewittchen**, welches hier in Amerika durch den Disneyfilm* *Snow White and the Seven Dwarfs* besonders berühmt wurde. Da Sie alle dieses Märchen

gut kennen, geben wir hier eine Nacherzählung* eines der
weniger bekannten Grimmschen* Märchens.

Eine alte Frau machte das Feuer zurecht und zündete es mit 10
Stroh an. Sie wollte Bohnen kochen. Ein Strohhalm* und eine
Bohne fielen auf den Boden hinab. Später kam eine glühende
Kohle neben sie zu liegen.

„Was fangen wir nun an?" sprach die Kohle.

„Weil wir dem Tode so glücklich entronnen* sind," antwortete 15
die Bohne, „wird es gescheit* sein, in ein anderes Land hinaus-
zuziehen."

Der Vorschlag gefiel den beiden anderen. Bald kamen sie an
einen kleinen Bach. Da keine Brücke da war, streckte sich der
Strohhalm von einem Ufer zum andern. Die Kohle trat auf ihn 20
wie auf eine Brücke. Plötzlich aber blieb sie stehen und der
Strohhalm fing an zu brennen, zerbrach* in zwei Stücke und fiel
in den Bach hinunter. Die Kohle fiel ihm nach, und beide gaben
den Geist auf.

Die Bohne lachte und lachte darüber und hörte nicht auf, bis 25
sie zerplatzte*. Glücklicherweise kam ein Schneider vorbei, der
Nadel und Zwirn* herausholte und die Bohne wieder zusammen-
nähte. Weil der Schneider schwarzen Zwirn gebraucht hatte,
haben alle Bohnen jetzt eine schwarze Naht*.

*Kinder- und Hausmärchen fairy
  tales for children and the home
*herausgeben publish
*Schneewittchen Snow White
*der Disneyfilm film produced by
  Walt Disney
*die Nacherzählung, -en retelling
*Grimmsch (of the) Grimms,
  Grimms'
*der Strohhalm, -e (blade of)
  straw
*entrinnen, a, o (ist) escape
*gescheit smart, clever
*zerbrechen, a, o, i break
*zerplatzen (ist) burst, split
*der Zwirn thread
*die Naht, ⁼e seam

EXERCISES

I. Answer with complete German sentences: (1) Wo hoffte
Lotte, eine Stellung zu bekommen? (2) Was kann sie tun, wenn
das nicht geht? (3) Tut sie das gern? (4) Ist es langweilig bei
ihrem Onkel? (5) Schwimmt man dort in einem See? (6) Sind
ihr Onkel und ihre Tante junge Leute? (7) Warum muß sie
schreien, wenn sie sie anredet? (8) Was machten die Brüder

Grimm? (9) Nennen Sie eines der bekanntesten deutschen Märchen. (10) Womit zündete die Frau das Feuer an? (11) Warum machte sie ein Feuer? (12) Wie kamen der Strohhalm und die Bohne zusammen? (13) Wollten die beiden anderen tun, was die Bohne vorschlug? (14) Wie machte der Strohhalm eine Brücke über den Bach? (15) War die Bohne traurig (sad), als die zwei ins Wasser hinunterfielen?

II. Give the principal parts of: anfangen, anzünden, aufgeben, aufhören, bemerken, gebrauchen, herausholen, herausziehen, hinunterfallen, versuchen.

III. Give synopses of: (1) Die alte Frau macht das Feuer zurecht. (2) Es bedeutet viel Arbeit für mich. (3) Die Studenten ziehen in die Welt hinaus. (4) Der Professor wiederholt das Wort. (5) Sie zündet das Feuer mit Stroh an.

IV. Fill in the correct forms of the verbs called for (the position of the prefix is not indicated!): (1) Die Studenten (einsteigen, *past perf.*) __ schon in das Auto __. (2) Sie (hinausfahren, *past*) __ aus der Stadt. (3) Vier von ihnen (hineingehen, *past*) __ in einen Wald (woods) und (versuchen, *past*) __ etwas für ein Feuer zu finden. (4) Wir (anfangen, *pres. perf.*) __ neulich __, Deutsch in unserem täglichen Leben (gebrauchen, *infinitive with* zu) __. (5) Er (herausziehen, *pres. perf.*) __ nur einen alten Schuh aus dem Wasser __. (6) Du (hineintreten, *fut.*) __ in das Zimmer allein __. (7) Wir (bemerken, *pres. perf.*) __ oft __, daß der Krieg nie (aufhören, *pres.*) __. (8) Es ist nicht immer leicht, ein Feuer (anzünden, *infinitive with* zu) __.

V. Translate into German: (1) Mr. Semmler didn't need a salesgirl. (2) Fortunately Lotte had already driven here. (3) This time we will try to use the typewriter. (4) If the reason is good, we will gladly cease. (5) He fell down into the lake and was pulled out by his friends. (6) Then he planned to swim across to the other bank. (7) Our uncle drove here last week. (8) When she gave up her position she didn't give us her reason. (9) He screamed when I began to answer him. (10) Did they laugh when he stopped?

VOCABULARY

(From now on separable prefixes will be indicated by a hyphen.)

(das) **Ame′rika** America
an-fangen, i, a, ä begin
antworten answer
an-zünden light, ignite
auf-geben, a, e, i give up
auf-hören stop, cease
der **Bach, ⸗e** brook
bald soon
bekannt well known
bemerken notice
die **Bohne, -n** bean
brennen burn
die **Brücke, -n** bridge
dabei while doing it
draußen out there
gebrauchen use
glücklich lucky, fortunate
glühen glow
heraus-holen take out
hinab-fallen, fiel, gefallen, fällt (ist) fall down
hinaus-gehen, ging, gegangen (ist) go out
hinaus-ziehen, zog, gezogen (ist) move out
hinunter-fallen, ie, a, ä (ist) fall down

kennen be acquainted with
die **Kohle, -n** coal
langweilig boring
das **Märchen, -** fairy tale
nach-fallen, ie, a, ä (ist) fall after
die **Nadel, -n** needle
sammeln collect
der **Schneider, -** tailor
die **Schreibmaschine, -n** typewriter
schwarz black
schwimmen, a, o swim
der **See, -n** lake
segeln sail
Semmler *proper name*
sofort at once
stehen-bleiben, ie, ie (ist) stop
die **Stellung, -en** job
strecken stretch, extend
das **Stroh** straw
das **Ufer, -** bank
die **Verkäuferin, -nen** salesgirl
versuchen try
der **Vorschlag, ⸗e** suggestion
zurecht-machen fix
zusammen-nähen sew together

LESSON 18

Numerals

18.1 Cardinal and ordinal numerals. A cardinal numeral is one that expresses quantity, that answers the question *How many?* An ordinal numeral expresses position in a numerical sequence, it answers the question *Which one(s)?*

18.2 Cardinal numerals. The cardinal numerals in German are:

eins	elf	einundzwanzig	hundertundeins
zwei	zwölf	zweiundzwanzig, etc.	zweihundert
drei	dreizehn	dreißig	tausend
vier	vierzehn	vierzig	eine Million'
fünf	fünfzehn	fünfzig	eine Milliar'de (billion)
sechs	sechzehn	sechzig	eine Billion' (trillion)
sieben	siebzehn	siebzig	
acht	achtzehn	achtzig	
neun	neunzehn	neunzig	
zehn	zwanzig	hundert	

The word for *zero* is **null**.

(a) Of these numerals **eins** is regularly declined, exactly like the indefinite article. Actually the indefinite article is an unstressed form of the numeral, just as *a* and *an* are unstressed de-

[132]

velopments of the numeral *one*. The numeral is frequently indicated in German by spaced type.

Ich habe nur e i n Buch.

(b) Occasionally **-er** is added to the genitive and **-en** to the dative of **zwei** and **drei,** but these numerals can be considered in general as indeclinable. The remaining numerals are not ordinarily declined, until **eine Million,** which is used simply as a noun with four cases, singular and plural.

(c) A cardinal numeral is written as one word.

einunddreißig *31*   **dreitausendsechshundert** *3600*

18.3 Ordinal numerals. The ordinals are formed by adding **-t** to the cardinal **zwei,** and to **vier** through **neunzehn** (note, however, **der siebte, der achte**), and by adding **-st** to the cardinal from **zwanzig** on. **Der erste** and **der dritte** are irregular.

der erste	der neunte
der zweite	der zehnte
der dritte	der elfte
der vierte	der zwanzigste
der fünfte	der einundzwanzigste
der sechste	der dreißigste
der sieb(en)te	der hundertste
der achte	der tausendste

The ordinals are declined like adjectives.

der erste Mann	ein zweiter Mann	diese dritte Maschine
des ersten Mannes	eines zweiten Mannes	dieser dritten Maschine
etc.	etc.	etc.

18.4 Cardinal and ordinal compounds. To the cardinal may be added **-mal** and **-erlei,** to the ordinal **-ens.** The meaning of such words will be clear from these examples:

> **einmal, zweimal** *once, twice*
> **zweierlei, dreierlei** *two sorts of, three sorts of*
> **erstens, zweitens, drittens** *firstly, secondly, thirdly; in the first, second, third place*

[*133*]

18.5   Fractions. Fractions are formed by adding -el to the ordinal for the denominator and using a cardinal for the numerator. *A half* is **eine Hälfte; halb** is used as an adjective.

3/5 **drei Fünftel**   7/20 **sieben Zwanzigstel**   **ein halbes Jahr**

18.6   Special items. In working with numerals certain facts are to be remembered.

(a) The four arithmetical processes are expressed as follows:

$2 + 2 = 4$ **zwei und zwei ist vier**
$16 - 9 = 7$ **sechzehn weniger neun ist sieben**
$3 \cdot 6 = 18$ **dreimal sechs ist achtzehn**
$24 : 8 = 3$ **vierundzwanzig geteilt** or **dividiert durch acht ist drei**

(b) A number followed by a point is an ordinal.

der 3. Mai = der dritte Mai

(c) The comma is regularly used for decimal separation.

$3,6 + 8,2 = 11,8$ **drei Komma sechs und acht Komma zwei ist elf Komma acht**

18.7   Expressions of time. Time of day is expressed on the whole the same way in both languages. In German the half hour always and the quarter hours frequently are expressed *toward* the next hour. The following examples should make this clear.

at 8:00 **um acht (Uhr)**
7:30 **halb acht**
10:15 **viertel nach zehn** or **viertel (auf) elf**
11:45 **dreiviertel (auf) zwölf** or **viertel vor zwölf**
3:20 **zwanzig Minuten nach drei** or **drei Uhr zwanzig**
6:35 **fünfundzwanzig Minuten vor sieben** or **sechs Uhr fünfund-dreißig**
a.m. **vormittags**
p.m. **nachmittags**

All methods of public transportation and many other things in Germany are run on *twenty-four hour time.* Thus a train may leave at **siebzehn Uhr zwanzig** (5:20 p.m.) and a theater performance may start at **halb zwanzig** (7:30 p.m.). The former time will appear on a timetable as **17:20**, and the latter will appear on the printed program, for example, as **½20 Uhr.**

18.8   Dates. A date is expressed in German by placing the ordinal number as an adjective before the name of the month. If the date is expressed as a number it is followed by a period. See § 18.6 (b).

der 21. März

The date of a letter is usually expressed in the accusative case (definite time when) with or without **den.**

New York, (den) 5. Mai 1957

18.9   Use of *je*. Je gives distributive force.

Wir haben je ein Buch. *We have a book each.* (There are as many books as there are people.)

GESPRÄCH

Herr Krause: Ach, Braun, es ist gut, daß ich Sie treffe. Wie spät ist es eigentlich nach Ihrer Uhr?
Herr Braun: Zwanzig vor acht.
Krause: Dann muß ich mich aber beeilen. Meine Uhr geht nämlich zur Abwechslung wieder mal nicht, und ich habe noch keine 5 Zeit gehabt, sie zum Uhrmacher zu bringen.
Braun: Tja, das ist so eine Sache! Meine geht selten richtig. Ein paar Tage lang geht sie nach, dann geht sie auf einmal vor. Also, ob sie jetzt richtig geht, weiß ich nicht.
Krause (lacht): Na, das ist ja einfach knorke*. Da komm' ich 10 also heute entweder zu früh oder zu spät im Büro an. Auf Wiedersehen!
Braun (auch lachend): Auf Wiedersehen!

*knorke fine, excellent, "dandy"

LESESTÜCK

Das Jahr hat vier Jahreszeiten. Diese sind der Frühling, der Sommer, der Herbst und der Winter. Der Frühling beginnt gewöhnlich am 21. März, der Sommer am 21. Juni, der Herbst am

22. September und der Winter am 21. Dezember. Zuweilen
5 beginnt der eine oder der andere am 20. oder am 22. des Monats
(der Herbst am 21. oder am 23.). Der März, der April und der
Mai sind also Frühlingsmonate, und der Juni, der Juli und der
August sind Sommermonate. Was sind der September, der Ok-
tober und der November? Natürlich sind sie Herbstmonate, und
10 die Wintermonate sind der Dezember, der Januar und der
Februar.

Der April, der Juni, der September und der November haben
je dreißig Tage. Der Februar ist der einzige Monat, der nur acht-
undzwanzig Tage hat. Die übrigen haben je einunddreißig. Wenn
15 die Jahreszahl* durch vier teilbar* ist, haben wir ein Schaltjahr*.
Dann hat der Februar noch einen Tag, also neunundzwanzig im
ganzen.

Die ersten sechs Tage der Woche heißen der Sonntag, der
Montag, der Dienstag, der Mittwoch, der Donnerstag und der
20 Freitag. In Norddeutschland heißt der siebte Tag der Sonnabend
und in West- und Süddeutschland heißt er der Samstag.

Jeder Tag dauert vierundzwanzig Stunden. Sechzig Minuten
sind eine Stunde und sechzig Sekunden sind eine Minute. Es
sind also dreitausendsechshundert Sekunden in einer Stunde, und
25 86 400 in einem Tag. Wieviele Sekunden sind in einem Jahr?
Mehr als dreißig Millionen.

George Washington, der erste Präsident der Vereinigten
Staaten, wurde am 22. Februar 1732 geboren und starb am 14.
Dezember 1799. Er war 67 Jahre alt, als er starb. Der sechzehnte
30 Präsident lebte vom 12. Februar 1809 bis zum 14. April 1865. Wie
hieß er?

Hier sind noch ein paar Daten. Weihnachten fällt auf den 25.
Dezember und der Danksagungstag auf den letzten Donnerstag
im November. Ostern ist der erste Sonntag nach dem ersten Voll-
35 mond an oder nach dem 21. März. Unsere Unabhängigkeitserklärung wurde am 4. Juli 1776 unterzeichnet. Den wievielten
haben wir heute*? Um das zu beantworten, muß man einen
Kalender ansehen.

*die **Jahreszahl**, -en date
*teilbar divisible
*das **Schaltjahr**, -e leap year

*Den wievielten haben wir
heute? What is the date today?

EXERCISES

I. Answer with complete German sentences: (1) Warum hat Krause keine Uhr? (2) Wer repariert (repairs) Uhren? (3) Wie spät ist es nach Brauns Uhr? (4) Warum weiß Krause nicht, ob er zu früh oder zu spät ins Büro kommt? (5) Welches Jahr haben wir jetzt? (6) Welche Jahreszeit haben wir jetzt? (7) Was ist die nächste Jahreszeit? (8) Was war die vorige Jahreszeit? (9) Den wievielten haben wir heute? (10) Den wievielten hatten wir gestern?

II. Read in German:

$5 + 3 = 8$	$17 - 6 = 11$	$7 \cdot 4 = 28$
$8 + 5 = 13$	$53 - 4 = 49$	$16 \cdot 3 = 48$
$26 + 28 = 54$	$75 - 24 = 51$	$14 \cdot 12 = 168$
$106 + 281 = 387$	$324 - 182 = 142$	$3,2 \cdot 1,6 = 5,12$
$16,8 + 14,7 = 31,5$	$107,3 - 54,9 = 52,4$	$624 \cdot 8 = 4992$

$9 : 3 = 3$
$34 : 17 = 2$
$144 : 6 = 24$
$3520 : 64 = 55$
$144,57 : 7,9 = 18,3$

III. Read the following times in German (when there is more than one way give all possible ways):

11:00	9:30	8:45	1:53	3:37
6:23	12:15	12:30	2:20	3:30

IV. (a) Express the following dates in German:

October 12, 1492	June 15, 1215	April 23, 1921
September 4, 1647	July 14, 1789	December 1, 1878

(b) Read the following as dates in letters:

May 7, 1949   October 2, 1923   February 9, 1951

VOCABULARY

die **Abwechslung, -en** alternation;   **an-kommen, kam, gekommen**
zur ___ for a change   (ist) arrive

der **April'** April
der **August'** August
beantworten answer
sich **beeilen** hurry
der **Danksagungstag** Thanksgiving Day
der **Dezem'ber** December
der **Dienstag, -e** Tuesday
der **Donnerstag, -e** Thursday
auf **einmal** suddenly
fallen auf, ie, a, ä (ist) come on (*of dates*)
der **Februar** February
der **Frühlingsmonat, -e** spring month
gehen, ging, gegangen (ist) go, run (*of a timepiece*)
heißen, ie, ei be named
der **Herbst, -e** fall, autumn
der **Herbstmonat, -e** fall month
die **Jahreszeit, -en** season
der **Januar** January
je each
der **Juli** July
der **Juni** June
der **Kalen'der, -** calendar
der **Mai** May
der **März** March
die **Million', -en** million
der **Monat, -e** month
der **Montag, -e** Monday

nach-gehen, ging, gegangen (ist) be slow
noch in addition
der **Novem'ber** November
ob whether, if
der **Okto'ber** October
das **Ostern** Easter
der **Präsident', -en, -en** president
die **Sache; das ist so eine ___** that's the way things are
die **Sekun'de, -n** second
selten rare
der **Septem'ber** September
der **Sommermonat, -e** summer month
der **Sonnabend, -e** Saturday
spät late; **wie ___ ist es** what time is it?
tja = ja yes
übrig remaining
die **Unabhängigkeitserklärung** Declaration of Independence
unterzeichnen sign
der **Vollmond, -e** full moon
vor-gehen, ging, gegangen (ist) be fast
die **Weihnachten** (*pl.*) Christmas
wieviele how many
der **Winter, -** winter
der **Wintermonat, -e** winter month

LESSON 19

Modal auxiliaries, present and past tenses

19.1 Modal auxiliaries. Six verbs exist in German which in themselves do not express an action or a condition, but in some way vary the aspect of another verb. These are called "modal auxiliaries." In English *can*, *may*, and *must* exist as modal auxiliaries; *shall* still has such uses (as in the Ten Commandments), but *will* is used now for the most part only as the auxiliary of the future tense. The six verbs with their principal parts are given below. An explanation of the use of the two past participles will be given in Lesson 20.

dürfen	durfte	hat gedurft, dürfen	darf
können	konnte	hat gekonnt, können	kann
mögen	mochte	hat gemocht, mögen	mag
müssen	mußte	hat gemußt, müssen	muß
sollen	sollte	hat gesollt, sollen	soll
wollen	wollte	hat gewollt, wollen	will

19.2 Present and past tenses. The present tense of each of the modals is irregular. The past tense is derived from the second of the principal parts like a weak verb. **Dürfen** will suffice as an example.

ich darf	ich kann	ich mag
du darfst	du kannst	du magst
er darf	er kann	er mag
wir dürfen	wir können	wir mögen
ihr dürft	ihr könnt	ihr mögt
sie dürfen	sie können	sie mögen

ich muß	ich soll	ich will
du mußt	du sollst	du willst
er muß	er soll	er will
wir müssen	wir sollen	wir wollen
ihr müßt	ihr sollt	ihr wollt
sie müssen	sie sollen	sie wollen

ich durfte	wir durften
du durftest	ihr durftet
er durfte	sie durften

19.3 Meanings. Each of the modals has a fundamental meaning and most of them have one or more connotations which call for a different English translation.

(a) **Dürfen** means *to be permitted to.* Notice that it has passive force. In this meaning it is often translated by *may.* In English, if a person is forbidden or not permitted to do something we say *He must not do it.* This form in German involves **dürfen**.

> **Darf ich fragen?** *May I ask?*
> **Er durfte nicht heiraten.** *He wasn't allowed to get married.*
> **Das darf er nicht tun.** *He must not do that.*

(b) **Können** means *can, to be able, to know how.*

> **Können Sie das nicht in der Woche machen?** *Can't you do that during the week?*
> **Können Sie Tennis spielen?** *Do you know how to play tennis?*

(c) **Mögen** today ordinarily means *to like* or *to like to.* An older meaning, rendered by *may,* is preserved in certain types of phrases, but in these only, and gives the idea of possibility. (See also Lesson 26.)

> **Ich mag frohe Gesichter um mich.** *I like cheerful faces around me.*
> **Das mag wahr sein.** *That may be true.*

[*140*]

(d) **Müssen** means *must, to have to.* Sometimes it has the force of *not being able to help* doing something.

> **Warum müssen Sie dabei sein?** *Why must you be present?*
> **Ich mußte lachen.** *I couldn't help laughing* or *I had to laugh.*

(e) **Sollen** means *to be to, to be expected to.* Sometimes, as in the Ten Commandments, it has the force of *shall.* It is also used to express a claim that is made about the subject of the sentence. In the subjunctive (see Lessons 23 and 26) it expresses moral obligation.

> **Es sollte vorgestern geschehen.** *It was (supposed) to be done day before yesterday.*
> **Du sollst nicht stehlen.** *Thou shalt not steal.*
> **Unsere Gesellschaft soll in gutem Ruf stehen.** *Our company is said to have a good reputation.*

(f) **Wollen** expresses the idea of *wanting to.* Wanting to involves *intention,* whereas wishing and desiring do not necessarily involve it. Therefore, **wollen** frequently is used with the meaning *to intend to, to be going to, to be about to.* Finally, it may express a claim that the subject of the sentence makes about himself.

> **Er will sie nicht allein auswählen.** *He doesn't want to select her by himself.*
> **Wir wollen eine neue Sekretärin anstellen.** *We are going to hire a new secretary.*
> **Sie will sehr intelligent sein.** *She claims to be very intelligent.*

19.4 Dependent infinitive. As can be seen in the examples above, the dependent infinitive is used without **zu** after the modals and is placed at the end of the clause. However, the infinitive may be understood rather than expressed, as in English. This is especially true with verbs of motion, as **gehen, kommen, fahren.**

> **Wollen Sie das machen? Ja, ich will es.** *Do you want to do that? Yes, I want to.*
> **Ich muß ins Büro.** *I must go to my office.*

19.5 Modals with a passive infinitive. In German, just as in English, the modals cannot be put into the passive. To form a passive construction with them one must use the passive infinitive. This is formed by taking the past participle of the verb used with the modal together with the infinitive of **werden.** The two words are then regarded as one unit.

Active: **Die Frau kann den Mann sehen.** *The woman can see the man.*

Passive: **Der Mann kann von der Frau gesehen werden.** *The man can be seen by the woman.*

GESPRÄCH

Herr Westermann: Guten Morgen, Herr Reinhold. Ein herrlicher Tag, nicht wahr?

Herr Reinhold: Jawohl. Und trotzdem muß ich ins Büro, obgleich es Samstag ist.

5 **Westermann:** Das ist schade. Darf ich fragen, warum?

Reinhold: Wir wollen eine neue Sekretärin anstellen*, und heute kommen die Bewerberinnen*.

Westermann: Können Sie das nicht in der Woche machen, statt daß Sie sich ein gutes Wochenende dadurch verderben?

10 **Reinhold:** Es sollte vorgestern geschehen, aber der Chef* mußte plötzlich nach Chicago und ist erst gestern abend zurückgekommen.

Westermann: Wenn der Chef da ist, warum müssen Sie denn dabei sein?

15 **Reinhold:** Weil die Sekretärin eher für mich arbeitet als für den Chef. Er will sie also nicht allein auswählen.

Westermann: Werden viele kommen?

Reinhold: Es kann sein. Das Gehalt ist ziemlich gut. Dazu soll unsere Gesellschaft in gutem Ruf stehen. Die vorige Sekretärin

20 war ja neun Jahre bei uns.

Westermann: Und dann hat sie sich verheiratet, nicht wahr? Na, diesmal wählen Sie sich eine aus, die alt und häßlich ist! Die jungen und schönen schauen sich doch immer nur nach einem Mann um*.

25 **Reinhold:** Das ist schon wahr. Und doch mag ich frohe Gesichter um mich, und es schadet nichts, wenn sie auch schön sind.

Westermann: Hoffentlich kriegen Sie, was Sie wollen. Auf
Wiedersehn, Herr Reinhold!
Reinhold: Auf Wiedersehn!

*an-stellen hire   *der Chef, -s boss
*die Bewerberin, -nen applicant   *sich um-schauen look around

LESESTÜCK

Will ein deutsches Kind auf die Universität, so muß es im Alter
von zehn Jahren die Volksschule* verlassen und nach Bestehen
einer Prüfung in eine höhere Schule eintreten. Diese höhere
Schule, in der das Studium neun Jahre dauert, heißt ein Gymnasium*.   5

Hiervon gibt es drei Haupttypen*: das klassische oder alt-
sprachliche Gymnasium, das neusprachliche Gymnasium und
das mathematisch-naturwissenschaftliche Gymnasium. Diese
unterscheiden sich durch die verschiedene Betonung der Fremdsprachen und der naturwissenschaftlichen Fächer. In dem klas- 10
sischen Gymnasium müssen Griechisch, Latein und eine moderne
Fremdsprache studiert werden. In dem neusprachlichen Gymnasium muß der Student auch drei Fremdsprachen belegen*,
aber hiervon dürfen zwei (in manchen Ländern alle drei)
moderne sein. Und in dem mathematisch-naturwissenschaftlichen 15
Gymnasium braucht der Student nur zwei Fremdsprachen zu
belegen, wovon in manchen Ländern beide moderne sein dürfen.
In diesem Gymnasium werden aber Mathematik und die Naturwissenschaften besonders betont. Außerdem gibt es natürlich in
allen drei Gymnasien noch die üblichen Fächer wie Geschichte, 20
Deutsch, Literatur usw.

Zum Schluß muß der Student dann eine Reifeprüfung* (auch
Abitur* genannt) bestehen. Wenn er diese besteht, so kann er
sich—ganz egal* was für ein Gymnasium er besucht hat—irgend
eine Universität aussuchen und dort studieren, was er will.   25

Obwohl, wie schon früher gesagt, der deutsche Universitätsstudent viel mehr Freiheit hat als der amerikanische, ist das nicht
der Fall im Gymnasium. Hier muß der Student sechs Tage die
Woche in die Schule, wo er viel Arbeit und wenig Freiheit hat.
Das Resultat ist, daß nur ungefähr dreißig Prozent von denen,   30

die mit zehn Jahren anfingen und später auf eine Universität wollten, den neunjährigen Kursus und die Reifeprüfung bestehen.

35 Da nur ungefähr fünfzehn Prozent der deutschen Jugend diese Gymnasien besuchen können und da, wie oben gesagt, nur ungefähr dreißig Prozent von diesen zum formellen höheren Studium weitergehen können, so sieht man—man mag darüber denken, wie man will—daß es nicht leicht ist, in Deutschland Universitätsstudent zu werden. Und das soll der Fall in fast ganz Europa sein.

*die **Volksschule, -n** primary school (*keep the German word*)

*das **Gymna'sium, -sien** secondary school (*keep the German word*)

*der **Haupttyp, -en** main type

*belegen enroll in

*die **Reifeprüfung, -en** final examination

*das **Abitur', -e** final examination (*keep the German word*)

*ganz egal' no matter

EXERCISES

I. Answer with complete German sentences: (1) Was für ein Tag war es? (2) Wohin mußte Herr Reinhold? (3) Wen wollten sie anstellen? (4) An welchem Tag der Woche war es? (5) Wie war das Gehalt der Sekretärin? (6) Warum verließ die vorige Sekretärin ihre Stellung? (7) Woran denken die jungen und schönen Mädchen? (8) Warum will Herr Reinhold keine alte, häßliche Sekretärin haben? (9) In was für eine Schule muß das deutsche Kind, das auf die Universität will? (10) Wie alt ist es, wenn es in diese Schule eintritt? (11) Wie lange ist der Kursus? (12) Was für eine Prüfung muß der Student bestehen, bevor er auf die Universität darf? (13) In welchem Alter kann er gewöhnlich auf die Universität? (14) Wie mag man über das deutsche System denken? (15) Wo soll es ungefähr gerade so schwer sein, Universitätsstudent zu werden, wie in Deutschland?

II. Fill in the blank spaces with the forms called for: (1) Herr Reinhold (had to) ___ in sein Büro gehen. (2) Herr Westermann (was permitted) ___ seine kranke Frau besuchen. (3) Die neue Sekretärin (is said to) ___ sehr schön sein. (4) Der Professor (likes) ___ keine schlechten Studenten. (5) (Do you want) ___

ein gutes Gehalt? (*3 forms*) (6) Du (must not) __ hier bleiben.
(7) Zuerst (was able to) __ sie Beethoven nicht finden. (8) Der
Mann (claims to) __ ein großer Komponist sein. (9) Karl (was
to) __ nicht lange in Berlin bleiben. (10) (Can't you) __ zu
Hause bleiben? (*3 forms*)

III. Translate into German: (1) He could not find a good room
for me. (2) My uncle wants to stay at home all summer. (3) His
sister was about to leave the house when her husband arrived.
(4) Do you like him? (*3 forms*) (5) She claims to be very musical. (6) You must not do that without him. (*3 forms*) (7) I
have to read this book today, but my brother had to read it yesterday. (8) It is said to be very difficult to become a university
student in Europe.

VOCABULARY

das **Alter,** - age
altsprachlich classical-language
amerika'nisch American
aus-suchen seek out
aus-wählen choose, select
bestehen, -stand, -standen pass
das **Bestehen** passing
besuchen attend
betonen emphasize
die **Betonung** emphasis
dabei present
diesmal this time
dürfen be permitted, may
eher rather
ein-treten, a, e, i (ist) enter
das **Fach, ̈er** subject
der **Fall, ̈e** case
froh happy, cheerful
das **Gehalt, ̈er** salary
die **Gesellschaft, -en** company
das **Gesicht, -er** face
griechisch Greek
häßlich ugly
heißen, ie, ei be called
hiervon of this, of these
höher higher
irgend ein any (at all)

die **Jugend** youth
Latein' Latin
mancher many a; *pl.* many, some
mathematisch-naturwissenschaft-
  lich mathematical-scientific
modern' modern
mögen may
naturwissenschaftlich scientific
neunjährig nine years'
neusprachlich modern-language
obwohl although
das **Resultat', -e** result
der **Ruf** reputation
schaden harm, hurt
die **Sekretä'rin, -nen** secretary
das **Studium, -dien** study
trotzdem nevertheless
üblich usual
der **Universitätsstudent, -en, -en**
  university student
unterscheiden, ie, ie differentiate
usw. = undsoweiter etc.
verderben, a, o, i spoil
sich verheiraten get married
weiter-gehen, ging, gegangen
  (ist) go on
das **Wochenende, -n** week-end

LESSON 20

Remaining tenses of the modal auxiliaries

20.1 Present and past perfect tenses. The present and the past perfect tenses of the modal auxiliaries are formed by using the auxiliary verb **haben** with the past participle of the modal. There are two past participle forms, and the use of one or the other depends on the presence of a dependent infinitive.

20.2 Perfect tenses without a dependent infinitive. If no dependent infinitive is used, the perfect tenses are formed with the regular (ge . . . t) past participle. No matter how obviously it is understood, the fact that the infinitive is not actually present in the sentence calls for the regular past participle.

> **Das habe ich nie gekonnt.** *I could never do that.*
> **Er hat auf die Universität gewollt.** *He wanted to go to the university.*

20.3 Perfect tenses with a dependent infinitive. If the dependent infinitive is actually present, then the alternate past participle that resembles the infinitive in form MUST be used. The dependent infinitive precedes this past participle.

> **Er hat dann nachgeben müssen.** *Then he had to give in.*
> **Willi hatte sich waschen müssen.** *Willi had had to wash himself.*

This combination of the dependent infinitive and the alternate past participle is frequently referred to as a "double infinitive." One feature of the double infinitive is that it must always come last in the clause. The form of **haben** precedes it immediately in a subordinate clause.

> **Er erklärte, daß er dann hat nachgeben müssen.** *He explained that he had to give in then.*

20.4 Future tense.† The future tense of the modals is formed as for any other verb.

> **Er wird es nicht wollen.** *He will not want it.*

When there is a dependent infinitive this precedes the infinitive of the modal, and the two must stand together at the end of the clause, even in a subordinate clause.

> **Er wird nicht gehen wollen.** *He will not want to go.*

20.5 Double infinitive with other verbs. There are a few other verbs that have the double infinitive construction, the most important being **lassen. Sehen** and **hören** are also frequently found. The word order statements given in § 20.3 apply to these verbs also.

> **Er hat sein Buch in Europa drucken lassen.** *He had his book printed in Europe.*
> **Ich habe so oft davon sprechen hören.** *I have so often heard talk about that.*

GESPRÄCH

Professor Huber: Guten Tag, Braun. Na, freuen Sie sich auf die Osterferien*?

Braun: Tja, ich weiß nicht. Mit den Ferien ist das eine eigene Sache. Da gibt's immer viel mehr zu tun als sonst.

Huber: Wieso denn?

Braun: Na, z. B., jeder Professor sagt: „Ah, Sie haben ja nächste Woche Ferien, da können Sie sich mal vorbereiten, über dieses oder jenes zu referieren*." Oder sie sagen für die folgende

5

† The future perfect is not discussed.

[147]

Woche eine Prüfung an*, so daß man die Ferien doch nicht recht
10 genießen kann.

Huber: Ja, aber mein lieber Braun, Sie wollen doch Wissenschaftler* werden! Dann müssen Sie sich den Gedanken an
Ferien im gewöhnlichen Sinn aus dem Kopf schlagen. Denn für
den rechten Wissenschaftler ist die Arbeit das Wichtigste.

15 Braun: Aber jeder Mensch muß doch mal Ferien haben!

Huber: Jeder Mensch muß mal Abwechslung haben. Aber das
bedeutet nicht notwendigerweise* Spielen oder Faulenzen*. Und
das ist der Unterschied zwischen einem wissenschaftlichen Beruf
und einem anderen: der Wissenschaftler arbeitet sogar in den
20 Ferien und in den sogenannten Freistunden.

Braun: Ich glaube, dasselbe hatte der Vater mir sagen wollen,
als er mir sagte: „Wenn du nur Dummheiten im Kopf hast, dann
schlage dir den Gedanken an die Wissenschaft aus dem Kopf!"

Huber: Ja, Ihr Herr Vater hatte ganz recht. Die Wissenschaft
25 ist keine geduldige Kuh, die sich melken* läßt, wenn es einem
gerade paßt. Die Wissenschaft ist ein neidisches Weib, das einen
ganz in Anspruch nimmt. Wer das nicht verstehen will oder
kann, der soll sich lieber einen anderen Beruf wählen. Nun, ich
muß nach Hause, meine Frau wartet mit dem Essen. Fröhliche
30 Ostern und einen schönen Gruß an Ihren Herrn Vater.

*die **Osterferien** (*pl.*) Easter holidays
***referieren** give a report
***an-sagen** announce

*der **Wissenschaftler**, - scientist
***notwendigerweise** necessarily
*das **Faulenzen** loafing
***melken** milk

LESESTÜCK

Der kleine Willi hatte sich an diesem Tage besser als gewöhnlich
waschen müssen, denn die Klasse sollte von dem Direktor mündlich geprüft werden. Auch durfte Willi nicht den alltäglichen
braunen Anzug anziehen, sondern mußte den sonntäglichen, den
5 blauen tragen. Es dauerte lange, bevor Willi endlich zum Frühstück erschien, und dann mochte er nichts essen, denn er war zu
aufgeregt*. Die Mutter redete ihm aber zu* und endlich hat er
dann doch nachgeben müssen und hat etwas gegessen und ge-
trunken. Auf dem Wege zur Schule traf er dann mehrere Schul-

kameraden, und sie konnten nur von einem reden: „Was wird 10
der Mann wohl fragen?"

Als der Vater am Abend nach Hause kam, fragte er den Sohn:
„Na, Willi, wie war denn die Prüfung?" „Ach," antwortete Willi,
„ich hatte zuerst solche Angst, denn ich hatte so viel über den
Direktor reden hören. Aber es war gar nicht so schlimm, denn er 15
war freundlich und fromm." „Freundlich und fromm? Wieso?"
„Ja, nach jeder Antwort, die ich geben mußte, hat er nur immer
die Hände gefaltet und hat gesagt: „Ach du lieber Gott, ach du
lieber Gott!' "

*auf-regen excite   *zu-reden urge

EXERCISES

I. Answer with complete German sentences: (1) Zu welcher
Jahreszeit kommt Ostern? (2) Warum freut sich Braun nicht
recht auf die Osterferien? (3) Was ist der Unterschied zwischen
einem rechten Wissenschaftler und einem anderen? (4) Was soll
Braun tun, wenn er das Spielen oder Faulenzen mehr als die
Arbeit mag? (5) Warum muß Professor Huber nach Hause?
(6) Warum hatte sich Willi eines Tages besser als gewöhnlich
waschen müssen? (7) Was hat er an diesem Tage nicht tragen
dürfen? (8) Warum hat er zuerst das Frühstück nicht gewollt?
(9) Wen traf Willi auf dem Wege zur Schule? (10) Wann hat
Willi dem Vater seine Erfahrung (experience) mit der Prüfung
erzählen müssen.

II. Give synopses, omitting the future perfect: (1) Ich muß in
die Schule. (2) Können Sie das nicht machen? (3) Er will das
nicht tun. (4) Der Wissenschaftler darf nicht faulenzen. (5)
Mögen Sie das nicht? (6) Er läßt sich ein neues Haus bauen.

III. Fill in the correct forms of the verbs called for: (1) Elise
(wollen, *pres. perf.*) ___ oft Berlin sehen ___. (2) Herr Reinhold
(müssen, *past perf.*) ___ am Samstag in die Stadt ___. (3) Die
neue Sekretärin (können, *fut.*) ___ alles sehr schnell lernen ___.
(4) Niemand (sehen, *pres. perf.*) ___ die Kinder spielen ___.
(5) Ich weiß, daß er bald (wollen, *fut.*) ___ schlafen ___. (6) Der

Student (können, *past perf.*) __ es einfach nicht verstehen __.
(7) Es war schade, daß der Professor sein Auto (müssen, *past perfect*) __ verkaufen __. (8) Mein Bruder (lassen, *pres. perf.*) __ das Paket zur Post bringen __.

IV. Translate into German: (1) It was that (that was it) that Braun's father had wanted to say. (2) This little girl has never been allowed to swim. (3) The director had not wanted to go. (4) The student has had his laundry sent home. (5) Who hasn't cared for that? (6) Frieda had not been able to find a good room. (7) Miss Schroeder has never wanted to work in summer. (8) I believe that he will be able to do it if you help him. (9) No one has ever wanted that. (10) He did not know how to write (*use present perfect*).

VOCABULARY

die **Abwechslung, -en** variation
alltäglich everyday
die **Angst;** __ **haben** be afraid
der **Anspruch; in** __ **nehmen** lay claim to
die **Antwort, -en** answer
bedeuten mean
der **Beruf, -e** profession
bevor before
blau blue
braun brown
der **Direktor, -en** director
die **Dummheit, -en** stupidity
eigen peculiar
falten fold
die **Ferien** (*pl.*) vacation, holidays
die **Freistunde, -n** leisure hour
fröhlich happy
fromm pious
das **Frühstück, -e** breakfast
geduldig patient
der **Gruß, ⸗e** greeting
der **Kopf, ⸗e** head
die **Kuh, ⸗e** cow

lieber preferably, rather
mehrere several
mündlich oral
nach-geben, a, e, i give in
neidisch envious
passen suit
prüfen examine
schlagen, u, a, ä; aus dem Kopf __ get out of one's head
der **Schulkamerad, -en, -en** schoolmate
der **Sinn, -e** sense, mind
sonntäglich Sunday
sonst usual
das **Spielen** play(ing)
verstehen, -stand, -standen understand
der **Weg, -e** way
das **Weib, -er** woman
wieso how so
die **Wissenschaft** knowledge
wissenschaftlich scholarly, learned
zuerst at first

LESSON 21†

Irregular weak verbs; wissen

21.1 Irregular weak verbs. There are eight weak verbs that are irregular in their principal parts but which derive the tense forms from these according to rule. They are:

brennen	**brannte**	hat gebrannt	**brennt** *to burn*
kennen	**kannte**	hat gekannt	**kennt** *to know*
			(see § 21.3)
nennen	**nannte**	hat genannt	**nennt** *to name*
rennen	**rannte**	ist or hat gerannt	**rennt** *to run*
senden	**sandte** *or*	hat gesandt	**sendet** *to send*
	sendete	*or* gesendet	
wenden	**wandte** *or*	hat gewandt	**wendet** *to turn*
	wendete	*or* gewendet	
bringen	**brachte**	hat gebracht	**bringt** *to bring*
denken	**dachte**	hat gedacht	**denkt** *to think*

The present and past tenses of **denken** will serve as a model for all.

ich denke	wir denken	ich dachte	wir dachten
du denkst	ihr denkt	du dachtest	ihr dachtet
er denkt	sie denken	er dachte	sie dachten

† For the alphabet in German print, see Introduction.

21.2 Wissen, *to know*, is not only irregular in its principal parts but also in the present tense. The principal parts are:

wissen   wußte   hat gewußt   weiß

The present and past tenses are:

ich weiß	wir wissen	ich wußte	wir wußten
du weißt	ihr wißt	du wußtest	ihr wußtet
er weiß	sie wissen	er wußte	sie wußten

21.3 Difference between *wissen* and *kennen*. In German, as in the Romance languages, a distinction is made between knowledge of acquaintance and factual knowledge. The former is rendered by **kennen**, the latter by **wissen**. Wissen usually has as its direct object a clause or a pronoun representing a clause.

> **Ich kenne diesen Herrn nicht, aber ich weiß, wo er wohnt.** *I don't know this gentleman, but I know where he lives.*
> **Wissen Sie, wer hier war? Nein, das weiß ich nicht.** *Do you know who was here? No, I don't (know that).*

GESPRÄCH

Heinrich: Nun, Otto, fährst du zu Weihnachten nach Hause?

Otto: Ich glaube kaum. Ich habe jetzt eine Stellung bei Herrn Lehmann. Ich darf keine zwei Wochen wegbleiben.

Heinrich: Das habe ich nicht gewußt. Was tust du da?

5 **Otto:** Ich arbeite vier Stunden nachmittags als Gehilfe. Natürlich werde ich dafür bezahlt, aber die Hauptsache* ist, daß ich dabei in der Praxis* lerne, wie man ein Geschäft führt.

Heinrich: Herrn Lehmann kenn' ich nicht. Vor zwei Jahren habe ich eine gewisse Else Lehmann kennengelernt. Ist sie vielleicht eine

10 Tochter?

Otto: Nein, er hat keine Tochter. Wenigstens hat er nie eine erwähnt, und er bringt das Gespräch sehr oft auf seine Familie.

Heinrich: Die Familie selbst kennst du also nicht?

Otto: Noch nicht. Aber ich bin Weihnachten zum Essen eingeladen.

15 **Heinrich:** Und am nächsten Tag kommst du dann zu uns hinaus, gelt*?

Otto: Weiß das denn deine Mutter? Und ist es nicht zu umständlich für sie?

Heinrich: Ich habe das schon mit der Mutter besprochen. Sie freut
sich drauf, denn sie kennt dich ja von den letzten Osterferien und sagt, 20
du paßt ausgezeichnet zur Familie.
Otto: Nun, das ist nett von ihr. Sage ihr bitte, daß ich gern komme.
Aber jetzt muß ich mich trollen*, sonst komm' ich zu spät.

*die Hauptsache, –n main thing   *gelt = nicht wahr isn't it, etc.
*die Praxis practice   (*turns a statement into a question*)
                       *sich trollen "take off," hurry

LESESTÜCK

Im 17. Jahrhundert führten die Länder Europas einen fürchterlichen
Krieg gegeneinander. Da dieser Krieg von 1618 bis 1648 dauerte,
nannte man ihn den Dreißigjährigen Krieg. Deutschland war der
Schauplatz* dieses Krieges. Am Ende lag Deutschland verheert* da.
Städte waren zerstört, Dörfer niedergebrannt, Menschen und Tiere 5
getötet. Wo die Soldaten hinkamen, verwüsteten* sie alles, und sie
kamen fast durch ganz Deutschland.

    Der Roman **Simplicius Simplicissimus** von Christoffel von
Grimmelshausen gibt uns ein sehr lebendiges Bild von diesen Zeiten.
Grimmelshausen erlebte den Krieg selber, und sein Roman enthält 10
viel Autobiographisches. Der Roman erschien im Jahre 1669. Er
erzählt von einem Jungen, der Simplicius Simplicissimus genannt
wurde, weil er so einfältig zu sein schien. Soldaten kamen in sein
Dorf, raubten oder verbrannten alles, und der Junge lief in den
Wald weg. Jahrelang irrte er umher*, wurde von Soldaten ge- 15
stohlen und erlebte alle Schrecken des Krieges. Seine Wanderungen
brachten ihn bis nach Asien hin, aber endlich wandte er sich nach
seinem Dorf zurück* und ließ sich da nieder.

*der Schauplatz, ⸚e scene   *umher-irren (ist) roam about
*verheeren lay waste   *sich zurück-wenden turn back
*verwüsten ravage

EXERCISES

I. Answer with complete German sentences: (1) Warum kann
Otto nicht nach Hause fahren? (2) Arbeitet Otto bei Herrn

Lehmann den ganzen Tag? (3) Was will er lernen? (4) Spricht
Herr Lehmann gern von seiner Familie? (5) Wann geht Otto
zu den Lehmanns? (6) Wohin soll er am nächsten Tag gehen?
(7) Weiß Heinrichs Mutter von der Einladung? (8) Woher
kennt Heinrichs Mutter Otto? (9) In welchem Jahr fing der
Dreißigjährige Krieg an? (10) Wo wurde dieser Krieg geführt?
(11) Was machten die Soldaten in diesem Krieg? (12) Wer war
der Verfasser des *Simplicissimus?* (13) In welchem Jahrhundert
lebte er? (14) Warum nannte man den Jungen „Simplicius"?
(15) Was erzählte Grimmelshausen in diesem Roman?

II. Give the principal parts of: brennen, kennen, nennen, rennen,
senden, wenden, denken, bringen, wissen.

III. Conjugate in the present and past tenses: kennen, denken,
bringen, wissen.

IV. Give synopses of: (1) Er kennt Herrn Lehmann nicht. (2)
Sie bringen das Gespräch sehr oft darauf. (3) Meine Mutter
weiß das schon. (4) Die Soldaten brennen die Dörfer nieder.
(5) Er wendet sich nach seinem Dorf zurück.

V. Translate into German: (1) Otto must not stay away six days.
(2) Heinrich had not known that his friend was working. (3)
Heinrich has known Otto for three years. (4) Otto brought the
conversation around to the business that he was learning. (5)
Otto has thought of his family every year at Christmas. (6) The
Thirty Years' War was waged in the seventeenth century. (7)
The soldiers burned down every village in the region. (8) There
were soldiers everywhere in Germany. (9) The boy was called
Simplicius, but he was not really simple-minded. (10) He did not
settle down in Asia, but returned to his village.

VOCABULARY

(das) **Asien** Asia
autobiographisch autobiograph-
  ical
das **Dorf, ⁼er** village
dreißigjährig thirty years'

einfältig simple-minded
das **Ende, -n** end
enthalten, ie, a, ä contain
erleben experience
erwähnen mention

führen conduct, wage (war)
gegeneinander against one another
der **Gehilfe, -n, -n** assistant
das **Geschäft, -e** business
Grimmelshausen, Christoffel von *proper name*
hinaus-kommen, a, o (ist) come out
hin-bringen, brachte, gebracht bring
jahrelang for years
der **Junge, -n, -n** boy
kennen-lernen become acquainted with
leben'dig lively, vivid
Lehmann *proper name*
nachmittags in the afternoon

nieder-brennen, brannte, gebrannt burn down
sich **nieder-lassen, ie, a, ä** settle down
der **Schrecken, -** terror
Simplicius Simplicissimus *proper name*
stehlen, a, o, ie steal
die **Tochter, ⸗** daughter
töten kill
umständlich bothersome, a nuisance
der **Wald, ⸗er** woods
die **Wanderung, -en** wandering
weg-bleiben, ie, ie (ist) stay away
weg-laufen, ie, au, äu (ist) run away
zerstören destroy

LESSON 22

Comparison of adjectives and adverbs

22.1 Comparative and superlative. The comparative of an adjective or an adverb indicates an increased degree of what is expressed by the positive; the superlative expresses the highest degree. The comparative is regularly used to express the relationship between two objects, the superlative to express the relationship between three or more. For example:

Positive	Comparative	Superlative
small	smaller	smallest

New Jersey is a small state, Delaware is smaller, but Rhode Island is the smallest state in the Union.

22.2 Formation of the comparative and the superlative. There is only one way to form the comparative and superlative in German. The comparative stem is formed by adding -er to the positive; the superlative stem is formed by adding -(e)st to the positive.

schnell	schneller	der schnellste
reich	reicher	der reichste
sorgfältig	sorgfältiger	der sorgfältigste

(a) Some of the more common adjectives of one syllable add umlaut in the comparative and superlative. These forms are indicated in the vocabulary thus: **arm**(¨), which means it is compared: **arm, ärmer, der ärmste.**

(b) **Hoch** changes **ch** to silent **h** in the comparative: **höher.**

(c) Adjectives that end in **-e** drop this before the comparative ending: **weise, weiser.**

(d) Adjectives that end in **-el, -en,** and **-er** drop this e before the comparative ending: **edel, edler.**

(e) The following adjectives have an irregular comparison:

gut	besser	der beste
viel	mehr	der meiste
groß	größer	der größte
nah(e)	näher	der nächste

22.3 Inflection of adjectives.

(a) When used attributively (see § 9.1 (b)), the comparative and superlative are declined like the positive, the endings being added to the **-er** and **-st,** respectively.

der größere Mann   mein liebster Onkel
des größeren Mannes   meines liebsten Onkels
    etc.   *etc.*

(b) When used as a predicate adjective (see § 1.6), the comparative is used in the stem form.

Er ist viel älter als ich. *He is much older than I.*

The superlative is not used in the stem form. Therefore a form obtained by putting **am** before the adjective and adding the weak adjective ending **-en** to it is used for the predicate adjective in the superlative.

Der Baum ist im Sommer am grünsten. *The tree is greenest in the summer.*

NOTE. There is a fine distinction between the usage just discussed and that in which an adjective in the predicate modifies a noun that is *understood* after it. In the latter case it is an attributive adjective and treated as such.

Von allen Männern ist ein Verliebter der dümmste. *Of all men, the one in love is the stupidest.* (**Mann** is understood after **dümmste.**)

22.4 Comparison of adverbs. The comparative of an adverb is formed by adding -er to the positive. The superlative is the **am . . . sten** form.

ruhig	ruhiger	am ruhigsten

Gern is compared irregularly:

gern	lieber	am liebsten

Lieber with a verb indicates preference for one of two and **am liebsten** for one of three or more.

Er hat lieber weggehen wollen. *He preferred to go away.*
Am liebsten möchte ich ihm dein Zimmer geben. *I'd like best to give him your room.*

NOTE. Adverbs do not have inflectional endings. **Gut** is an adverb in the following:

ein gut erzogenes Kind *a well brought up child*

22.5 *Wie* and *als*. After the positive **wie,** *as,* is used; after the comparative **als,** *than,* is used.

so groß wie *as large as*   **größer als** *larger than*

22.6 *Immer* and *um* with a comparative. With the comparative, **immer** expresses the idea worded in English with a repetition of the comparative.

Er ist immer reicher geworden. *He became richer and richer.*

Degree of difference is expressed with the preposition **um.**

um ein kleines größer *larger by a small amount*

22.7 Absolute comparative. The absolute comparative of the adjective is used in the same way as *rather* plus an adjective in English. It expresses slightly less than the positive. We have one remnant still in English: an *elderly* person is not as old as an *old* person. Only the fact that the context shows no comparison being made indicates that the comparative is being used absolutely.

Wird er längere Zeit bei uns bleiben? *Will he stay a rather long time with us?*

22.8   Absolute superlative. The absolute superlative is a different form of the adverb used to express a very high degree, but not to imply a comparison. It is formed with **auf . . . ste.**

Du wirst es ohne Zweifel aufs schnellste zeigen. *You will without doubt show it extremely fast (with greatest speed).*

22.9   Position of adverbs.

(a) **Time and place.** In English it sounds wrong to say, "He was yesterday here." That is because adverbs of place precede those of time in English. In German adverbs of time precede those of place and phrases of time precede those of place.

Er war gestern hier. *He was here yesterday.*
Man kann im Sommer an die Küste fahren. *You can go to the coast in summer.*

(b) **Negatives. Nicht** and **nie** come as near the end of the clause as possible if a complete negative statement is being made.

Das Mädchen hat ihm diesmal nicht geschrieben. *The girl didn't write to him this time.*

However, if a positive statement is being made in which a certain element is being negated, the **nicht** (or **nie**) precedes that element.

Nicht die größte Stadt ist die Hauptstadt, sondern eine viel kleinere. *Not the biggest city is the capital, but a much smaller one.*
Ein nie zu vergessendes Erlebnis ist mir neulich passiert. *A never to be forgotten event happened to me recently.*

GESPRÄCH

Mutter: Karl, weißt du, wer zu Besuch kommt?
Karl: Wie soll ich das wissen? Man erzählt mir nie was*. Wer?
Mutter: Der Onkel Albert. Er hat sein Geschäft im Westen verkauft und will sich hier im Osten niederlassen.

5 **Karl:** Wird er längere Zeit bei uns bleiben?

Mutter: Nein, nur zehn Tage oder so was*. Dann fährt er weiter.

Karl: Ist er denn viel älter als du, daß er sich schon zurückzieht?

Mutter: Du weißt doch, daß ich die jüngste in der Familie bin, fünfzehn Jahre jünger als er. Aber mit dem Alter hat das in diesem
10 Fall nichts zu tun. Es verhält sich* vielmehr so. Einen gescheiteren* Menschen hat's kaum gegeben. Und niemand hat je ein Geschäft besser oder sorgfältiger führen können als er. So ist er immer reicher geworden, bis er sich endlich sagte: „Jetzt habe ich genug! Jetzt höre ich auf!"

15 **Karl:** Warum hat er sich denn nie verheiratet?

Mutter: Als junger Mann hat er sich in das reizendste Mädchen verliebt, das ich je gesehen habe. Aber damals waren wir alle sehr arm, vielleicht waren wir die ärmste Familie in unserer kleinen Stadt. Er hat lieber weggehen wollen, als sie bitten, seine Armut
20 mit ihm zu teilen.

Karl: Und sie? Hat sie nicht warten können . . . oder wollen?

Mutter: Ich habe gesagt, daß er gescheit ist. Aber diesmal hat er sich wirklich dumm benommen*. Er ist einfach weggegangen, ohne ihr ein Wort zu sagen. Sie war natürlich beleidigt. Es war die alte
25 Geschichte!

Karl: Von allen Männern ist ein Verliebter wohl der dümmste! Na, warte nur, wenn ich einmal verliebt bin, mach' ich's gescheiter.

Mutter: Wenn du einmal verliebt bist, wirst du's ohne Zweifel aufs schnellste zeigen. Aber jetzt lassen wir diesen Blödsinn*. Hilf mir das
30 Zimmer für den Onkel fertig machen. Am liebsten möchte* ich ihm dein Zimmer geben. Was sagst du? Es ist nur auf eine kurze Zeit.

Karl: Na, wenn's absolut sein muß, schön.

*was = etwas something	*sich benehmen, a, o, i behave
*so was = so etwas some such thing	*der Blödsinn nonsense
*sich verhalten, ie, a, ä be like	*möchte should like
*gescheit smart, clever	

LESESTÜCK

Vor dem zweiten Weltkrieg (1939-1945) bestand Deutschland aus achtzehn Ländern. Darunter war Preußen* das größte und Bayern* das zweitgrößte, obgleich es viel kleiner war als Preußen. Heutzutage gibt es kein Preußen mehr und so ist Bayern, welches etwas

größer als der Staat West Virginien ist, das größte Land der 5
Deutschen Bundesrepublik*, obwohl es an Einwohnerzahl* dem
Industriegebiet* Nordrhein=Westfalen* bei weitem nachsteht*. So
hat dieses letztere, welches ungefähr 1/12 so groß wie Kalifornien
ist, 2,5 Millionen mehr Einwohner als dieser Staat.

Die Bundesrepublik hat zehn Länder und, abgesehen von* West 10
Berlin, eine Bevölkerung von rund 48 700 000. Während vor dem
Krieg Berlin die Hauptstadt des Reiches war — sie war auch die
größte Stadt — gibt es in der Bundesrepublik dreiunddreißig
Städte, die größer sind als Bonn, der Sitz der westdeutschen Regie=
rung. Also ist in Westdeutschland die Hauptstadt nicht die größte 15
Stadt. Diese ist Hamburg mit rund 1 700 000 Einwohnern. Die
zweitgrößte ist München mit beinahe einer Million. West Berlin mit
seiner Bevölkerung von rund 2 200 000 ist natürlich die größte
Stadt des gesamt* deutschen Territoriums.

In der Deutschen Demokratischen Republik, wie der östliche Teil 20
Deutschlands genannt wird, gibt es nur fünf Länder. Darunter ist
die Mark* Brandenburg der Fläche nach das größte, aber Sachsen*,
eines der kleineren Länder, das größte an Bevölkerung. Die Haupt=
stadt dieses östlichen Teils von Deutschland ist Ost Berlin mit rund
1 200 000 Einwohnern. Die Einwohnerzahl der DDR ist ungefähr 25
17 200 000.

Während der Westen Deutschlands eine Demokratie ist, ist der
Osten nur eine Scheindemokratie*. Denn hier leben die Menschen
unter der Diktatur* der kommunistischen Partei. Und jeder von
den vielen Flüchtlingen aus dem Osten sagt, er wollte lieber in West= 30
deutschland betteln gehen als in dem sogenannten Arbeiter= und
Bauernparadies* bleiben.

---

*(das) **Preußen** Prussia
*(das) **Bayern** Bavaria
*die **Bundesrepublik** Federal Republic
*die **Einwohnerzahl, —en** (number of) population
*das **Industrie'gebiet, —e** industrial district
***Nordrhein=Westfalen** region of the Lower Rhine and Westphalia
***nach=stehen, stand, gestanden** be be-hind
*abgesehen von disregarding
*gesamt total
*die **Mark, —en** (a word indicating a former border territory) march
*(das) **Sachsen** Saxony
*die **Scheindemokratie, —n** pseudo-democracy
*die **Diktatur'** dictatorship
*das **Arbeiter= und Bauernparadies** workers' and farmers' paradise

EXERCISES

I. Answer with complete German sentences: (1) Wer kommt zu Besuch? (2) Wie lange bleibt er zu Besuch? (3) Wo hat Onkel Albert gewohnt? (4) Warum hat er sein Geschäft verkauft? (5) Warum hat er sich nie verheiratet? (6) Wessen Zimmer möchte die Mutter dem älteren Bruder am liebsten geben? (7) Was war das größte Land Deutschlands vor dem zweiten Weltkrieg? (8) Welches ist heutzutage größer, Preußen oder Bayern? (9) Welches ist das größte Land der DDR? (10) Wo will der Flüchtling lieber leben, in Nordrhein-Westfalen oder in Sachsen? (11) Was ist größer, Bayern oder Kalifornien? (12) Welche Stadt ist größer, Hamburg oder die Hauptstadt der DDR? (13) Wieviel mehr Menschen hat West Berlin als Hamburg? (14) Wieviel mehr Menschen hat Nordrhein-Westfalen als Kalifornien? (15) Welches deutsche Land ist ungefähr so groß wie unser Staat West Virginien?

II. Give the comparative and superlative of: fest, fleißig, gut, spät, verschieden, dunkel, lang, viel, nah, gern.

III. (a) Supply the correct forms of the comparative in the blanks: (1) Onkel Albert ist der (alt) ⸺ Sohn der Familie. (2) Der (jung) ⸺ Mann läuft (schnell) ⸺ als der ältere. (3) Ich fahre (gern) ⸺ an den See. (4) Seine Mutter wohnt in der (klein) ⸺ Stadt. (5) Der Onkel ist wohl (reich) ⸺ als der Vater.

(b) Supply the correct forms of the superlative in the blanks: (1) Im Juli und August ist das Wetter (warm) ⸺. (2) Das geschah in der (kurz) ⸺ Nacht im Jahr. (3) Diese Romane sind mir alle zu dumm, (gern) ⸺ lese ich keinen. (4) Von allen Studenten arbeitet er (fleißig) ⸺. (5) Welcher Tag ist (lang) ⸺?

IV. Translate into German: (1) Uncle Albert has lived longer in the west than in the east. (2) The prettiest girl is not always the most capable. (3) A good teacher always speaks most clearly. (4) The air is cooler in the mountains. (5) The second World War was the most terrible that has ever been waged. (6) The light is brightest in summer. (7) Miss Schroeder plays tennis much better than her brother. (8) Most men prefer to eat at home. (9) These are the tallest trees in the forest. (10) Mrs. Schmidt can visit a friend in Chicago or one in New York, but she likes best to stay here.

VOCABULARY

absolut' absolute
die Armut poverty
beleidigen offend
bestehen, -stand, -standen (aus) consist (of)
betteln beg
bitten, bat, gebeten ask, request
Bonn *place name*
(das) Brandenburg Brandenburg
die Demokratie' democracy
demokra'tisch democratic
der Einwohner, - inhabitant
die Fläche, -n area
Hamburg *place name*
je ever
kurz short
letzter latter
kein . . . mehr no more
München Munich
niemand nobody
östlich eastern
die Partei', -en party

die Regierung, -en government
das Reich, -e empire
reizend charming
die Republik', -en republic
rund in round numbers
sorgfältig careful
das Territo'rium, -rien territory
verkaufen sell
sich verlieben (in) fall in love (with); verliebt in love
vielmehr rather
weg-gehen, ging, gegangen (ist) go away
weiter-fahren, u, a, ä (ist) travel on
der Weltkrieg, -e world war
westdeutsch West German
das Zimmer, - room
sich zurück-ziehen, zog, gezogen retire
der Zweifel, - doubt
zweitgrößt second largest

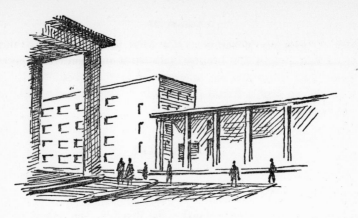

LESSON 23

Formation of the subjunctive

23.1 Subjunctive mood. In many languages there is a set of verb forms used to express ideas rather than facts. There are vestiges of these forms still extant in English in such phrases as *Long live the king! So be it! If he were here,* etc. In each of these phrases a fact is not expressed, for if it were the indicative would be used and the phrases would be *The king lives long, It is so, He is here.* In the first of the three phrases a wish is expressed; in the second either a wish or a command; and in the third a statement is given that is contrary to the actual fact.

23.2 Subjunctive tenses. We call this set of forms the subjunctive mood. In German there are four tenses and two sets of forms to each tense in the subjunctive. The four tenses are present, past, future, and future perfect. For each tense there is a type I and a type II. The subjunctive forms are used in several ways, as will be explained in the next three lessons.

23.3 Subjunctive endings. All eight sets of forms involve one and the same set of endings.

-e	-en
-est	-et
-e	-en

23.4 Present subjunctive I. The present subjunctive I is formed by adding these endings to the infinitive stem for all verbs except **sein.**

ich	sei	habe	werde	sage	fahre	lese	könne
du	seiest	habest	werdest	sagest	fahrest	lesest	könnest
er	sei	habe	werde	sage	fahre	lese	könne
wir	seien	haben	werden	sagen	fahren	lesen	können
ihr	seiet	habet	werdet	saget	fahret	leset	könnet
sie	seien	haben	werden	sagen	fahren	lesen	können

23.5 Present subjunctive II of regular weak verbs. The present subjunctive II of all regular weak verbs is derived from the second principal part, the endings being added to the past stem.

ich sagte	wir sagten	ich antwortete	wir antworteten
du sagtest	ihr sagtet	du antwortetest	ihr antwortetet
er sagte	sie sagten	er antwortete	sie antworteten

23.6 Present subjunctive II of irregular weak verbs, of *werden*, of *wissen*, and of the modals. The first singular of each of these sets of forms is:

ich hätte	ich sendete	ich würde	ich dürfte
ich brennte	ich wendete	ich wüßte	ich könnte
ich kennte	ich brächte		ich möchte
ich nennte	ich dächte		ich müßte
ich rennte			ich sollte
			ich wollte

The remaining forms follow the pattern given in § 23.5.

23.7 Present subjunctive II of strong verbs. The present subjunctive II of strong verbs is derived from the second principal part. To this are added the endings and the umlaut whenever possible.

ich	wäre	säße	bliebe	trüge
du	wärest	säßest	bliebest	trügest
er	wäre	säße	bliebe	trüge
wir	wären	säßen	blieben	trügen
ihr	wäret	säßet	bliebet	trüget
sie	wären	säßen	blieben	trügen

23.8 Irregularities in the present subjunctive II of some strong verbs. A few strong verbs do not have the same vowel in the present subjunctive II as in the second principal part. For example:

stünde (or stände)   hülfe

23.9 Compound tenses. The remaining tenses are compound forms. The past I and II is formed with the past participle and the present I and II of the auxiliary of the perfect. The future is formed with the present infinitive and the present I and II of **werden,** and the future perfect with the perfect infinitive and the forms of **werden.**

I	II
ich habe gesessen du habest gesessen *etc.*	ich hätte gesessen du hättest gesessen *etc.*
ich werde sitzen du werdest sitzen *etc.*	ich würde sitzen du würdest sitzen *etc.*
ich werde gesessen haben du werdest gesessen haben *etc.*	ich würde gesessen haben du würdest gesessen haben *etc.*
ich sei gegangen du seiest gegangen *etc.*	ich wäre gegangen du wärest gegangen *etc.*
ich werde gehen du werdest gehen *etc.*	ich würde gehen du würdest gehen *etc.*
ich werde gegangen sein du werdest gegangen sein *etc.*	ich würde gegangen sein du würdest gegangen sein *etc.*

23.10 Model synopses. A synopsis of a verb in the subjunctive consists of eight forms, two types of each of the four tenses.

I	II
Mein Onkel lebe lange.	Mein Onkel lebte lange.
Mein Onkel habe lange gelebt.	Mein Onkel hätte lange gelebt.
Mein Onkel werde lange leben.	Mein Onkel würde lange leben.
Mein Onkel werde lange gelebt haben.	Mein Onkel würde lange gelebt haben.
Er komme nach Hause.	Er käme nach Hause.
Er sei nach Hause gekommen.	Er wäre nach Hause gekommen.
Er werde nach Hause kommen.	Er würde nach Hause kommen.
Er werde nach Hause gekommen sein.	Er würde nach Hause gekommen sein.

EXERCISES

I. Conjugate in the present subjunctive I and II: sein, haben, werden, antworten, fahren, sitzen, können, wissen.

II. Give the third singular present indicative and the third singular present subjunctive I and II of: besprechen, treffen, zurück-geben, müssen, verlassen, heiraten, schlagen, helfen, kennen, ziehen.

III. Give synopses in the indicative and subjunctive of the following: (1) Das kleine Kind (bitten) seine Mutter um ein Stück Brot. (2) Du (kommen) mit uns hinaus. (3) Das Fräulein (wollen) im Hotel bleiben (*omit the fut. perf. forms*). (4) Er (aufnehmen) das Buch. (5) Die Frau (sehen) den jungen Mann nicht. (6) Frau Schmidt (verkaufen) ihrem Bruder ihr Auto. (7) Was (denken) die Leute wohl darüber? (8) (Legen) Sie das Buch auf den Tisch? (9) Wo (liegen) das Geld? (10) Die Frau (können) es nicht (*omit the fut. perf. forms*).

LESSON 24

Conditional sentences; wishes contrary to fact

24.1 Conditional sentences. There is a certain kind of sentence in which one statement is made to be dependent on another for its truth or falsity. In the sentence *We will be there if we can find the time,* the first statement is true or false depending on whether we can find the time or not. Such a statement is called a conditional sentence.

24.2 Real conditions. If the statement refers to the future we speak of a real condition, for the situation expressed in the *if* clause has neither become a fact nor turned out to be contrary to fact. In German we find the present indicative in the **wenn** clause and either the present or the future in the main clause (result clause).

> **Sie werden besser studieren, wenn Sie im Kühlen sitzen.** *You will study better if you sit where it is cool.* or
> **Sie studieren besser, wenn Sie im Kühlen sitzen.**

24.3 Conditions contrary to fact. Another type of conditional statement refers either to the present moment or to the past time. The situation expressed in the *if* clause has turned out to be contrary to fact. When we say either *If he were here* or *If he had been here*, we know that he is not here or that he was not here. Such a sentence is called a condition contrary to fact. In German in all statements of conditions contrary to fact the subjunctive is used, since an idea, and not a fact, is being stated (§ 23.1), and type II is always used.

24.4 Tenses in conditional sentences.

(a) If the sentence refers to the **present** moment the present subjunctive II is used in the **wenn** clause, and in the result clause either the present subjunctive II or the future subjunctive II is used. There is no difference in meaning between the use of the present and of the future in the result clause, the difference is stylistic.

> Ich würde es tun, wenn ich hier nicht bleiben müßte. *I would do it if I didn't have to stay here.* or
> Ich täte es, wenn ich hier nicht bleiben müßte.

(b) If the sentence refers to the **past**, the past subjunctive II is used in the **wenn** clause, and either the past subjunctive II or the future perfect II is used in the result clause. Again the difference in usage in the result clause is stylistic.

> Ich würde sie gebeten haben, wenn ich sie öfter gesehen hätte. *I would have asked her if I had seen her oftener.* or
> Ich hätte sie gebeten, wenn ich sie öfter gesehen hätte.

24.5 Omission of *wenn*. In English the word *if* can be omitted, though it is still understood, in such sentences as *Were he my friend I would help him, Had they had a little more money they would have succeeded.* Note that the omission of *if* is indicated by putting the verb first. In German **wenn** may be omitted at any time and very frequently is. The omission of **wenn** is indicated by placing the verb first in the clause instead of last. The following result clause is almost invariably introduced by **so** (or **dann**).

> Wäre er mein Freund, so würde ich ihm helfen.
> Hätten sie ein bißchen mehr Geld gehabt, so wäre es ihnen gelungen.
> Ist er wirklich mein Freund, dann wird er mir helfen.

24.6 Wishes. A wish for the present or the past that is *impossible of fulfillment* is expressed in both languages simply by using the *if* or **wenn** clause as a separate exclamation, with *only* or **nur** added.

> **Wenn's nur nicht so heiß wäre!** *If it only weren't so hot!*
> **Wenn ich mich nur darauf vorbereitet hätte!** *If I had only prepared myself for it!*

Here, too, the *if* or **wenn** may be omitted. In literary style such a wish may be introduced by *that* or **daß**.

> **Wäre es nur nicht so heiß!** *Were it only not so hot!*
> **Hätte ich mich nur darauf vorbereitet!** *Had I only prepared myself for it!*
> **O, daß dieser Krieg nie gewesen wäre!** *Oh, that this war had never been!*

24.7 Possibility. The subjunctive is frequently used to express possibility or probability. This subjunctive is often called the *potential* and is always type II.

> **Das wäre aber schön.** *That would be nice.*
> **Das könnte Robert doch tun.** *But Robert could do that.*
> **Ich würde sehr gern mit Ihnen gehen.** *I'd like very much to go with you.*

24.8 Subjunctive with future conditions. In German as in English a conditional statement referring to the future is occasionally toned down by using the forms of a contrary to fact condition.

> **Wenn Sie um drei Uhr vorbeikämen, würde ich mich wohl verlocken lassen.** *If you should come past at three, I probably could be enticed.*

GESPRÄCH

Anna: Heute ist es wirklich heiß, gelt?

Georg: Das kann man wohl sagen. Ich glaube, ich gehe heute nachmittag ins Kino.

Anna: Was wird gespielt?

5 **Georg:** Keine Ahnung, aber da haben sie Klimaanlage*. Wenigstens kann ich bequem sitzen. Wollen Sie mit?

Anna: Ich würde gerne mitkommen, wenn ich mich nicht auf eine Prüfung vorbereiten müßte.

Georg: Warum haben Sie das gestern abend nicht gemacht? Da war es schön kühl. 10

Anna: Ich würde es auch gemacht haben, wenn zwei Freundinnen mich nicht besucht hätten. Die sind fast den ganzen Abend bei mir geblieben. Ich würde sie gebeten haben, ein bißchen früher wegzugehen, wenn sie nicht von so weit her gekommen wären. Aber wir sehen uns so selten. 15

Georg: Vielleicht werden Sie doch besser studieren können, wenn Sie vorher zwei Stunden im Kühlen gesessen haben.

Anna: Hebe dich weg von mir, Satan*.

Georg: Nein, ich meine es im Ernst. Denn von jetzt bis Mitternacht werden Sie gewiß bei dieser Hitze nicht studieren können. 20

Anna: Ja, Sie haben vielleicht recht. Wenn Sie um drei Uhr bei mir vorbeikämen, würde ich mich wohl verlocken* lassen. Oder ist Ihnen das zu spät?

Georg: Nein, es ist mir vollkommen gleich, wann ich hingehe. Wenn's nur nicht so furchtbar heiß geworden wäre! Denn ich muß jetzt ein 25 Geständnis machen, ich muß mich auch auf eine Prüfung vorbereiten.

Anna: Sie Schlimmer!* Da es aber einmal abgemacht* ist, können wir's nicht ändern. Also bis um drei!

Georg: Auf Wiedersehn!

*die **Klimaanlage** air conditioning
*Hebe **dich weg von mir, Satan.** Get thee behind me, Satan.
*verlocken entice

*Sie **Schlimmer!** You wicked fellow!
*ab=machen make an agreement, settle

LESESTÜCK

Als die Verbündeten* Napoleon besiegten und dann nach Elba verbannten, hätten sie sich nie träumen lassen, daß der französische Kaiser sie jemals* wieder bedrohen* würde. Denn wenn sie an diese Möglichkeit gedacht hätten, so hätten sie ihn gewiß gleich von Anfang an stärker bewachen* lassen. 5

Er entfloh also und kam zurück nach Frankreich, wo er binnen zwei Monate eine Armee von 130 000 zusammenstellte. Die Verbündeten unter Wellington stellten sich ihm zuletzt bei Waterloo

entgegen*, und hier wurde am 18. Juni 1815 die entscheidende und
10 blutige Schlacht von Belle Alliance geschlagen*.

Zuerst schienen die Franzosen zu gewinnen, so daß Wellington,
der Nachschub* von dem preußischen* General Blücher erwartete,
mit der Uhr in der Hand gesagt haben soll: „Wenn doch nur Blücher
käme! Oder wenigstens die Nacht!" Ohne diesen Nachschub — das
15 wußte er — würde er nämlich die Schlacht verlieren.

Da kam dann endlich Blücher doch noch zur rechten Zeit, und die
Macht des Friedensfeindes*, wie man Napoleon im verbündeten
Lager nannte, wurde gründlich vernichtet. Wäre Blücher nicht zur
rechten Zeit gekommen und hätte Napoleon gesiegt, wer weiß, was
20 dann geschehen wäre.

*die Verbündeten Allies	*schlagen, u, a, ä fight
*jemals ever	*der Nachschub reinforcements
*bedrohen threaten	*preußisch Prussian
*bewachen guard	*der Friedensfeind, –e enemy of the
*sich entgegen=stellen oppose	peace

EXERCISES

I. Answer with complete German sentences: (1) Ist es heute
heiß? (2) Wohin geht Georg am Nachmittag? (3) Ist es kühl im
Kino? (4) Warum muß Anna studieren? (5) Wer war den
vorigen Abend bei ihr? (6) Was hätte sie getan, wenn sie die
Freundinnen öfters gesehen hätte? (7) Um wieviel Uhr soll
Georg bei ihr vorbeikommen? (8) Welches Geständnis hat Georg
zu machen? (9) Will Anna trotzdem mit ihm ins Kino gehen?
(10) Wer hat Napoleon nach Elba verbannt? (11) Was hätten
diese sich nie träumen lassen? (12) Was hätten sie getan, wenn
sie Napoleon noch weiter gefürchtet (feared) hätten? (13) Was
soll Wellington in der Schlacht bei Waterloo vor der Ankunft
Blüchers gesagt haben? (14) Was wäre geschehen, wenn Napoleon die Schlacht gewonnen hätte?

II. Rewrite the following sentences, changing the English to
German: (1) I would go to the movies, wenn ich das Geld finden
könnte. (2) Ich hätte fleißiger studiert, if I had understood the
book. (3) Die Studenten werden morgen aufs Land fahren, if
the weather remains beautiful. (4) Ich würde meine Prüfungen

[*172*]

besser machen, if I prepared myself for them. (5) George would have gone past Anna's house, wenn er den Weg nicht zu lang gefunden hätte. (6) She will ask her friends to eat with her, wenn sie nicht weggehen. (7) We would not hear the professor, wenn der Saal größer wäre. (8) Wir würden es gesehen haben, if the auto had moved. (9) Frau Heinze würde nicht spinnen können, if the room did not have a light. (10) Napoleon could have won the battle, wenn Blücher nicht zur rechten Zeit gekommen wäre.

III. Restate 1-9 of the sentences you formed in II, using the other possible verb form in the result clause.

IV. Restate these sentences, putting the **wenn** clause first.

V. Restate these sentences, omitting **wenn**.

VI. Translate into German: (1) Could he have done that? (2) If the boy were in love he would show it. (3) If only this rain would stop soon. (4) If he had arrived earlier, we would have had time to go to the movies. (5) My (ach), but that would have been nice!

VOCABULARY

die Ahnung, –en idea	das Geständnis, –ffe confession
ändern change	gewinnen, a, o win
der Anfang, ⸚e beginning	gleich immediately
die Armee', –n army	gründlich thorough
Belle Alliance *place name*	heiß hot
bequem comfortable	die Hitze heat
besiegen conquer	der Kaiser, – emperor
binnen (*gen. or dat.*) within	kühl cool
Blücher *proper name*	das Lager, – camp
Elba *name of an island*	meinen mean
entfliehen, o, o (ift) escape	mit along
entscheiden, ie, ie decide	mit=kommen, a, o (ift) come along
der Ernst seriousness, earnest	die Mitternacht, ⸚e midnight
erwarten expect, await	die Möglichkeit, –en possibility
franzö'sisch French	die Nacht, ⸚e night
die Freundin, –nen (female) friend	die Schlacht, –en battle
furchtbar fearful	siegen be victorious
der General, ⸚e general	träumen dream

[*173*]

verbannen banish
verlieren, o, o lose
vernichten annihilate
vollkommen complete
von ... an from ... on
vorbei=kommen, a, o (ist) come past

vorher before
wann when
weit far
wenigstens at least
zusammen=stellen put together

LESSON 25

Indirect discourse

25.1 Direct and indirect discourse. There are two kinds of quotations. A *direct quotation* is one given in the exact words of the original speaker. It is placed betweeen quotation marks in writing and printing.

He said, "I went there yesterday."
He asked, "Do you want this now?"

An *indirect quotation* indicates what the original speaker said —his original remark can even be figured out from the indirect quotation—but the exact words of the original speaker are not given. The change involves the form of the verb and possibly the pronouns in the original statement or question.

He said that he had gone there the day before.
He asked if we wanted this now.

25.2 Indirect quotations with the indicative. If the verb introducing the indirect quotation in German is in the present tense, if it is in the first person of any tense, or if it is a verb like **wissen** that would introduce a factual statement, then the verb of the indirect quotation is likely to be in the indicative and the usage will parallel English.

[*175*]

Ich sagte, daß es kühl war.
Man sagt, daß er sehr krank ist.
Wissen Sie, wer das geschrieben hat?

25.3 Indirect quotations with the subjunctive. If, however, the introductory verb is in a tense referring to the past and is not otherwise included in § 25.2, then the subjunctive is used for the indirect quotation. This is to indicate that the person quoting is not giving a fact, but only an idea, namely, what someone else has said or thought or hoped or feared.

25.4 Use of types I and II. There are two different stylistic usages of the subjunctive in indirect quotations, the literary and the colloquial. In literary usage the tendency is strong to use type I of the subjunctive whenever possible. Colloquial usage prefers type II; reflections of this are sometimes found in literary usage.

The same tense of the original statement is kept, the past, present perfect, and the past perfect tenses of the direct statement all becoming the past subjunctive I. This is radically different from English, which changes the tense and not the mood.

> Er sagte: „Ich tue es gern." becomes Er sagte, daß er es gern tue. *He said that he would do it gladly.*
>
> Er sagte: „Der Professor war hier." becomes Er sagte, daß der Professor hier gewesen sei. *He said that the professor had been here.*

If the resultant form, taken with its subject, is identical with an indicative form, then the corresponding type II form must be used.

> Er sagte: „Das haben wir nie gesehen." becomes Er sagte, daß sie das nie gesehen hätten. (daß sie . . . gesehen haben is indicative and hence cannot be used.) *He said that they had never seen that.*

25.5 Indirect questions. To introduce an indirect question in English made from a direct question formed by placing the verb first, we use *if* or *whether*. In German **ob** is used. Both languages in turning into an indirect question a direct one formed by an interrogative word use this same word to introduce it.

Wir fragten: „Ist die Handschrift vollständig?" becomes **Wir fragten, ob die Handschrift vollständig sei.** *We asked if the manuscript was complete.*

Hildebrand fragte: „Wer ist dein Vater?" becomes **Hildebrand fragte, wer sein Vater sei.** *Hildebrand asked who his father was.*

25.6 Indirect commands. In English a command is rendered indirectly in one of two ways

He told me to close the window.
He said that we should study more.

German uses the second way only, and the auxiliary verb is usually **sollen.**

Er sagte mir, daß ich das Fenster zumachen solle.
Er sagte, daß wir mehr studieren sollten.

25.7 Omission of *daß.* The conjunction **daß** may be omitted in an indirect quotation. If it is, the verb is placed second.

Er sagte, sie hätten das nie gesehen. *He said they had never seen that.*

25.8 Omission of introductory verb. Because the subjunctive of indirect discourse is readily recognizable, the introductory verb may not be expressed. Furthermore the indirect statement may go beyond the end of the sentence, or even of the paragraph, without further introductory verbs. See the **Lesestück** for examples.

GESPRÄCH

Frau Serlo: Ach, das ist aber nett von Ihnen, daß Sie mal vorbei kommen!

Frau Kranz: Ja, mein Mann und ich hatten schon lange vor, Sie zu besuchen. Aber er ist ja so viel auf Reisen. Jetzt ist er wieder weg. Da dachte ich plötzlich heute morgen: „Es ist so ein schöner Tag, ich 5 fahre mal 'naus* in die Vorstadt* und besuche Frau Serlo in ihrem neuen Haus." Ich glaube, Sie dachten schon, wir hätten Sie ganz und gar vergessen.

Frau Serlo: Ganz offen gesprochen, wir waren sehr enttäuscht, daß

10 Sie nicht mal herauskamen. Die Fahrt ist natürlich etwas umständlich, aber mein Mann sagte, so umständlich sei sie doch nicht, daß Sie
nicht mal kommen könnten, zumal da Sie einen Wagen haben. Aber
nun sind Sie ja doch gekommen, da können wir hübsch plaudern.
Frau Kranz: Ihr Haus ist reizend, und so ein großer Garten! Da
15 sind wir in der Stadt arm dran*.
Frau Serlo: Nun, es ist nicht alles Gold, was glänzt. Es ist wahr,
wir haben eine herrliche Anlage*, aber es ist doch gar einsam hier.
Bis jetzt ist noch niemand von den alten Bekannten gekommen, uns
zu besuchen.
20 **Frau Kranz:** Na, für Städter ist eine Fahrt in die Vorstadt immer
so eine Sache. Aber da ich jetzt einmal hier war, und da mein Mann
ja sowieso so viel weg ist, kann ich ja öfters kommen.
Frau Serlo: Ach, wenn Sie das doch nur täten! Dann wäre mir
schon so geholfen. Und dann könnten Sie ja vielleicht auch manchmal
25 hier übernachten*. So hätten Sie die lange Fahrt nicht zweimal
am selben Tag.
Frau Kranz: Ja, das ginge leicht.
Frau Serlo: Also, abgemacht! Und nun kommen Sie, ich zeige
Ihnen das Haus.

*'naus = hinaus   *die Anlage, –n grounds
*die Vorstadt suburbs   *übernachten spend the night
*arm dran poorly off

LESESTÜCK

Hildebrand und Hadubrand

In einer sehr alten deutschen Handschrift* ist uns ein Bruchstück*
der Sage von dem Kampf zwischen Vater und Sohn erhalten. Diese
Handschrift ist selbst mehr als tausend Jahre alt, aber die Sage ist
viel älter und weit verbreitet.
5   Der Dichter des „Hildebrandsliedes", wie es genannt wird, begann
das Gedicht mit den Worten, er habe gehört, daß sich die zwei
Männer zwischen zwei Heeren begegnet seien. Da hätten sie sich zum
Kampf bereitet, ohne einander zu erkennen. Hildebrand, der Vater,
habe den anderen gefragt, wer sein Vater sei. Wenn er das wisse,
10 dann wisse er alles andere. Hadubrand habe geantwortet, daß sein

Vater Hildebrand geheißen habe und daß der mit König Dietrich vor vielen Jahren nach Osten geflohen sei. Seine Frau und sein Kind hätten seitdem gar nichts von ihm gehört.

Jetzt habe sich der Vater zu erkennen gegeben, aber der Sohn habe es nicht glauben wollen. Er sei überzeugt, daß er seinen Vater nie 15 wieder lebendig sehen werde, der andere sei nur ein Feigling und wolle den Kampf vermeiden.

Wie gesagt, die Handschrift ist nicht vollständig. Wir lesen nur noch, daß der Vater zornig wurde, als der andere ihn einen Feigling nannte, und daß es an den Kampf ging. Wir wissen nicht, wer der 20 Sieger war. Aber in einer altnordischen* Sage lesen wir, daß Hildebrand seinen eigenen Sohn erschlagen* hatte. Denselben Ausgang hat die Handlung auch in anderen ähnlichen Geschichten, z. B. in der von Sohrab und Rustum.

Die Frage, ob diese Handschrift einmal vollständig gewesen sei, 25 läßt sich nicht mit einem kategorischen „ja" oder „nein" beantworten. Wir vermuten aber, daß der ursprüngliche Dichter das Werk vollendet hat.

*die **Handschrift,** –en manuscript   *altnordisch Old Norse
*das **Bruchstück,** –e fragment   *erschlagen, u, a, ä slay

EXERCISES

I. Answer with complete German sentences: (1) Worüber freut sich Frau Serlo? (2) Warum ist Frau Kranz gerade heute hinausgefahren? (3) Wie ist eine Fahrt in die Vorstadt gewöhnlich? (4) Warum ist Frau Serlo trotz ihres neuen Hauses unglücklich? (5) Wie alt ist die Geschichte von dem Kampf zwischen Vater und Sohn? (6) Wie alt ist die Handschrift des Hildebrandsliedes? (7) Finden wir die ganze Geschichte in dieser Handschrift? (8) Wo begegneten sich Hildebrand und Hadubrand? (9) Was wollte Hildebrand wissen? (10) Wann war Hildebrand nach Osten geflohen? (11) Floh er allein? (12) Hörte seine Frau oft von ihm? (13) Was dachte Hadubrand, als Hildebrand sich zu erkennen gab? (14) Was machte der Vater, als der Sohn ihn einen Feigling nannte? (15) Warum dürfen wir glauben, daß Hadubrand erschlagen wurde?

[*179*]

II. Translate into English: (1) Anna sagte, daß zwei Freundinnen bei ihr geblieben seien. (2) Georg sagte ihr, sie solle zwei Stunden im Kühlen sitzen. (3) Manche Leute dachten früher, Bücher lesen sei gefährlich. (4) Karls Mutter glaubte, er wisse schon von dem Besuch. (5) Er fragte sie, ob der Onkel eine längere Zeit da bleibe. (6) Otto sagte, daß Herr und Frau Lehmann ihn schon eingeladen hätten. (7) Wenn die Soldaten erschienen, glaubte man immer, sie würden alles rauben oder verbrennen. (8) Herr Reinhold sagte, daß die vorige Sekretärin sehr tüchtig geworden sei. (9) Haydn glaubte, seine Musik habe vielen Leuten das Leben gerettet. (10) Der Arzt fragte den Mann, ob er glaube, daß seiner Frau durch das Rezept geholfen worden sei.

III. Turn each of the following direct quotations into an indirect one: (1) Herr Pfeiffer fragte Herrn Schmidt: „Ist Ihre Frau immer noch in Kalifornien?" (2) Herr Schmidt antwortete: „Sie besucht eine alte Freundin in Chicago." (3) Er sagte auch: „Sie werden sich wohl viel zu sagen haben." (4) Heinrich fragte: „Was gibt es heute zu essen?" (5) Robert sagte: „Wir wollen lieber beim Fenster sitzen." (6) Als Karl wegging, sagte Elsa: „Kaufe mir auch eine Karte für das Konzert!" (7) Die Sage erzählte: „Die zwei hatten einander so lieb." (8) Lotte sagte: „Ich habe ihn nie arbeiten sehen." (9) Rudolf fragte Otto: „Um welches Stipendium hast du dich beworben?" (10) Die Freunde dachten sich: „Wir werden Beethoven einen neuen Anzug kaufen."

VOCABULARY

der **Ausgang**, ⸚e conclusion
bekannt acquainted
bereiten prepare
Dietrich Theodoric
einander one another
enttäuschen disappoint
erhalten, ie, a, ä preserve
etwas somewhat
die **Fahrt**, –en trip, drive
der **Feigling**, –e coward
fliehen, o, o (ist) flee

ganz und gar completely
gar very, quite; — **nichts** nothing at all
das **Gedicht**, –e poem
glänzen glitter
das **Gold** gold
Hadubrand *proper name*
die **Handlung**, –en plot, action
das **Heer**, –e army
heraus-kommen, a, o (ist) come out
Hildebrand *proper name*

[180]

das **Hildebrandslied** Lay of Hildebrand
hinaus=fahren, u, a, ä (ift) drive
  out
hübfch nice
katego'rifch categorical
leben'dig alive
offen frank
Ruftum *proper name*
die **Sage,** –n legend
feitdem since then
der **Sieger,** – victor
Sohrab *proper name*
fowiefo as it is
der **Städter,** – city person

überzeugen convince
umftändlich roundabout
vermeiden, ie, ie avoid
vermuten presume
vollenden complete
vollftändig complete
vor=haben, hatte, gehabt, hat plan,
  intend
der **Wagen,** – auto
wahr true
weit wide
zornig angry
zumal especially
zwifchen between

LESSON 26

Other uses of the subjunctive; **als ob;** *sollen and* **mögen**

26.1 Commands. To express a command that something be done, the present subjunctive type I is frequently used in the first plural, in the third singular, and, of **sein** only, in the third plural. In the first plural the subjunctive is recognizable as such only because the verb is first.

> **Laufen wir ein bißchen schneller.** *Let's run a bit faster!*
> **Man fülle eine Probierröhre mit Wasser.** (*Let one*) *fill a test tube with water.*
> **Man nehme dieses Rezept in die Apotheke.** *Someone take this prescription* (*This prescription is to be taken*) *to the drugstore.*
> **Als Dichtungen dieser Art seien eine altnordische Sage und die Geschichte von Sohrab und Rustum genannt.** *As poems of this type let us mention an Old Norse legend and the story of Sohrab and Rustum.*

26.2 Moral obligation. The present and past subjunctive II of **sollen** are used to express moral obligation, English *should* or *ought to* and *should have* or *ought to have.*

> **Wir sollten sie bald besuchen.** *We ought to* (or *should*) *visit them soon.*

[182]

Ich hätte sie schon gestern lesen sollen. *I ought to have* (or *should have*) *read it yesterday.*

26.3 Wishes. The present subjunctive I is used in set phrases to express a realizable wish, such as the well-known toast:

> **Er lebe hoch!** *Here's long life to him!*
> **So sei es!** *So be it!*
> **Er ruhe sanft!** *May he rest in peace!*

26.4 Clauses with *als ob* and *als wenn*. The present and past subjunctive, usually type II, are used in clauses beginning with **als ob** and **als wenn,** *as if.*

> **Es sieht aus, als ob es regnen könnte.** *It looks as if it might rain.*
> **Er tat, als wenn er nie davon gehört hätte.** *He acted as if he had never heard of it.*

The **ob** or **wenn** may be omitted. Then the verb follows directly after **als** instead of coming at the end of the clause.

> **Es sieht aus, als könnte es regnen.**
> **Er tat, als hätte er nie davon gehört.**

26.5 Special phrasing. The subjunctive II is used often to tone down a blunt statement or request. The present subjunctive II of **mögen** is used regularly to express a want or desire politely.

> **Wenn Sie das sagten, würden Sie sich wohl irren.** *If you were to say that you might be mistaken.*
> **Dürfte ich Sie darum bitten?** *Might I ask you for it?*
> **Ich möchte ein Glas Wasser, bitte.** *I'd like a glass of water, please.*
> **Möchten Sie mit uns fahren?** *Would you like to ride with us?*

GESPRÄCH

Georg: Laufen wir ein bißchen schneller, Hermann! Es sieht aus, als ob es bald regnen könnte.

Hermann: Fahren wir dann lieber mit dem Autobus! Warum sollten wir bei dieser Hitze laufen? Ich möchte auch nicht müde nach Hause kommen, ich habe eine Menge Arbeit zu tun.

Georg: Du sprichst, als wärest du der einzige, der zu arbeiten hätte!

Hermann: Und wenn ich fragen darf, was hast du so Wichtiges* zu erledigen?

5

Georg: Vier Kapitel in meinem Handbuch* der Chemie. Eigentlich
10 hätte ich zwei davon schon gestern lesen sollen, aber ich bin nicht
dazu gekommen. Jetzt habe ich noch zwei!
Hermann: Bei mir ist es die Mathematik. Für morgen müssen wir
drei Lehrsätze* auswendig lernen, und die wollen mir nicht in den
Kopf.
15 Georg: Aber da fährt der Autobus schon vorbei! Wir müssen eine
halbe Stunde auf den nächsten warten. Also, was machen wir?
Hermann: Laufen, natürlich.
Georg: Ich möchte bloß wissen, warum ich immer den Autobus
versäume.
20 Hermann: Das dürfte* wohl die Tücke des Objekts* sein. Ohne
Frage könnte es nie an dir liegen!

*was . . . so Wichtiges what that is so important	*dürfte might
*das Handbuch, ⁼er manual	*die Tücke des Objekts′ malice of the inanimate thing
*der Lehrsatz, ⁼e theorem	

LESESTÜCK

Karl Maria von Weber wurde von einem Leipziger* Kritiker*
namens Müller in bissiger* Weise verfolgt. Weber wurde ganz
unglücklich hierüber und fragte einen Freund, was er in dieser Sache
tun könne. Der Freund schrieb lakonisch zurück: „Man erdichte*
5 deinen Tod." Weber zerbrach sich hierüber den Kopf. Aber dann zog
er in ein kleines süddeutsches* Dorf, schrieb Berichte über seine letzten
Tage, und ließ diese von dem Freund an die hervorragendsten Zeitun-
gen abschicken*. Diese druckten sie nicht nur ab*, sondern schmückten sie
noch mit Würdigungen. Und, wie das nun einmal so im Leben ist,
10 die glänzendsten unter ihnen waren diejenigen von Müller. Dieser,
durch das frühe Hinscheiden* entwaffnet, nannte Weber einen Für-
sten unter den deutschen Komponisten, dem er ein ehrendes Andenken
bewahren werde. Einige Wochen später traf Müller in Leipzig auf
— Weber. Er traute seinen Augen nicht. Aber Weber grüßte
15 freundlich und sagte: „Ja, ja, Herr Müller, ich lebe noch. Dafür
sind S i e tot."

*Leipziger (of) Leipzig	*bissig savage, biting
*der Kritiker, – critic	*erdichten invent

[184]

füdbeutſch South German   *ab=druden* reprint
ab=ſchiden send off   *das Hinſcheiden* death

EXERCISES

I. Answer with complete German sentences: (1) Warum will Georg schneller gehen? (2) Warum will Hermann das nicht? (3) Hat Georg auch eine Menge Arbeit zu tun? (4) Was studiert Georg? (5) Was für eine Schwierigkeit hat Hermann? (6) Wie oft fahren die Autobusse vorbei? (7) Was möchte Georg wissen? (8) Wie erklärt Hermann das? (9) Wer war Karl Maria von Weber? (10) Warum war er unglücklich? (11) An wen wandte er sich? (12) Was sagte ihm dieser? (13) Was machte Weber also? (14) Wann schrieb Müller eine glänzende Würdigung? (15) Was hätte sich Müller nie gedacht?

II. Translate into German: (1) Let's go to the concert this evening. (2) I'd like to go, but I have no money. (3) The girl acted as if she had never gone to the theater. (4) Might I ask if you have money? (5) The newspapers ought not to have believed Weber when he said that he was dead. (6) Lotte should visit her aunt more frequently. (7) Otto talks as if he knew the family well. (8) If Uncle Albert were to sell his business he would leave the west. (9) Would you like to see our new house? (10) Let this sentence be the last.

VOCABULARY

als ob as if
das Andenken memory
aus=ſehen, a, e, ie look
auswendig by heart
der Bericht, –e report
bewahren preserve, keep
bloß mere
die Chemie' chemistry
ehren honor
entwaffen disarm
erledigen finish, do
der Fürſt, –en, –en prince
hervorragend prominent

das Kapi'tel, – chapter
lakoniſch laconic
Leipzig *place name*
liegen, a, e, an be due to
namens by name
ſchmüden adorn
tot dead
trauen (dat.) trust
verfolgen persecute
verſäumen miss
die Würdigung, –en appreciation
zerbrechen, a, o, i crack
zurüd=ſchreiben, ie, ie write back

[185]

APPENDIX A

The modified adjective construction

27.1 A particularly troublesome construction is that involving an *adjective that modifies a noun and in turn is modified by a number of words.* Because this is found so frequently with a present or past participle it is often referred to as the "participial construction." It is the same construction that we have in English in such phrases as:

> *A glass filled with sand . . .*
> *The amount of the second element replacing the one in question . . .*
> *The substances readily soluble in their solvents . . .*

27.2 The difficulty in German arises for the English-speaking person from the fact that the word order is almost completely reversed. In a brief phrase, however, English has the same order as German, which is (1) limiting adjective if one is used, (2) modifiers of the attributive adjective, (3) attributive adjective itself, (4) the noun. We say in English *a well-intended remark, a kindly disposed person,* but as soon as the phrase attains any length we have limiting adjective—noun—attributive adjective—modifiers, as illustrated in § 27.1.

27.3 The construction causes trouble in German, too, because it is used with great frequency in essay style and sometimes attains considerable length. The solution of the difficulty is really a matter of recognition, and practice is necessary for this. Only a few easier examples are given here, with translations, to give the student his first acquaintance with the modified adjective construction.

> **Ein mit Sand gefülltes Glas** . . . *A glass filled with sand* . . .
> **Die das betreffende Element ersetzende Menge des zweiten**

Elements . . . *The amount of the second element replacing the element in question* . . .

Die leicht in ihren Lösungsmitteln löslichen Stoffe . . . *The substances readily soluble in their solvents* . . .

Eine mit Materie ausgefülltes Gebiet . . . *a region filled with matter* . . .

Ein einziger, als solcher direkt erkennbarer Kristall . . . *a single crystal directly recognizable as such* . . .

Diese langsam durch das Land fahrenden Züge . . . *These trains which travel slowly through the country* . . .

Die den Leuten dieser Stadt eigene Redeweise . . . *The way of speaking peculiar to the people of this city* . . .

Seine nicht leicht zu beschreibende Methode . . . *His method not easily to be described* . . . (The present participle with zu has future passive meaning.)

27.4 Each of the phrases above can also be rendered as a noun modified by a relative clause. The results of this change are:

Ein Glas, das mit Sand gefüllt ist . . .
Die Menge des zweiten Elements, die das betreffende Element ersetzt . . .
Die Stoffe, die leicht in ihren Lösungsmitteln löslich sind . . .
Ein Gebiet, das mit Materie ausgefüllt ist . . .
Ein einziger Kristall, der als solcher direkt erkennbar ist . . .
Diese Züge, die langsam durch das Land fahren . . .
Die Redeweise, die den Leuten dieser Stadt eigen ist . . .
Seine Methode, die nicht leicht zu beschreiben ist . . .

EXERCISE

I. Change to a noun modified by a relative clause: (1) eine drei Jahre dauernde und mit Krieg erfüllte Zeit . . . (2) die in Frieden und Unschuld lebenden Menschen . . . (3) der schon vor zwei Wochen in Europa unterzeichnete Friedensvertrag (peace treaty) . . . (4) die wegen der schlechten Landstraßen langsame Reise . . . (5) das durch eine Flamme erhitzte Gasgemisch . . . (6) der die Gase stark komprimierende Kolben . . . (7) der im vorigen Jahrhundert lebende österreichische Dichter . . . (8) die durch vier teilbare Jahreszahl . . . (9) das in zwei Elemente zerfallende (decomposing) Radium . . . (10) die in einem luftleeren Raum zu stellende Glocke (bell) . . .

APPENDIX B

The infinitive

Although most of the uses of the infinitive have already been discussed, a review of these uses is given here and one or two more are added.

28.1 The infinitive is regularly used with **zu**. The student must learn to associate the preposition with the verb form and then learn those situations in which **zu** is not used, as for instance after a modal auxiliary. With a separable prefix the **zu** comes between the prefix and the verb and the whole is written as one word, as **hinauszugehen** and **anzusehen**.

28.2 The infinitive regularly follows all words involved in the construction. See §§ 12.3, 15.7c, 15.7d, 19.4.

28.3 The present infinitive is used to form the future tense and the perfect infinitive to form the future perfect tense. In each case it is added to the present tense of **werden**. This applies to both the indicative and the subjunctive. See §§ 12.1, 12.2, 23.9. The infinitive is here used without **zu**.

28.4 The infinitive, used without **zu,** is dependent on a modal auxiliary. In this usage the perfect infinitive is often found, and very frequently the passive infinitive. See §§ 19.5, 20.3, 20.4.

28.5 The infinitive may be capitalized and used as a neuter noun. See § 7.6b.

28.6 The infinitive of a transitive verb used with **zu** after a form of **sein** usually has passive force. See § 15.7c.

28.7 Um . . . zu is used with the infinitive to express purpose. Um starts the phrase and the infinitive with **zu** comes last.

> **Er ging früh hin, um einen guten Platz zu bekommen.** *He went early in order to get a good seat.*
> **Um ein A zu bekommen, muß man fleißig studieren.** *To get an A you must study hard.*

28.8 The infinitive is sometimes used to give a sharp command.

> **Alles hierbleiben!** *Everybody stay here!*
> **Den Hut abnehmen!** *Take off your hat!*

28.9 The infinitive with **zu** can follow a noun or an adjective.

> **kein Brot zu essen** *no bread to eat*
> **Das ist leicht zu verstehen.** *That is easy to understand.*

28.10 Only three prepositions can be followed by the infinitive with **zu: (an)statt, ohne,** and **um.**

> **Anstatt eine Antwort zu geben, ging er weg.** *Instead of giving an answer he left.*
> **Er schrieb einen langen Brief, ohne ein Wort darüber zu sagen.** *He wrote a long letter without saying a word about it.*

If any other preposition is involved it must be compounded with **da(r)-,** which anticipates the following infinitive phrase.

> **Die Schwierigkeit besteht darin, den Stoff flüssig zu behalten.** *The difficulty consists in keeping the substance liquid.*
> **Ich bin nie dazu gekommen, diese Bücher zu lesen.** *I never got around to reading these books.*

APPENDIX C

Word formation

29.1 Word formation from the simple words of the language takes place in three ways. As time goes on the student should develop a feeling for word formation that in many cases will enable him to recognize the meaning of a derivative. In the following paragraphs these three ways are only mentioned and not discussed at any length.

29.2 Many words are formed by change in the root of the word, or the root may be used without change. Thus we have the noun **der Fluß**, *river*, which is connected with the verb **fließen**, *flow*, and we have the noun **der Lauf**, *run* or *course*, which is connected with the verb **laufen**. At the beginning, at any rate, the student has to rely on his dictionary or vocabulary for the meaning of these words.

29.3 The second group of words is formed by the use of prefixes and suffixes.

(a) Separable and inseparable prefixes of verbs have already been discussed (Lesson 17). These same prefixs are found in nouns and adjectives connected with these verbs.

> **die Bemerkung (bemerken)** *remark*
> **der Ausgang (ausgehen)** *exit, conclusion*
> **anfänglich (anfangen)** *original*

Two more common prefixes are **un-** and **ur-**. **Un-** is the negative prefix, as in English; **ur-** gives the meaning of *very old, original, primitive*.

> **unmöglich** *impossible*
> **der Urwald** *forest primeval, virgin forest*
> **uralt** *very old, ancient*

(b) Adjective suffixes include:

-bar—the equivalent of English *-able, -ible*. It is usually added to verb stems, as **lesbar,** *readable, legible.*

-en, -ern—added to nouns to indicate material, as **golden,** *golden;* **hölzern,** *wooden.*

-er—forms an indeclinable adjective when added to the name of a city, as **Berliner.**

-ig, -isch, -lich—correspond to English *-y, -ish, -ly,* although the translation is not always obtained by the use of these English suffixes: **abhängig,** *independent;* **chemisch,** *chemical;* **möglich,** *possible.*

-los—the equivalent of English *-less,* as **grundlos,** *groundless, without reason.*

-sam—corresponding to English *-some,* as **einsam,** *lonesome, lonely.*

(c) Noun suffixes have already been mentioned (§ 7.8). To those mentioned may be added **-e,** which forms nouns of quality from certain adjectives. Such nouns are feminine, and if the plural exists it is formed by adding **-n.**

die Größe *size, magnitude*   **die Röte** *redness*

Another suffix is **-schaft,** which usually forms abstract nouns. These are feminine and the plural ends in **-en.**

die Landschaft *landscape*   **die Freundschaft** *friendship*

29.4 The third group of words is formed by combining two or more separate words. Some of these compounds, particularly the long ones, are not listed in dictionaries, and the student must know how to break them up to look up the meanings of the component parts.

A word formed in this way is grammatically the same as the last part. **Der Rohstoff,** *raw material,* is a masculine noun with the plural in **-e** because **Stoff** is a masculine noun with the plural in **-e. Widerspruchsfrei,** *free of contradiction,* is an adjective because **frei** is one.

The last part of the compound is the basic part as far as meaning is concerned and is limited by the parts preceding it. This is also true of English: a *penknife* is a certain kind of knife, one originally used for sharpening quill pens; a *watermelon* is

[*191*]

a kind of melon. Thus, **ein Schulmädchen** is a *girl*, **eine Mädchen-schule** is a *school*.

As in English the first part of the compound carries the primary accent.

If the first of the two parts of a compound ends with a consonant doubled and the second part begins with the same consonant, the compound drops one of the three.

> **die Metallegierung,** *alloy*, from **das Metall** and **die Legierung**
> **der Mittag,** *noon*, from **die Mitte** and **der Tag**

If two or more compounds have one part in common, it is customary not to repeat this part, but to indicate its omission with a hyphen.

> **Regen-, Fluß- und Seewasser** for **Regenwasser, Flußwasser und Seewasser,** *rain, river, and sea water*
> **Kristallflächen oder -kanten** for **Kristallflächen oder Kristallkanten** *crystal surfaces or crystal edges*

Notice also:

> **Schreib- und andere Fehler** for **Schreibfehler und andere Fehler** *typographical errors and other errors*

APPENDIX D

Principal parts of strong verbs

Here is a list of some of the most important strong verbs with their principal parts, arranged according to classes.

I. (a)	bleiben	blieb	ist geblieben	bleibt	remain
	meiden	mied	hat gemieden	meidet	avoid
	scheiden	schied	hat geschieden	scheidet	separate
	scheinen	schien	hat geschienen	scheint	shine, seem
	schreiben	schrieb	hat geschrieben	schreibt	write
	schreien	schrie	hat geschrien	schreit	yell, cry
	schweigen	schwieg	hat geschwiegen	schweigt	be silent
	steigen	stieg	ist gestiegen	steigt	climb
	treiben	trieb	hat getrieben	treibt	drive
(b)	beißen	biß	hat gebissen	beißt	bite
	gleichen	glich	hat geglichen	gleicht	resemble, be like
	greifen	griff	hat gegriffen	greift	seize
	leiden	litt	hat gelitten	leidet	suffer
	reißen	riß	hat gerissen	reißt	tear
	reiten	ritt	ist *or* hat geritten	reitet	ride
	schneiden	schnitt	hat geschnitten	schneidet	cut
	schreiten	schritt	ist geschritten	schreitet	stride, step
	streiten	stritt	hat gestritten	streitet	quarrel

[193]

II.

biegen	bog	hat gebogen	biegt	bend
bieten	bot	hat geboten	bietet	offer
fliegen	flog	ist *or* hat geflogen	fliegt	fly
fliehen	floh	ist geflohen	flieht	flee
fließen	floß	ist geflossen	fließt	flow
frieren	fror	hat gefroren	friert	freeze
genießen	genoß	hat genossen	genießt	enjoy
gießen	goß	hat gegossen	gießt	pour
heben	hob	hat gehoben	hebt	lift
riechen	roch	hat gerochen	riecht	smell
schießen	schoß	hat geschossen	schießt	shoot
schließen	schloß	hat geschlossen	schließt	close
verlieren	verlor	hat verloren	verliert	lose
ziehen	zog	ist *or* hat gezogen	zieht	move; pull

III. (a)

binden	band	hat gebunden	bindet	tie
finden	fand	hat gefunden	findet	find
gelingen	gelang	ist gelungen	gelingt	succeed
klingen	klang	hat geklungen	klingt	sound
singen	sang	hat gesungen	singt	sing
sinken	sank	ist gesunken	sinkt	sink
springen	sprang	ist gesprungen	springt	jump
trinken	trank	hat getrunken	trinkt	drink
zwingen	zwang	hat gezwungen	zwingt	compel

(b)

beginnen	begann	hat begonnen	beginnt	begin
gewinnen	gewann	hat gewonnen	gewinnt	win, gain
schwimmen	schwamm	ist geschwommen	schwimmt	swim

Appendix D

IV.

Infinitive	Present	Preterite	Perfect	Meaning
brechen	bricht	brach	hat gebrochen	break
empfehlen	empfiehlt	empfahl	hat empfohlen	recommend
gelten	gilt	galt	hat gegolten	be valid
helfen	hilft	half	hat geholfen	help
kommen	kommt	kam	ist gekommen	come
nehmen	nimmt	nahm	hat genommen	take
sprechen	spricht	sprach	hat gesprochen	speak
stehlen	stiehlt	stahl	hat gestohlen	steal
sterben	stirbt	starb	ist gestorben	die
treffen	trifft	traf	hat getroffen	hit, meet
werden	wird	wurde	ist geworden	become
werfen	wirft	warf	hat geworfen	throw
bitten	bittet	bat	hat gebeten	request

V.

Infinitive	Present	Preterite	Perfect	Meaning
essen	ißt	aß	hat gegessen	eat
geben	gibt	gab	hat gegeben	give
geschehen	geschieht	geschah	ist geschehen	happen
lesen	liest	las	hat gelesen	read
liegen	liegt	lag	hat gelegen	lie
messen	mißt	maß	hat gemessen	measure
sehen	sieht	sah	hat gesehen	see
sitzen	sitzt	saß	hat gesessen	sit
treten	tritt	trat	ist or hat getreten	step, kick
vergessen	vergißt	vergaß	hat vergessen	forget
fahren	fährt	fuhr	ist or hat gefahren	travel, ride; drive

VI.

Infinitive	Present	Preterite	Perfect	Meaning
schlagen	schlägt	schlug	hat geschlagen	beat
tragen	trägt	trug	hat getragen	carry, wear
wachsen	wächst	wuchs	ist gewachsen	grow
waschen	wäscht	wusch	hat gewaschen	wash

VII.

Infinitive	Past	Perfect	Present	English
braten	briet	hat gebraten	brät	roast
fallen	fiel	ist gefallen	fällt	fall
fangen	fing	hat gefangen	fängt	catch
halten	hielt	hat gehalten	hält	hold
hangen	hing	hat gehangen	hängt	hang
heißen	hieß	hat geheißen	heißt	be named
lassen	ließ	hat gelassen	läßt	let, leave
laufen	lief	ist gelaufen	läuft	run
raten	riet	hat geraten	rät	advise
rufen	rief	hat gerufen	ruft	call
schlafen	schlief	hat geschlafen	schläft	sleep
stoßen	stieß	hat gestoßen	stößt	hit, bump

Irregular

gehen	ging	ist gegangen	geht	go
sein	war	ist gewesen	ist	be
stehen	stand	hat gestanden	steht	stand
tun	tat	hat getan	tut	do

GERMAN-ENGLISH VOCABULARY

The genitive singular of a noun is indicated only for those masculine nouns which add -n or -ns.

The principal parts of strong and irregular verbs are indicated. A separable prefix is indicated by the hyphen following.

Adjective-adverbs are listed as adjectives, unless the adverbial meaning is not clear.

Numerals are not listed, but are to be found in Lesson 18.

A

ab-drucken reprint
der Abend, -e evening; see **heute**
das Abendessen, - supper, evening meal
aber but, however
abgesehen von disregarding
ab-hängen, hing, gehangen (von) depend (upon)
das Abitur', -e final examination
ab-machen agree upon, settle
ab-schicken send off
absolut' absolute
ab-wechseln alternate
die Abwechslung, -en variation; **zur ___** for a change
ach oh
der Ackerbau agriculture
ähnlich similar
die Ahnung, -en idea
der Alkohol, -e alcohol
all, alle all
allein' alone
allerlei all sorts of things
allgemein general
alltäglich everyday
als than; when
als ob as if
also so, therefore, well, that is

alt (¨) old
das Alter, - age
altnordisch Old Norse
altsprachlich classical-language
(das) Ame'rika America
amerika'nisch American
sich amüsieren have fun, have a good time
an to, at, on
das Andenken memory
ander other
ein andermal another time
ändern change
anders different, differently
anderthalb one and a half
die Anekdo'te, -n anecdote
die Anerkennung recognition
der Anfang, ⸗e beginning
an-fangen, i, a, ä begin
an-gehören belong
angenehm pleasant
die Angst fear; **___ haben** be afraid
an-gucken peer at
an-kommen, a, o (ist) arrive
die Ankunft, ⸗e arrival
die Anlage, -n grounds
die Anordnung, -en arrangement
an-reden speak to

[197]

an-regen stimulate
an-sagen announce
an-sehen, a, e, ie look at
der Anspruch claim; in — nehmen lay claim to
die Anstalt, -en institution
anständig good, respectable
anstatt instead of
an-stellen hire
sich an-strengen exert oneself
die Antwort, -en answer
antworten (*dat.*) answer
an-ziehen, zog, gezogen put on
der Anzug, ⸗e suit
an-zünden light, ignite
die Apothe′ke, -n drugstore
der Apothe′ker, - druggist
der Appetit′ appetite
der April′ April
die Arbeit, -en work, labor
arbeiten work
das Arbeiter- und Bauernparadies
paradise for the laborer and
farmer
die Arbeitsfrau, -en cleaning
woman
sich ärgern be annoyed
arm (¨) (an) poor (in)
die Armee′, -n army
die Armut poverty
die Art, -en type, kind
der Arzt, ⸗e doctor
(das) Asien Asia
auch also, too
auf on, up, at, for (a period of
time)
der Aufenthalt stay
auf-fressen, a, e, i eat up
auf-geben, a, e, i give up
auf-gehen, ging, gegangen (ist)
go up
auf-hören stop, cease
auf-regen excite
auf-springen, a, u (ist) jump up

auf-stehen, stand, gestanden (ist)
get up
auf-treiben, ie, ie scrape up
auf-treten, a, e, i (ist) appear
das Auge, -n eye
der August′ August
aus out of, from
der Ausflug, ⸗e excursion
der Ausgang, ⸗e conclusion
ausgezeichnet excellent, splendid
aus-machen; nichts — not to
matter
der Ausschank, ⸗e *place where
drinks are served, usually for
the waiters only*
aus-sehen, a, e, ie look
außen; von — from the outside
außer beside
äußer external; das Äußere external appearance
außerdem furthermore
äußerlich external
äußerst extreme
aus-steigen, ie, ie (ist) get out
aus-suchen seek out
aus-wählen choose, select
nach auswärts out, outward
auswendig by heart
sich aus-ziehen, zog, gezogen un-
dress
das Auto, -s auto
autobiographisch autobiographi-
cal
der Autobus, -se bus

B

der Bach, ⸗e brook
der Backstein, -e brick
bald soon
bange worried
barfuß barefoot
bauen build
der Bauer, -n farmer, peasant
der Baum, ⸗e tree

(das) **Bayern** Bavaria
beantworten answer
die **Beantwortung** answer
bedeuten mean; **bedeutend** significant
die **Bedeutung, -en** significance
bedrohen threaten
sich **beeilen** hurry
Beethoven *proper name*
befriedigen satisfy
begabt talented
begegnen (ist) meet (*dat.*)
der **Beginn** beginning
beginnen, a, o begin
begrenzt limited
der **Begriff, -e** concept
der **Behälter, -** container
behandeln treat
behaupten maintain, assert
bei with, at, by, in, in the case of, at the home of
die **beiden** the two
beieinander next to one another
beinahe almost
der **Beinbruch** breaking one's leg
das **Beispiel, -e** example; **zum —** for example
bekannt acquainted, well known
bekommen, a, o get
belegen enroll in
beleidigen offend
Belle Alliance *place name*
bemerken notice
benebelt befogged, tipsy
sich **benehmen, a, o, i** behave
bequem comfortable
bereiten prepare
der **Berg, -e** mountain
die **Bergakademie, -n** school of mines
der **Bericht, -e** report
der **Beruf, -e** profession
berühmt famous
beschäftigt busy
die **Beschwerde, -n** difficulty

besiegen conquer
besonders especially
besorgen take care of
besprechen, a, o, i discuss
bestehen, -stand, -standen pass; **— aus** consist of
das **Bestehen** passing
bestellen order
bestimmen determine; **bestimmt** definite
der **Besuch** visit
besuchen visit, attend
betonen emphasize
die **Betonung** emphasis
betrachten consider
betreiben, ie, ie operate
das **Bett, -en** bed
betteln beg
die **Bevölkerung, -en** population
bevor before
bewachen guard
bewahren preserve, keep
bewegen, bewog, bewogen move, induce
sich **bewerben, a, o, i (um)** apply (for)
die **Bewerberin, -nen** applicant
bezahlen pay (for)
die **Bibelübersetzung, -en** translation of the Bible
die **Bibliothek', -en** library
biegen, o, o turn
das **Bier, -e** beer
das **Bild, -er** picture
binden, a, u tie
binnen (*gen. or dat.*) within
die **Biologie'prüfung, -en** examination in biology
bis until
ein **bißchen** a bit
bissig savage, biting
bitte please
bitten, a, e ask, request
blau blue

bleiben, ie, ie (ist) stay; — bei stick to

der Bleistift, -e pencil

blenden dazzle

der Blick, -e glance

blitzblank clean and shining

der Blödsinn nonsense

bloß mere

Blücher *proper name*

blutig bloody

der Boden, = bottom, floor, soil

die Bohne, -n bean

Bonn *place name*

böse angry, evil

(das) Brandenburg Brandenburg

brauchbar usable

brauchen need

braun brown

brennen, brannte, gebrannt burn

bringen, brachte, gebracht bring

das Bruchstück, -e fragment

die Brücke, -n bridge

der Bruder, = brother

die Brüstung, -en railing

das Buch, =er book

die Buchhandlung, -en book store

büffeln work hard, grind

die Bühne, -n stage

das Bündel, - bundle

die Bundesrepublik Federal Republic

das Büro', -s office

C

der Charak'ter, -e character

der Chef, -s boss

die Chemie' chemistry

chemisch chemical

das College, -s college

D

da then, there; since

dabei present; while doing it

dabeistehend standing nearby

daher therefore

dahin to that place, there

damals at that time

damit with that

der Dank thanks

danke thanks, thank you

danken (*dat.*) thank

der Danksagungstag Thanksgiving Day

dann then; — und wann now and then

darauf thereupon

das that

daß that

das Datum, -ten date

dauern last

der Daumen, - thumb

das Davonlaufen; zum — enough to make you run away

dazu in addition

die Demokratie', -n democracy

demokra'tisch democratic

denken, dachte, gedacht (an) think (of); sich — imagine

denn for; *sometimes to be omitted in translation*

derselbe the same

deshalb therefore, that's why

das Detail', -s (*pronounced de-taij'*) detail

der Detektiv'roman, -e detective story

deutsch German, (das) Deutsch German

die Deutschstunde, -n German class

(das) Deutschland Germany

deutschsprechend German-speaking

der Dezem'ber December

d. h. = das heißt that is

der Dialekt', -e dialect

dichten write poetry

der Dichter, - poet

der **Film, -e** film, movie
die **Finanzierung** financing
finden, a, u find
die **Finsternis** darkness
die **Firma, -men** firm
die **Fläche, -n** area
die **Flamme, -n** flame
das **Fleisch** meat
fleißig industrious
fliehen, o, o (ist) flee
der **Flüchtling, -e** fugitive
folgen (ist; *dat.*) follow; __ **auf** follow on
fördern further, help
die **Form, -en** form
formell' formal
formen form, shape
fort away, gone; **in einem __** constantly
fort-gehen, ging, gegangen (ist) go away
fort-fahren, u, a, ä (ist) ride away
fort-laufen, ie, au, äu (ist) run away
fort-nehmen, a, o, i take away
fortwährend continuous
die **Frage, -n** question
fragen ask
(das) **Frankreich** France
der **Franzo'se, -n, -n** Frenchman
franzö'sisch French
die **Frau, -en** wife, woman, Mrs.
das **Fräulein, -** Miss, young lady
frech fresh
frei free; **im Freien** in the open, out of doors; __ **haben** be off, have off
die **Freiheit** freedom
die **Freistunde, -n** leisure hour
der **Freitag, -e** Friday
fremd strange
die **Fremdsprache, -n** foreign language
die **Freude, -n** pleasure
freuen make glad; **sich __** be glad; **sich __ auf** look forward to; **sich __ über** be glad about
der **Freund, -e** friend
die **Freundin, -nen** (female) friend
freundlich kind, friendly
der **Friede, -ns, -n** peace
der **Friedensfeind, -e** enemy of the peace
frisch fresh
froh happy, cheerful, glad
fröhlich happy
fromm pious
früh early; **früher** formerly
der **Frühling, -e** spring
der **Frühlingsmonat, -e** spring month
der **Frühlingstag, -e** spring day
das **Frühstück, -e** breakfast
frühstücken eat breakfast
sich fühlen feel
führen lead, conduct, wage (war)
füllen fill
die **Füllfeder, -n** fountain pen
der **Funken, -** spark
für for
die **Furcht (vor)** fear (of)
furchtbar fearful
fürchten fear
fürchterlich fearful, frightful, terrible
der **Fürst, -en, -en** prince
der **Fuß, ⸗e** foot
das **Futter** fodder

G

die **Gabel, -n** fork
der **Gang** motion, operation
ganz whole, all, complete; quite; **im ganzen** on the whole; __ **und gar** completely
gar very, quite; __ **nicht** not at all; __ **nichts** nothing at all
der **Garten, ⸗** garden

der **Gärtner**, - gardener
das **Gas**, -e gas
das **Gasgemisch**, -e gas mixture
die **Gasmaschine**, -n gas engine
der **Gast**, ⁼e guest
das **Gasthaus**, ⁼er inn
geben, a, e, i give; **es gibt** there
    is, there are
geboren born
gebrauchen use
der **Gedanke**, -ns, -n (**an**) thought
    (of)
das **Gedicht**, -e poem
geduldig patient
die **Gefahr**, -en danger
gefährlich dangerous
gefallen, ie, a, ä please
Gefrorenes ice cream
gegen against
gegeneinander against one an-
    other
gegenüber facing
das **Gehalt**, ⁼er salary
gehen, ging, gegangen (ist) go;
    run (*of a timepiece*); **wie geht
    es Ihnen** how are you; **das geht**
    that's possible; **richtig __** be
    right (*timepiece*)
der **Gehilfe**, -n, -n assistant
gehörig proper, suitable
der **Geist**, -er spirit, ghost
das **Geld** money
gelehrt learned
gelingen, a, u (ist) succeed
gelt *turns a statement into a ques-
    tion*
gelten, a, o, i hold true
die **Gemeinschaft**, -en community,
    congregation
das **Gemisch**, -e mixture
der **General**, ⁼e general
genießen, o, o enjoy
der **Genitiv'** genitive
genug enough
genügen suffice

der **Genuß**, **Genüsse** pleasure, en-
    joyment
geographisch geographic
gerade exactly, just
germanisch Germanic
gern(e) gladly; *with a verb gives
    the idea of* "to like to"
gesamt total
das **Geschäft**, -e business
geschehen, a, e, ie (ist) happen,
    be done
gescheit smart, clever
die **Geschichte**, -n story, history
das **Geschlecht**, -er race
die **Gesellschaft**, -en company;
    __ **leisten** keep company
das **Gesicht**, -er face
das **Gespräch**, -e conversation
das **Geständnis**, -se confession
gestern yesterday
gewinnen, a, o win; __ **an** gain
    in
gewiß certain
gewöhnlich usual, ordinary
glänzen glitter; **glänzend** brilliant
das **Glas**, ⁼er glass
die **Glasscherbe**, -n piece of
    broken glass
der **Glaube**, -ns, -n belief
glauben (**an**) think, believe (in)
der **Glaubenskampf**, ⁼e religious
    war, religious struggle
gleich same; immediately; **es ist
    mir __** it makes no difference
    to me
glücklich happy, lucky, fortunate
glücklicherweise fortunately
glühen glow
das **Gold** gold
der **Gott**, ⁼er God, god; __ **sei
    Dank** thank God
die **Götterdämmerung** twilight of
    the gods
Gottfried von Straßburg *proper
    name*

gottverlassen godforsaken

greifen, i, i (nach) reach (for)

griechisch Greek

Grimmelshausen, Christoffel von *proper name*

Grimmsch (of the) Grimms, Grimms'

die Grippe flu, grippe

groß (¨) large, great

das Grün green

der Grundgedanke, -ns, -n basic thought

gründlich thorough

grundverschieden fundamentally different

der Gruß, ⸗e greeting

grüßen greet

gut good, kind; all right

das Gymnasium, -sien secondary school; *use German word*

H

haben, hatte, gehabt, hat have

Hadubrand *proper name*

halb half

die Hälfte, -n half

hallo hello

der Halsbruch breaking one's neck

halten, ie, a, ä stop; nichts ⸺ auf think nothing of

Hamburg *place name*

die Hand, ⸗e hand

das Handbuch, ⸗er manual

die Handlung, -en plot, action

die Handschrift, -en manuscript

hart (¨) hard

Hartmann von Aue *proper name*

häßlich ugly

häufig frequent

die Hauptsache, -n main thing

hauptsächlich chief, main

die Hauptstadt, ⸗e capital

der Haupttyp, -en main type

das Haus, ⸗er house; nach Hause home; zu Hause at home

die Hausarbeit housework

heben, o, o lift

das Heer, -e army

heiß hot

heißen, ie, ei be named, be called

helfen, a, o, i (*dat.*) help

hell light

her ago

herab′ down

herab-fallen, ie, a, ä (ist) fall down

heraus-geben, a, e, i publish

heraus-holen take out

heraus-kommen, a, o (ist) come out

der Herbst, -e fall, autumn

der Herbstmonat, -e fall month

der Hering, -e herring

der Herr, -n, -en gentleman, Mr., *not to be translated before a noun of rank or title;* mein ⸺ sir

herrlich splendid, glorious

die Herrschaften (*pl.*) gentlemen

herrschen rule

her-stellen produce

hervorragend prominent

das Herz -ens, -en heart

heute today; ⸺ abend this evening; ⸺ morgen this morning; ⸺ nachmittag this afternoon

heutig present-day

heutzutage in these days

hier here

hierüber about this

hiervon of this, of these

Hildebrand *proper name*

das Hildebrandslied Lay of Hildebrand

der Himmel, - heaven

hinab-fallen, ie, a, ä (ist) fall down

hinauf′ up

hinauf-gehen, ging, gegangen (ist) go up

hinaus-fahren, u, a, ä (ist) drive out

hinaus-gehen, ging, gegangen (ist) go out

hinaus-kommen, a, o (ist) come out

hinaus-wandern (ist) wander out

hinaus-ziehen, zog, gezogen (ist) move out

hin-bringen, brachte, gebracht bring

hin-gehen, ging, gegangen (ist) go there

das Hinscheiden death

hin-stellen put

hinunter-fallen, ie, a, ä (ist) fall down

die Hitze heat

hoch (¨) high

die Hochschule, -n institution of higher learning

hoffentlich I hope (so)

das Hofkonzert, -e court concert

holen get, fetch

hören hear, listen

hübsch nice

das Hühnchen, - little chicken

die Hühnerbrühe chicken broth

hungrig hungry

intensiv' intensive

interessant' interesting

das Interes'se, -n (an) interest (in)

inzwischen meanwhile

irgend ein any (at all)

irgendwo somewhere (or other)

sich irren be mistaken

(das) Ita'lien Italy

J

ja yes; indeed

das Jahr, -e year

jahrelang for years

die Jahreszahl, -en date

die Jahreszeit, -en season

das Jahrhundert, -e century

der Januar January

jawohl yes, indeed; very good

je each; ever

jeder each, every

jemals ever

jemand someone

jetzt now

die Jugend youth

der Juli July

jung (¨) young

der Junge, -n, -n boy

der Juni June

I

die Idee', -n idea

ihr you; her, their

Ihr your

immer always; — noch still

in in, into

indem in that

das Industrie'gebiet, -e industrial region

infolge as a result of

inkorrekt incorrect

innerhalb within

K

der Kaffee coffee

das Kaffeehaus, =er café

der Käfig, -e cage

der Kaiser, - emperor

der Kalen'der, - calendar

(das) Kalifornien California

kalt (¨) cold

der Kampf, =e fight, struggle

das Kapi'tel, - chapter

kaputt' broken, out of order

die Karte, -n map, menu

der **Kartof'felkloß,** ⸗e potato
dumpling
katego'risch categorical
der **Katholik',** -en, -en Catholic
katho'lisch catholic
kaufen buy
kaum hardly, scarcely
kein not a, no, not any
der **Kellner,** - waiter
kennen, kannte, gekannt be acquainted with, know; ⸺ **lernen**
become acquainted with, meet
das **Kind,** -er child
Kinder- und Hausmärchen fairy
tales for children and home
der **Kindergarten,** ⸗ garden of
children
das **Kino,** -s movies
die **Kirche,** -n church
die **Kirchensteuer,** -n church tax
klar clear
die **Klasse,** -n class (*in the sense
of* form *or* class group)
der **Klassiker,** - classical writer
klassisch classical
kleiden dress
klein small, little
die **Klimaanlage** air conditioning
knorke fine, excellent, "dandy"
kochen cook
die **Kohle,** -n coal
der **Kolben,** - piston
kommen, a, o (ist) come
der **Kommunis'mus** communism
kommuni'stisch communistic
der **Komponist',** -en, -en composer
komprimieren compress
die **Konfession',** -en creed
konfessionell' pertaining to creed
konfessions'los without denomination, non-churchgoing
der **König,** -e king
können, konnte, gekonnt, kann
can, be able

konsequent' consistent, logical
die **Konzentrierung,** -en concentration
das **Konzert',** -e concert
der **Kopf,** ⸗e head
kosten cost
der **Krach,** -e crash
die **Kraft,** ⸗e force
krank (¨) sick
die **Kreide,** -n chalk
der **Krieg,** -e war
kriegen get, catch
der **Kritiker,** - critic
der **Kronleuchter,** - chandelier
die **Küche,** -n kitchen
der **Kuchen,** - cake
die **Kuh,** ⸗e cow
kühl cool
das **Kultur'volk,** ⸗er highly civilized people
die **Kunsthochschule,** -n academy
of art
die **Künstlerin,** -nen artist
der **Kursus,** -se course
kurz (¨) short
die **Kusi'ne,** -n (female) cousin

L

das **Laborato'rium,** -rien laboratory
lachen laugh
der **Laden,** ⸗ store
das **Lager,** - camp
lako'nisch laconic
das **Land,** ⸗er land, country
der **Länderteil,** -e part of the
country
landeswirtschaftlich of agriculture
lang long
lange long, for a long time
langsam slow
langweilig boring
lassen, ie, a, ä let, leave, allow

das **Latein'** Latin
laufen, ie, a, ä (ist) run
leben live, be alive
das **Leben,** - life
leben'dig alive, lively, vivid
leer empty
sich **legen** lie down
die **Legen'de, -n** legend
Lehmann *proper name*
die **Lehre, -n** teaching, rule
lehren teach
der **Lehrer,** - teacher
der **Lehrsatz, ∴e** theorem
leicht easy
leid; das tut mir __ I'm sorry
about that
leiden, litt, gelitten suffer
leider unfortunately
leihen, ie, ie borrow
Leipzig *place name*
Leipziger (of) Leipzig
leisten afford; **Gesellschaft __**
keep company
leiten conduct, direct
Lenoir *proper name*
lernen learn
lesen, a, e, ie read
das **Lesestück, -e** reading selection
letzt last
letzter latter
das **Licht, -er** light
lieb dear
die **Liebe, -n** love; **meine __** my
dear girl
lieber preferably, rather
der **Liederabend, -e** evening of
song
liegen, a, e lie, be situated; **__ an**
be due to
der **Likör', -e** liquor
die **Linsensuppe** lentil soup
die **Lippe, -n** lip
die **Literatur', -en** literature

das **Lokal', -e** place
(das) **London** London
der **Londoner,** - Londoner
los the matter
die **Luft** air
die **Lungenentzündung** pneu-
monia
die **Lust, ∴e** desire
lustig gay
Luther *proper name*
der **Lyriker,** - lyric poet

M

machen do, make
die **Macht, ∴e** power
das **Mädchen,** - girl, waitress
der **Mai** May
die **Majestät', -en** majesty
mal = einmal once; *frequently to*
be omitted in translation
das **Mal, -e** time
man one
mancher many a; *pl.* many, some
manchmal often
der **Mann, ∴er** man, husband
der **Mantel, ∴** topcoat
das **Märchen,** - fairy tale
marinieren marinate
die **Mark, -en** border territory,
march
der **März** March
die **Maschi'ne, -n** engine
das **Material', -ien** material
die **Mathematik'** mathematics
mathematisch-naturwissenschaft-
lich mathematical-scientific
die **Mauer, -n** wall
die **Medizin', -en** medicine
mehr more; **kein . . . __** no more
mehrere several
die **Meile, -n** mile
mein my
meinen mean

die **meisten** most

meistens mostly, for the most part, usually

meistenteils usually, generally

der **Meister, -** master

melken milk

die **Menge, -n** amount, large amount

der **Mensch, -en, -en** person, human being

merken notice

messen, a, e, i measure

das **Messer, -** knife

mindestens at least

die **Minu'te, -n** minute

das **Mira'kel, -** miracle

mit with; along

miteinander with one another

mit-fahren, u, a, ä (ist) ride along

mit-gehen, ging, gegangen (ist) go along, walk along

mit-kommen, a, o (ist) come along

das **Mittagessen, -** noon meal, lunch

die **Mitte, -n** middle

das **Mittel, -** (**gegen**) remedy (for)

mittelalterlich medieval

(das) **Mitteldeutschland** Central Germany

mittelhochdeutsch Middle High German

die **Mitternacht, ⸗e** midnight

der **Mittwoch, -e** Wednesday

modern' modern

mögen, mochte, gemocht, mag like, care to, may

möglich possible

die **Möglichkeit, -en** possibility

der **Monat, -e** month

der **Mond, -e** moon

der **Montag, -e** Monday

morgen tomorrow

der **Morgen, -** morning; **heute morgen** this morning

das **Motiv', -e** motif

der **Motor, -en** motor

müde tired

München Munich

mündlich oral

munter cheerful

die **Musik'** music

musika'lisch musical

die **Musik'-Hochschule, -n** academy of music

der **Musik'kritiker, -** music critic

müssen, mußte, gemußt, muß have to, must

die **Mutter, ⸗** mother

die **Mythologie'** mythology

N

na well; —— **schön** oh, all right

nach after, to, according to

nach-geben, a, e, i give in

die **Nacherzählung, -en** retelling

nach-fallen, ie, a, ä (ist) fall after

nach-gehen, ging, gegangen (ist) be slow

nachher afterward

der **Nachmittag, -e** afternoon

nachmittags in the afternoon

der **Nachschub** reinforcements

nächst next

nach-stehen, stand, gestanden be behind

die **Nacht, ⸗e** night

das **Nachthemd, -en** nightshirt

die **Nadel, -n** needle

die **Nähe** vicinity; **in der** —— nearby

die **Naht, ⸗e** seam

der **Name, -ns, -n** name

namens by name, named

nämlich namely, you see

die **Nasenspitze, -n** tip of the nose
die **Nation', -en** nation
die **Natur', -en** nature
natürlich naturally
die **Naturwissenschaft, -en** natural science
naturwissenschaftlich scientific
neben beside
der **Neffe, -n, -n** nephew
nehmen, a, o, i take
neidisch envious
nein no
nennen, nannte, genannt name, call
nett nice
neu new
die **Neugierde** curiosity
neugierig curious
neuhochdeutsch New High German
neulich recently
neunjährig nine years'
neusprachlich modern-language
nicht not; ___ **mehr** no longer
die **Nichte, -n** niece
nichts nothing
nie never; **noch** ___ never yet
nieder-brennen, brannte, gebrannt burn down
(das) **Niederdeutschland** Low Germany
die **Niederlande** Netherlands
sich **nieder-lassen, ie, a, ä** settle down
niemand nobody
noch still, in addition; **immer** ___ still; ___ **nicht** not yet
nochmal once again
die **Nonne, -n** nun
(das) **Norddeutschland** North Germany
der **Norden** north
(das) **Nordrhein-Westfalen** region of the Lower Rhine and Westphalia

die **Nordseeküste** North Sea coast
notwendigerweise necessarily
der **Novem'ber** November
nun now; well
nur only

O

ob whether, if
(das) **Oberdeutschland** Upper Germany
der **Oberkellner, -** headwaiter
obgleich although
das **Objekt', -e** object
obwohl although
oder or
Odin *proper name*
der **Ofen, ⸗** stove
offen open, frank
offiziell' official
die **Öffnung, -en** opening
oft (¨) often
öfters frequently
ohne without
der **Okto'ber** October
der **Onkel, -** uncle
die **Oper, -n** opera
das **Orche'ster, -** orchestra
die **Orche'sterbrüstung, -en** orchestra railing
orga'nisch organic
der **Ort, -e** *or* ⸗**er** place, village
der **Osten** east
die **Osterferien** (*pl.*) Easter vacation
das **Ostern** Easter
(das) **Österreich** Austria
östlich eastern
die **Ostzone** East Zone

P

ein paar a couple
das **Paar, -e** pair

der **Pädagog′**, -en, -en pedagogue
die **Pädago′gik** pedagogy
pädago′gisch pedagogic(al)
das **Paket′**, -e package
der **Pakt**, -e pact
der **Pantof′fel**, - slipper
das **Papier′**, -e paper
(das) **Paris′** Paris
Pari′ser (of) Paris
die **Partei′**, -en party
passen fit, suit
Pech haben have trouble
die **Perio′de**, -n period
die **Pflanze**, -n plant
pflegen take care of
der **Phöbus-Palast** *name*
die **Physik′** physics
physika′lisch physical
das **Pianoforte**, -s piano
planen plan
der **Platz**, ⸗e seat
plaudern chat, talk
plötzlich sudden
poli′tisch political
die **Portion′**, -en portion
die **Post** mail, post office
präparieren prepare
der **Präsident′**, -en, -en president
die **Praxis** practice
(das) **Preußen** Prussia
preußisch Prussian
privat′ private
das **Problem′**, -e problem
problema′tisch problematical
der **Professor**, -en professor
das **Programm′**, -e program
Pros(i)t to your health
der **Protestant′**, -en, -en Protestant
protestan′tisch protestant
das **Prozent′**, -e per cent
prüfen examine
die **Prüfung**, -en examination, test
psychisch psychic
putzen clean, polish

R

das **Rad**, ⸗er wheel, bicycle
radikal′ radical
die **Ratte**, -n rat
rauben rob, plunder
recht right; all right; __ **haben** be right
die **Rede**, -n speech
reden talk
referieren give a report
die **Regel**, -n rule
regieren rule
die **Regierung**, -en government
regnen rain
reich rich
das **Reich**, -e empire
die **Reifenpanne**, -n flat tire
die **Reifeprüfung**, -en final examination
die **Reise**, -n trip
das **Reisegeld** (money for) fare
reisen (ist) travel
reizend charming
reklamieren reclaim
die **Religion′**, -en religion
die **Religions′gemeinschaft**, -en religious group
die **Republik′**, -en republic
der **Rest**, -e remainder
das **Restaurant′**, -s restaurant
das **Resultat′**, -e result
retten save
das **Rezept′**, -e prescription
richtig right, correct
die **Richtung**, -en direction
der **Ritter**, - knight
(das) **Rom** Rome
der **Roman′**, -e novel
die **Roman′tik** romanticism
Roswitha von Gandersheim *proper name*
der **Ruf** reputation
rufen, ie, u call
ruhen auf be based on

rund in round numbers
Rustum *proper name*

S

der Saal, Säle hall
die Sache, -n thing; das ist so eine
— that's the way things are
(das) Sachsen Saxony
die Sage, -n legend
sagen say; — wollen mean
der Salat' salad
sammeln collect
der Samstag, -e Saturday
der Satan Satan
der Sauerbraten beef soaked in
vinegar
der Sauerstoff oxygen
schade too bad
schaden harm, hurt
der Schall sound
das Schaltjahr, -e leap year
schauen look
der Schauplatz, ⁼e scene
die Scheindemokratie pseudo-
democracy
scheinen, ie, ie seem
schicken send
die Schlacht, -en battle
schlafen, ie, a, ä sleep; — gehen
go to bed
der Schlafrock, ⁼e dressing gown
die Schlafstube, -n bedroom
das Schlafzimmer, - bedroom
schlagen, u, a, ä fight; aus dem
Kopf — get out of one's head
schlecht bad, poor
schlimm bad, serious
der Schluß, -üsse conclusion
der Schmerz, -en pain
schmücken adorn
Schneewittchen Snow White
der Schneider, - tailor
schnell fast, quick
schon already

schön beautiful; all right, O. K.
schöpferisch creative
der Schreck fright
der Schrecken terror
schreiben, ie, ie write
die Schreibmaschine, -n typewriter
schreien, ie, ie yell, scream, shout
die Schriftsprache, -n literary language
der Schuh, -e shoe
die Schularbeit, -en homework
die Schule, -n school; in die —
to school
die Schulfreundin, -nen school
friend
der Schulkamerad, -en, -en schoolmate
schwarz (¨) black
schwätzen chatter
die Schweiz Switzerland
Schweizer (*indecl. adj.*) Swiss
schwer difficult, heavy, hard to
work
schwermütig depressed
die Schwierigkeit, -en difficulty
schwimmen, a, o (ist) swim
der See, -n lake
segeln sail
sehen, a, e, ie see
sehr very
sein, war, gewesen, ist (ist) be
sein his
seit since (*temporal*)
seitdem since then
die Seite, -n side
die Sekretä'rin, -nen secretary
die Sekun'de, -n second
selb same
selbst oneself, themselves; even
selten rare, infrequent
das Seme'ster, - semester
Semmler *proper name*
der Septem'ber September
die Serviet'te, -n napkin

setzen set; sich — sit down
sich himself, herself, *etc.*
sie she, they, it
Sie you
siegen be victorious
der Sieger, - victor
Simplicius Simplicissimus *proper name*
der Sinn, -e sense
die Situation', -en situation
der Sitz, -e seat
sitzen, saß, gesessen sit
so so, thus; such; — . . . wie as . . . as
sofort' at once
sogar' even
sogenannt so-called
der Sohn, ⸗e son
das Söhnchen, - little son
Sohrab *proper name*
solch such
der Soldat', -en, -en soldier
sollen, sollte, gesollt, soll be to, be supposed to, be said to
der Sommer, - summer
der Sommermonat, -e summer month
sondern but
der Sonnabend, -e Saturday
die Sonne, -n sun
der Sonntag, -e Sunday
sonntäglich Sunday
sonst otherwise, usually
die Sorge, -n worry
sorgfältig careful
sowie as well as
sowieso as it is
sowohl' (. . .) als both . . . and, as well as
sozial' social
sparen save
der Spaß, ⸗e; — machen give pleasure
spät late; wie — ist es? what time is it?

spazieren-gehen go for a walk
die Speisekarte, -n menu
speisen eat
die Spezial-Hochschule, -n special institute of higher learning
spielen play
das Spielen play(ing)
spinnen, a, o spin
die Sprache, -n language
sprechen, a, o, i speak
das Sprichwort, ⸗er proverb
der Staat, -en state
die Staatskirche, -n state church
die Stabilität' stability
die Stadt, ⸗e city
der Städter, - city person
städtisch (of the) city, municipal
stark (¨) strong
statt instead of
stecken stick, put
stehen, stand, gestanden, stand; — bleiben stop
stehlen, a, o, ie steal
die Stellung, -en job
sterben, a, o, i (ist) die
das Steuerrad, ⸗er steering wheel
still silent, quiet
das Stipen'dium, -dien scholarship
der Stoff, -e substance
die Straße, -n street
das Streben striving
die Strecke, -n distance
strecken stretch, extend
das Stroh straw
der Strohhalm, -e (blade of) straw
das Stück, -e piece, play, (moving) picture
der Student', -en, -en student
das Studentenleben, - student life
der Studentenstreich, -e student prank
die Studen'tin, -nen (female) student

der **Studienplan,** ⸗e course of studies
studieren study
das **Studium, -dien** study
der **Stuhl,** ⸗e chair
die **Stunde, -n** hour, lesson, class
suchen look for
süddeutsch South German
(das) **Süddeutschland** South Germany
der **Süden** south
die **Suppe, -n** soup
der **Suppenlöffel, -** soup spoon
die **Symphonie', -n** symphony

T

tadellos faultless
der **Tag, -e** day
täglich daily
die **Tante, -n** aunt
die **Tasse, -n** cup
technisch technical
der **Teil, -e** part; **zum** __ in part
teilbar divisible
teilen share
das **Tennis** tennis
der **Tennisplatz,** ⸗e tennis court
das **Tennisspiel, -e** game of tennis
der **Tenor',** ⸗e *or* **-e** tenor
das **Territo'rium, -rien** territory
der **Teufel, -** devil
das **Textbuch,** ⸗er textbook
Theophilus *proper name*
Thor *proper name*
tief deep
das **Tiefland,** ⸗er lowland
das **Tier, -e** animal
die **Tinte, -n** ink
(das) **Tirol** *province in W. Austria*
der **Tisch, -e** table
der **Titel, -** title
tja = ja yes
die **Tochter,** ⸗ daughter

der **Tod** death
der **Topf,** ⸗e pot
topogra'phisch topographical
tot dead
töten kill
traditionell' traditional
tragen, u, a, ä carry, wear
trauen (*dat.*) trust
der **Traum,** ⸗e dream
träumen dream
treffen, a, o, i meet, hit upon, come upon
treiben, ie, ie drive
trennen separate
treten, a, e, i (ist) step
trinken, a, u drink
sich **trollen** take off, go away
trotz in spite of
trotzdem nevertheless
tüchtig able, capable
die **Tücke** malice
tun, tat, getan do
der **Tunnel, -** tunnel
die **Tür, -en** door
die **Tüte, -n** paper bag

U

über over, about (*with acc.*)
überall everywhere
überhaupt in general
übermorgen day after tomorrow
übernachten spend the night
die **Übertragung, -en** translation
überzeugen convince
üblich usual
übrig remaining
das **Ufer, -** bank
die **Uhr, -en** watch; **acht** __ eight o'clock
der **Uhrmacher, -** jeweler, watch repair man
um around, at (*in time expressions*); __ . . . **zu** (*with infinitive*) in order to

der **Umgang** association
die **Umgangssprache** everyday language, colloquial language
umher-irren (**ist**) roam about
sich **um-schauen** (**nach**) look around (for)
umständlich bothersome, a nuisance, roundabout
die **Unabhängigkeitserklärung** Declaration of Independence
unangenehm unpleasant
unbefriedigt dissatisfied
unbeweglich immovable
und and
ungefähr about, approximately
unglücklich unhappy
die **Universität′, -en** university
die **Universitäts′bibliothek, -en** university library
der **Universitäts′student, -en, -en** university student
unmöglich impossible
die **Unschuld** innocence
unter among
unterscheiden, ie, ie differentiate
der **Unterschied, -e** difference
unterzeichnen sign
uralt ancient
ursprünglich original
usw. = **undsoweiter** and so forth, etc.

V

der **Vater, =** father
väterlich (paternal), parental
sich **verändern** change
verbannen banish
verbieten, o, o forbid
die **Verbindung, -en** compound
verbreiten spread
die **Verbreitung** dissemination
verbrennen, -brannte, -brannt burn
verbündet allied
verderben, a, o, i spoil

vereinigt united
verfolgen persecute
vergessen, a, e, i forget
der **Vergleich, -e** comparison
vergleichen, i, i compare
sich **verhalten, ie, a, ä** be like
verheeren devastate, lay waste
sich **verheiraten** get married
verkaufen sell
die **Verkäuferin, -nen** salesgirl
verkehren associate
verlassen, ie, a, ä leave
sich **verlieben** (**in**) fall in love (with); **verliebt in** love
verlieren, o, o, lose
verlocken entice
vermeiden, ie, ie avoid
vermuten presume
vermutlich presumed, imagined
vernachlässigen neglect
vernichten annihilate
versäumen miss
verschieden various, varied
sich **verschlafen, ie, a, ä** oversleep
verschlingen, a, u devour
verschreiben, ie, ie prescribe
der **Verstand** understanding
verstehen, -stand, -standen understand
der **Versuch, -e** attempt
versuchen try
vertrieben displaced
die **Verteilung, -en** distribution
verwandt relative
verwüsten ravage
viel much; **viele** many
vielleicht perhaps
vielmehr rather
die **Viertelstunde, -n** quarter of an hour
das **Volk, =er** people, race
die **Volksschule, -n** elementary school (*use the German word*)
vollenden complete
völlig complete, full

[215]

vollkommen complete
der Vollmond, -e full moon
vollständig complete
das Volu'men, -mina volume
von of, from, by; __ . . . an from . . . on
vor before, in front of
vorbei past
vorbei-kommen, a, o (ist) come past
vor-bereiten (auf) prepare (for)
der Vorfall, ᵕe incident
vor-gehen, ging, gegangen (ist) be fast
vorgestern day before yesterday
vor-haben, hatte, gehabt, hat plan, intend, have in mind
vorher before
vorig last, previous
die Vorlesung, -en lecture
der Vorschlag, ᵕe suggestion
vor-schlagen, u, a, ä suggest
vor-schreiben, ie, ie prescribe
die Vorspeise, -n appetizer
die Vorstadt suburbs
vor-stellen introduce
vor-wiegen, o, o predominate

W

wachsen, u, a, ä grow
das Wachstum growth
der Wagen, - wagon, auto
die Wahl, -en choice
wählen choose, select
wahr true; nicht __ (*turns a statement into a question*)
während during; while
der Wald, ᵕer woods
Walter von der Vogelweide *proper name*
der Wanderer, - wanderer, traveler
wandern (ist) wander, hike

die Wanderung, -en wandering
wann when
warm (¨) warm
warten (auf) wait (for)
warum why
was what; = etwas; so __ something like that; __ für (ein) what kind of (a)
die Wäsche laundry
waschen, u, a, ä wash
der Wasserfall, ᵕe waterfall
der Wasserstoff hydrogen
weder . . . noch neither . . . nor
weg away
der Weg, -e way; sich auf den __ machen start out
weg-bleiben, ie, ie (ist) stay away
wegen on account of
weg-gehen, ging, gegangen (ist) go away
sich weg-heben, o, o get away from
weg-laufen, ie, au, äu (ist) run away
weh tun, tat, getan hurt
wehrlos defenseless
das Weib, -er woman
die Weihnachten (*pl.*) Christmas
weil because
die Weile, -n while
die Weise, -n way, manner
weiß white
weit far, wide; so __ as far as
die Weiterentwicklung, -en further development
weiter-fahren, u, a, ä (ist) travel on
weiter-gehen, ging, gegangen (ist) go on
weiter-lesen, a, e, ie read on
welcher which, what
weltberühmt world famous
der Weltkrieg, -e world war

die **Weltliteratur** world literature

sich **wenden, wandte, gewandt an** turn to

wenig little; **wenige** few

wenigstens at least

wenn when, if; **__ auch** even if

wer who, whoever

werden, u, o, i (ist) become

werfen, a, o, i throw

das **Werk, -e** work

wert worth

weshalb why

westdeutsch West German

(das) **Westdeutschland** West Germany

der **Westen** west

das **Wetter** weather

wichtig important

wie how, like, as

wieder again

wiederholen repeat, review

das **Wiedersehen** seeing again; **auf __** goodbye

wiegen, o, o weigh

(das) **Wien** Vienna

Wiener (of) Vienna

wieso' how so

wieviel how much

wie viele how many

wievielt; den __en haben wir? what is the date?

wild wild

der **Winter, -** winter

der **Wintermonat, -e** winter month

wir we

wirklich real

die **Wirtschaftshochschule, -n** institute of commerce and finance

das **Wirtshaus, ̈er** inn, tavern

wissen, wußte, gewußt, weiß know

die **Wissenschaft** knowledge

der **Wissenschaftler, -** scientist, researcher

wissenschaftlich scholarly, learned

wo where

die **Woche, -n** week

das **Wochenende, -n** weekend

wohin' to what place, where

wohl indeed, probably; well

wohnen live, reside

der **Wolf, ̈e** wolf

Wolfram von Eschenbach *proper name*

wollen, wollte, gewollt, will want (to), be about to

das **Wort, -e** *or* ̈er word

wunderbar wonderful

wünschen wish

die **Würdigung, -en** appreciation

Z

der **Zahnarzt, ̈e** dentist

z. B. = zum Beispiel for example

zeigen show

die **Zeile, -n** line

die **Zeit, -en** time

das **Zeitalter, -** age

die **Zeitung, -en** newspaper

zerbrechen, a, o, i break to pieces, shatter, crack

zerplatzen (ist) burst, split

zerstören destroy

ziehen, zog, gezogen pull, draw; (ist) move, go

ziemlich fairly; **so __** pretty much, so so

das **Zimmer, -** room

die **Zimmertemperatur** room temperature

zornig angry

zu to, at; too

zuerst' at first

zuletzt' at the last, finally

zumal' especially

zurecht'-machen fix

zu-reden urge

zurück' back

zurück'-bringen, brachte, gebracht bring back

zurück'-kommen, a, o (ist) come back

zurück'-schreiben, ie, ie write back

sich zurück'-wenden, wandte, gewandt turn back

sich zurück'-ziehen, zog, gezogen retire

zusam'men-nähen sew together

zusam'men-stellen put together

zuvor' before, first

zuvor'-kommen, a, o (ist) get in ahead of

der Zuwachs (an) increase (in)

der Zweifel, - doubt

zweimal twice

zweitens in the second place

zweitgrößt second largest

der Zwirn thread

zwischen between

der Zylin'der, - cylinder

ENGLISH-GERMAN VOCABULARY

A

a, an ein
be able können, konnte, gekonnt,
  kann
about über, von; be ___ to wollen,
  wollte, gewollt, will gerade
act as if tun, als ob
afternoon der Nachmittag, -e;
  this ___ heute nachmittag
against gegen
ago vor
air die Luft
all all, alle; ganz
be allowed dürfen, durfte, ge-
  durft, darf
already schon
also auch
always immer
America das Amerika
American der Amerikaner, -
angry böse
answer antworten (dat.)
not anything nichts
arrive an-kommen, a, o (ist)
as . . . as so . . . wie; ___ if als
  ob
Asia das Asien
ask for bitten, a, e um
at zu (in time expressions)
attempt der Versuch, -e
aunt die Tante, -n

B

bad schlecht, schlimm
bank das Ufer, -
battle der Kampf, ⸚e

be sein, war, gewesen, ist (ist)
beautiful schön
become werden, u, o, i (ist)
bed; go to ___ schlafen gehen
beer das Bier, -e
before ehe
begin an-fangen, i, a, ä
believe (in) glauben (an)
between zwischen
book das Buch, ⸚er
boy der Junge, -n, -n
bright hell
bring bringen, brachte, gebracht;
  ___ around to bringen auf
brother der Bruder, ⸚
build bauen
burn verbrennen, -brannte,
  -brannt
business das Geschäft, -e
but aber, sondern
by von, bei

C

café das Kaffeehaus, ⸚er
be called heißen, ie, ei
can können, konnte, gekonnt,
  kann
capable tüchtig; ___ of fähig
care for mögen, mochte, gemocht,
  mag
catholic katholisch
cease auf-hören
century das Jahrhundert, -e
change sich ändern
child das Kind, -er
Christmas die Weihnachten
church tax die Kirchensteuer, -n

cinema das Kino, -s
city die Stadt, ˜e
claim wollen, wollte, gewollt, will
class die Klasse, -n; die Stunde, -n
classic writer der Klassiker, -
clean putzen
cleaning woman die Arbeitsfrau,
-en
clear klar
co-ed die Studentin, -nen
coffee der Kaffee
cold kalt (¨)
college das College, -s
combine sich verbinden, a, u
composer der Komponist, -en, -en
concert das Konzert, -e
considerable ziemlich
consist of bestehen, -stand,
-standen aus
conversation das Gespräch, -e
cool kühl
correct richtig
country das Land, ˜er; in the __
auf dem Lande
course der Kursus, -se
cup die Tasse, -n

D

darkness die Finsternis
day der Tag, -e; __ after tomorrow übermorgen
dead tot
develop werden, u, o, i (ist)
development die Entwicklung, -en
dialect der Dialekt, -e
dictator der Diktator, -en
difference der Unterschied, -e
difficult schwer
difficulty die Schwierigkeit, -en
diligent fleißig
director der Direktor, -en
do tun, tat, getan; machen
doctor der Arzt, ˜e
door die Tür, -en

drink trinken, a, u
drive here hierher-fahren, u, a, ä
(ist)
druggist der Apotheker, -
during während
dynamic dynamisch

E

early früh
east der Osten
eat essen, a, e, i
either . . . or entweder . . . oder
engine die Maschine, -n
Eskimo der Eskimo, -s
Europe das Europa
evening; this __ heute abend
ever je
every jeder
everything alles
everywhere überall
experiment das Experiment, -e

F

fall down hinab-fallen, ie, a, ä
(ist)
family die Familie, -n
farmer der Bauer, -n
fast schnell
father der Vater, ˜
fatiguing ermüdend
Faust theme das Faustmotiv
final endlich
find finden, a, u
first erst
flu die Grippe
follow folgen (ist; *dat.*)
foot der Fuß, ˜e
for für; denn
forest der Wald, ˜er
form die Form, -en
fortunately glücklicherweise
freedom die Freiheit
Frenchman der Franzose, -n, -n

frequently oft
friend der Freund, -e; die Freundin, -nen
friendly freundlich

however aber
hurt weh tun
husband der Mann, ⁼er
hydrogen der Wasserstoff

G

garden der Garten, ⁼
gas das Gas, -e; ⸺ **engine** die Gasmaschine, -n
general allgemein
German deutsch; Deutsch
Germany das Deutschland
get werden, u, o, i (ist)
girl das Mädchen, -
give geben, a, e, i; ⸺ **up** aufgeben
glad froh
gladly gern(e)
glass das Glas, ⁼er
go gehen, ging, gegangen (ist); fahren, u, a, ä (ist)
good gut
great groß (¨)

H

have haben, hatte, gehabt, hat; lassen, ie, a, ä; ⸺ **to** müssen, mußte, gemußt, muß
hear hören
heavy schwer
help helfen, a, o, i (*dat.*)
her ihr
here hier; hierher
highly civilized people das Kulturvolk, ⁼er
his sein
history die Geschichte, -n
hope (for) hoffen (auf)
home nach Hause; **at** ⸺ zu Hause
hot heiß
hour die Stunde, -n
house das Haus, ⁼er

I

I ich
ice cream Gefrorenes
if wenn
in in, an
individual einzeln
instead of (an)statt
interesting interessant
into in

J

jeweler der Uhrmacher, -

K

what kind of (a) was für (ein)
kitchen die Küche, -n
know wissen, wußte, gewußt, weiß; kennen, kannte, gekannt; ⸺ **how** können, konnte, gekonnt, kann

L

laboratory das Laboratorium, -rien
lady die Dame, -n
lake der See, -n
language die Sprache, -n
last dauern
last vorig, letzt
latter dieser
laugh lachen
laundry die Wäsche
learn lernen
leave verlassen, ie, a, ä
lecture die Vorlesung, -en
let lassen, ie, a, ä
library die Bibliothek, -en
life das Leben, -

light das Licht, -er
like mögen, mochte, gemocht, mag; — to gern *with verb*
literature die Literatur, -en
little klein
live wohnen, leben
long lang (¨); a — time lange
look forward to sich freuen auf
love; be in — verliebt sein
lowland das Tiefland, ¨er

M

machine die Maschine, -n
man der Mann, ¨er
many viele
material das Material, -ien
means; by — of durch
meet treffen, a, o, i
menu die Speisekarte, -n
mine mein
money das Geld
more mehr
morning der Morgen, -; this — heute morgen
most die meisten
motif das Motiv, -e
mountain der Berg, -e
movies das Kino, -s; at the — im Kino; to the — ins Kino
Mr. Herr
much viel
music die Musik
musical musikalisch
must müssen, mußte, gemußt, muß; — not dürfen nicht
my mein

N

near an, bei
need brauchen
never nie
new neu

newspaper die Zeitung, -en
nice nett
no kein
northern nördlich
North Germany das Norddeutsch-land
North Sea coast die Nordseeküste
not nicht; — a kein
nothing nichts
now jetzt
nowadays heutzutage

O

o'clock Uhr
of von
office das Büro, -s
often oft (¨)
on auf, an
one man
only nur
opera die Oper, -n
opposed gegen
order bestellen
original ursprünglich
our unser
oxygen der Sauerstoff

P

package das Paket, -e
paper das Papier, -e
parents die Eltern
part der Teil, -e
peace der Friede, -ns, -n
people die Leute
plan planen
play spielen
please gefallen, ie, a, ä (*dat.*)
poet der Dichter, -
poor arm (¨)
position die Stellung, -en
possible möglich
pot der Topf, ¨e
power die Macht, ¨e

predominant vorwiegend
prefer lieber *with verb*
prescription das Rezept, -e
pretty hübsch
probably wohl
problem das Problem, -e
process der Prozeß, -e
professor der Professor, -en
protestant evangelisch
pull out heraus-ziehen, zog, gezogen
put stellen

R

rain regnen
rain der Regen
raise heben, o, o
rather ziemlich
read lesen, a, e, ie
real wirklich
reason der Grund, ⸗e
recover sich erholen
region die Gegend, -en
relative verwandt
rely on sich verlassen, ie, a, ä auf
report; good ⸺s viel Gutes
return zurück-kehren (ist)
review wiederholen
rich reich
be right recht haben
room das Zimmer, -
rule die Regel, -n
run laufen, ie, au, äu (ist)

S

salesgirl die Verkäuferin, -nen
the same derselbe
say sagen; be said to sollen, sollte,
  gesollt, soll
school die Schule, -n; in ⸺ in der
  Schule; to ⸺ in die Schule
scream schreien, ie, ie
see sehen, a, e, ie

select wählen
sell verkaufen
semester das Semester, -
send schicken; ⸺ for rufen lassen
sentence der Satz, ⸗e
serious; nothing ⸺ nichts Schlimmes
settle down sich nieder-lassen, ie,
  a, ä
she sie
shine scheinen, ie, ie
show zeigen
simple-minded einfältig
since da
sister die Schwester, -n
sit sitzen, saß, gesessen; ⸺ down
  sich setzen
slow langsam
so so, also
soldier der Soldat, -en, -en
some einige
soon bald
southern südlich
South Germany das Süddeutschland
speak sprechen, a, o, i
in spite of trotz
standard German die deutsche
  Hochsprache
state der Staat, -en; ⸺ church
  die Staatskirche
stay bleiben, ie, ie (ist); ⸺ away
  weg-bleiben (ist)
stop auf-hören
story die Geschichte, -n
stove der Ofen, ⸗
student der Student, -en, -en
study lernen
such solcher
suit der Anzug, ⸗e
summer der Sommer, -
sun die Sonne, -n
swim schwimmen, a, o (ist);
  ⸺ across hinüber-schwimmen
  (ist)

T

table der Tisch, -e
take nehmen, a, o, i
talk sprechen, a, o, i; reden
tall hoch (¨)
teacher der Lehrer, -
tell erzählen
tennis das Tennis
terrible fürchterlich
test die Prüfung, -en
than als
that der, jener
the der; —— . . . —— je . . . desto
theater das Theater, -
their ihr
then dann, da
there dort, da; es; —— is, are es gibt
think of denken, dachte, gedacht an
thirty-years' dreißigjährig
this dieser
time die Zeit, -en; das Mal, -e; this —— diesmal
tired müde
to nach, zu
today heute
together zusammen
tomorrow morgen
too zu
train die Eisenbahn, -en
travel reisen (ist)
tree der Baum, ¨e
trip die Reise, -n
try versuchen
twilight of the gods die Götterdämmerung
the two die beiden
typewriter die Schreibmaschine, -n

U

uncle der Onkel, -
united vereinigt
university die Universität, -en; —— student der Universitätsstudent, -en, -en
until; not —— erst
use benutzen
usual gewöhnlich

V

very sehr
village das Dorf, ¨er
visit besuchen

W

wage (war) (Krieg) führen
wagon der Wagen, -
wait (for) warten (auf)
waiter der Kellner, -
wall die Mauer, -n
want (to) wollen, wollte, gewollt, will
war der Krieg, -e
watch die Uhr, -en
we wir
week die Woche, -n
well gut
west der Westen
western westlich
when als
whenever wenn
where wo, wohin
which welcher
while während
who wer
whole ganz
why warum
wife die Frau, -en
win gewinnen, a, o
window das Fenster, -
with mit
without ohne
woman die Frau, -en
word das Wort, -e *or* ¨er
work (on) arbeiten (an)

work die Arbeit, -en; das Werk, -e

world die Welt, -en; — war der
  Weltkrieg, -e

write schreiben, ie, ie

Y

year das Jahr, -e

yesterday gestern

you du, ihr, Sie

INDEX

Numbers refer to pages

[227]

INTERROGATIVE WORDS

wann	*when*	wo	*where*
warum	*why*	wofür	*for what, what for*
was	*what*	woher	*from where*
welcher	*which, what*	wohin	*to what place, where*
wem	*(to) whom*		
wen	*whom*	womit	*with what*
wer	*who*	worauf	*on what*
wessen	*whose*	woraus	*out of (or from) what*
wie	*how*	worin	*in what*
wieviel	*how much*	wovon	*of (or about) what*
wie viele	*how many*		

Ostsee
Nordsee
Kiel
Lübeck
Rostock
Hamburg
Wilhelmshaven
Bremen
Elbe
Weser
NEDERLAND
Hannover
Braunschweig
Bethel
Münster
Detmold
Clausthal
Essen
Paderborn
Hann-Münden
Göttingen
Halle
Düsseldorf
Wuppertal
Kassel
Jena
Köln
Rhein
Marburg
Werra
Fulda
Giessen
Aachen
Bonn
Königstein
Frankfurt A/M
Mosel
Main
Bamberg
LUXEMBOURG
Darmstadt
Würzburg
Erlangen
Trier
Mainz
Mannheim
Neckar
Nürnberg
Heidelberg
Neuendettelsau
Eichstätt
FRANKREICH
Karlsruhe
Regensbu
Stuttgart
Donau
Dillingen
Hohenheim
Tübingen
Augsburg
München
Freiburg
SCHWEIZ
ÖSTERR